To
_____

From
_____

Date
_____

Published by Christian Art Publishers
PO Box 1599, Vereeniging, 1930, RSA

© 2022
First edition 2022

Cover designed by Christian Art Publishers

Images used under license from Shutterstock.com

Unless otherwise indicated, Scripture quotations are taken from the Holy Bible, New International Version®, NIV® Copyright © 1973, 1978, 1984, 2011 by Biblica, Inc.® Used by permission. All rights reserved worldwide.

Scripture quotations marked NKJV are taken from the New King James Version®. Copyright © 1982 by Thomas Nelson. Used by permission. All rights reserved.

Scripture quotations marked NLT are taken from the Holy Bible, New Living Translation, copyright © 1996, 2004, 2015 by Tyndale House Foundation. Used by permission of Tyndale House Publishers, Inc., Carol Stream, Illinois 60188. All rights reserved.

Set in 12 on 15 pt Palatino LT Std
by Christian Art Publishers

Printed in China

ISBN 978-1-77637-075-7 (Faux Leather)
ISBN 978-1-77637-128-0 (Hardcover)

© All rights reserved. No part of this book may be reproduced in any form without permission in writing from the publisher, except in the case of brief quotations in critical articles or reviews.

22 23 24 25 26 27 28 29 30 31 – 10 9 8 7 6 5 4 3 2 1

A JOURNEY with JESUS

CHERIE HILL

CHRISTIAN ART PUBLISHERS

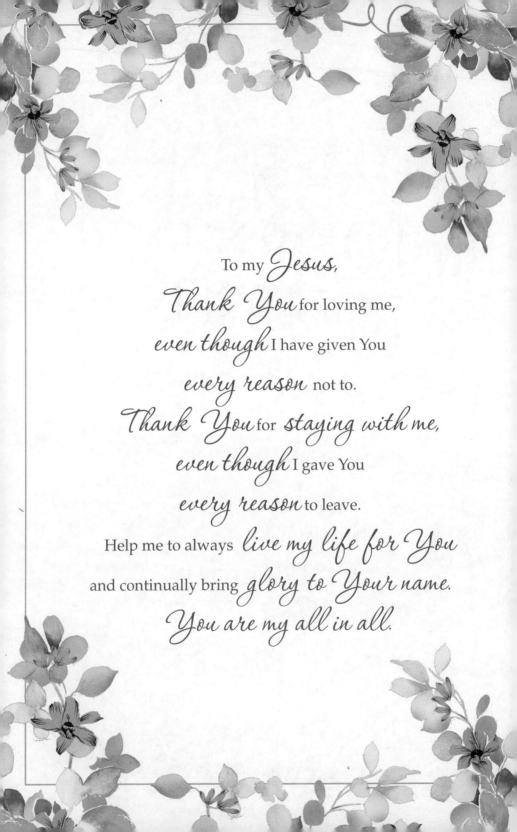

To my *Jesus*,
Thank You for loving me,
even though I have given You
every reason not to.
Thank You for *staying with me*,
even though I gave You
every reason to leave.
Help me to always *live my life for You*
and continually bring *glory to Your name*.
You are my all in all.

Table of Contents

Introduction 7

Section 1: THE STORM 8

Trusting God in Times of Trouble 10
Hope When Hope Seems Gone 24
Strength in the Spiritual Battle 38
God's Presence When You Feel Alone 54
Help When You're Hurting 68
God's Guidance through Uncertainty 82
Winning Over Worry and Fear 98

Section 2: "DON'T YOU CARE?" 112

Finding Faith through Your Doubt 114
Seeking God in Your Struggles 128
Facing Your Anger in Anxiety 142
Walking in God's Will 156
Worship through Your Worry 170
Contentment through the Chaos 184
Waiting On God 198

Section 3: IN THE BOAT 212

Rest with God 214
The Power of Your Prayers 228
Standing Firm in Faith 242
Experiencing the Goodness of God 256
Beyond Your Brokenness 270
Comfort in God's Constant Love 284
The Assurance of God's Abundance 298

Section 4: "PEACE, BE STILL" 312

Saved by Grace 314
In Pursuit of Peace 328
Joy in the Journey 342
The Significance of Your Suffering 356
Transformed by the Spirit 370
Blessing in Disguise 384
Expecting Miracles 399

Introduction

From the moment you pick up this book to the first word that you read, you begin a journey. It's not unlike the journey that the disciples took when they got into a boat with Jesus on the Sea of Galilee. And though your journey is different ... it is the same. Jesus is taking you to "the other side" – the other side of your doubt and fears, the other side of everything that is keeping you from moving forward in your faith. And you're going to want to take this journey.

You're going to want to experience the raging storms, the fear and desperation, and the doubt that consumes you with worry, because through it all, you're going to discover Jesus in your life in ways you never have before and your life will never be the same ... you'll be able to rest with Him, in the back of the boat, in His peace, through every storm of life.

Each day is going to reveal more about you and more about God. You'll find out that it's doubt that brings about greater faith and it's your storms of life that are the set up for God's greatest miracles in your life. You won't want to miss a single moment. No matter what you're facing in life, each page will take you through it.

You'll discover that God's love for you goes beyond all that you can hope for or imagine and you'll find that Jesus never leaves your side. Don't be tempted to give up on your faith, don't allow the wind and the waves to make you turn the other way ... just get into the boat and take this journey with Jesus.

SECTION 1

The Storm

As evening came, Jesus said to his disciples, "Let's cross to the other side of the lake." So they took Jesus in the boat and started out, leaving the crowds behind (although other boats followed). But soon a fierce storm came up. High waves were breaking into the boat, and it began to fill with water.

Mark 4:35-37 (NLT)

Do you feel as though you're in a raging storm of life? Storms of life seem to come out of nowhere, without warning, and suddenly you feel as though each breath might be your last.

With little delay, despair and hopelessness sets in and you realize there is no quick escape and nothing short of a miracle can save you. It's in the storm, when your faith seems to be failing you, and your soul is suffering beyond what you ever thought it could that you can rest assured. God has a miracle designed specifically for you – to secure your faith in ways He's never done before – but first, you must go *through* the storm. It's *in* the storm that you will find strength and peace, trusting in God's faithfulness which assures you that He wouldn't allow a storm if there wasn't a purpose for it. And though you feel as if God is failing you because you're trying to control the timing of His miracles … you need to trust God's schedule.

You may not understand God's ways, but you can trust them. His love, power, and faithfulness are not diminished by the wind and the waves. As the storm is threatening to take you under, know this: *Jesus is with you* – He knew the storm was coming, He is not surprised by it, and He *will* perform a miracle *in* it.

But right now, in the boat, with Jesus at your side, your faith is going to be tested, purified, and strengthened. *This* is where the journey with Jesus begins, but this is not how or where it ends.

TRUSTING GOD IN TIMES OF TROUBLE

"I have told you these things, so that in me you may have peace. In this world you will have trouble. But take heart! I have overcome the world."
JOHN 16:33

We tend to believe that God is unaware of the problems in our lives. When the waves of fear and desperation come crashing in on us, we let doubt and disbelief get the best of us and we forget what He's promised. Jesus assured us that we would have troubles. And He also promised that He's with us always.

Through all the joy and all the pain, through all the faith and all the doubt, through the darkest moments of our lives, He is always there to be Light and give hope. And sometimes it's the storms of your life that help you to see that Jesus is all you'll ever need because you will never know He is all you need, until He's all you've got.

There is not a single promise that God has not kept. Not a moment when He relinquished His control. God is always at work. And your storms of life are what will reveal, refine, strengthen, and perfect the areas in your life that are hindering your spiritual growth. God doesn't ask us to "blindly" trust Him. He reveals Himself through Scripture and works within our lives by fulfilling His promises to assure us that He is fully trustworthy.

Behind every storm there is a blessing – it's an opportunity to trust God, to know Him better, and to experience His miracles.

The question is: "Where are you in the boat right now?" Are you trusting God or treading water? Is your soul in despair or resting with Jesus? When He's promised that He has overcome the world, that means yours, too. And if He doesn't always calm the storm when and how you think He should … if He doesn't always rescue you from them, you can be sure by faith that He will take you through them.

God Help Me

*Listen to my prayer, O God, do not ignore my plea;
hear me and answer me ... "Oh, that I had the wings of
a dove! I would fly away and be at rest ... I would hurry
to my place of shelter, far from the tempest and storm."*
PSALM 55:1-2, 6, 8

JANUARY 1

There will be storms of life – storms that flood your spirit with disillusionment, despair and disappointment, but I am with you. And though the waves of the storm submerge your soul with agonizing fear, I have assured you there is nothing to fear. The hopelessness you feel does not mean hope is gone, not when your hope remains in Me. You are not alone – I have promised that I will never abandon you. Rest assured I knew the storm was coming, and though it was unexpected to you, I am right here with you and I will take you through it. I will never leave your side ... I am with you *in the boat*. When your thoughts are consumed with worry and distress capsizes your faith, keep your eyes on Me.

You may have lost your job, your health, or those you love, but all is not lost. Hoping in Me, hoping in faith, changes everything. Faith in Me makes the impossible possible. Don't allow the doubt and disbelief to overcome your faith. The storm does not affect My presence or My power. I never change. Do not allow the wind and the waves to convince you that I cannot hear you and that I am unaware of the storm that is threatening to take you under. I am with you so that you can have peace, and so that you can experience a miracle that I have prepared, uniquely, just for you.

FAITH THOUGHTS

You don't need to wait for Jesus ... you can tell the storm, "Peace, be still!" Keep your eyes on Him and don't let the wind and the waves distract your miracle-believing faith. Though He may be resting, He is at work ... preparing your heart for greater miracles than you can imagine.

JANUARY 2

A Prayer Away

We are hard pressed on every side,
but not crushed; perplexed, but not in despair.
2 CORINTHIANS 4:8

Though troubles come, though storms of life create destruction, there is no need to despair … you are held by Me. No matter how relentless and unending your storm, My love and power is greater. I am with you to strengthen your faith. It is by keeping your focus upon Me that you will refuse to give in to despair and hold on to the hope you are given through the promises of the Father. It is the Holy Spirit who will continually fill you with the Father's love and give you the strength to persevere.

It is My unrelenting love that will help you to overcome all your fears. It is love that beckoned Me to the Cross and overcame death and destruction, giving you eternal life. There is no greater power. Fix your eyes on Me and remember My strength to carry the Cross and suffer upon it. I died so you can live.

I sacrificed My life so that you could fully live and enjoy yours. When the walls of life come crashing in, when you are struggling to take just one more step of faith, remember that your miracle is only a prayer away … *Pray it.*

FAITH THOUGHTS

What is your greatest worry? What is your greatest fear? What is it that God cannot overcome when He has promised that He already has? Your foundation of faith sets the stage for God to show up and show off. If you're crushed and perplexed, focus on His love and rely on His power and presence.

When Troubles Come

*The LORD is good, a refuge in times of trouble.
He cares for those who trust in him.*
NAHUM 1:7

You tend to allow your troubles to threaten your trust. You doubt when you desperately need faith and choose to rely on your own strength, instead of Mine, in times of trouble. I am right here beside you. I am not surprised by your situation and there is nothing that I can't do. *Nothing.*

Through times of struggles and uncertainty, I need you to learn to come to Me, to be in My presence, and trust that I have everything under control. One of your miracles in this storm is that you can have peace, in Me, even as the storm rages around you. I know every detail of your circumstances. I know how your heart is breaking, I bottle every tear, and you've been promised that you will be given beauty for your ashes. Trust in My faithfulness and know that I am with you through the storm to give you faith, to keep you focused on the goodness and greatness of God. Your trust will come in diving deep into the promises that have been made to you and completely relying on My faithfulness.

The miracle I have prepared for you awaits the Father's will in determining when you are fully ready to receive it. The storm comes with great purpose – your heavenly Father would not allow it if it didn't. He is sovereign at all times, and there is nothing that catches Him by surprise. Do not allow the worries of your world to wear down your faith. Rise up in My strength and pray your way *through* the storm.

FAITH THOUGHTS

God is not surprised by your situation. He has everything under control even when it doesn't seem like it. What promise is God speaking to your heart today? Seek Him, seek His voice, and completely trust that He is faithful.

JANUARY 4

Loyal Love

Preserve me, O God, for in You I put my trust.
PSALM 16:1 (NKJV)

When your world is crashing down around you, I will keep your life from complete destruction. I was in the boat with the disciples, I knew the storm was coming, and I am with *you*. I even know the storms that are yet to come and I am preparing your faith. My miracles are waiting for your prayers – I'm waiting for your faith.

Though your desperation can cause you to feel overwhelmed to the point of trying to control only what I can, faith is a continual surrender of your own control and a confident, quiet trust in Me. When the storm is relentless, and battles are endless, My love and power prevail.

Storms will come to test your faith. Troubles will tempt you to give up and give in and you'll need to continually place your hope in Me. I allow the storms to test your faith, to strengthen it, to give you the opportunity to see My miracles. If you never had storms of life, you'd never see the miracle of their calming.

Your storm is so much more than what it appears on the surface. The wind and the waves are what you're focused on, but I am in charge of them and use them to give you proof of My faithfulness. Even though your faith grows weary, God never does, and above all, His love never fails.

FAITH THOUGHTS

Your troubles are not what God is focused on … it's your faith. He allows the storms of your life for purposes that go beyond what you can see at the moment. You will need to continually choose to have faith, to trust, to have hope in God's faithfulness.

Fixed Focus

JANUARY 5

For our light and momentary troubles are achieving for us an eternal glory that far outweighs them all. So we fix our eyes not on what is seen, but on what is unseen, since what is seen is temporary, but what is unseen is eternal.
2 CORINTHIANS 4:17-18

I know it seems like things will never change, like things are not getting any better, they are only getting worse … and prayer after prayer your faith grows more weary in the waiting. Only when you compare this present moment to the glory of eternity can you see My perspective on your situation. I am doing something. It's in this storm that you're sure you won't survive where you can rest assured that I have allowed it for purposes that go far beyond what you can understand. But if you trust Me, you will not only get through this, you will also find yourself experiencing miracles you never expected.

Life is a journey of faith, preparing you for eternity. When the storms of life relentlessly rage, you must remain focused on Me in the boat … focus on My peace. Don't allow your faith to get tossed about by the wind and the waves. Look to Me for your strength, find peace in the promises God has made to you and fix your heart and mind on the eternal hope and joy you've been promised.

There will be times when you feel as though you're walking through the valley of the shadow of death, but you can rest assured that no matter how hopeless things look, I am with you … leading you to lie down in green pastures … to rest beside *still waters*.

FAITH THOUGHTS

Are you focusing on your storm or on Jesus? Don't allow the wind and the waves of your circumstances to cast your faith into doubt. Be determined to keep your eyes on Jesus, so that you can experience His rest and His peace as you wait on His miracle in your boat.

January 6

Darkness into Light

"I will lead the blind by ways they have not known, along unfamiliar paths I will guide them; I will turn the darkness into light before them and make the rough places smooth. These are the things I will do; I will not forsake them."
ISAIAH 42:16

I realize that the unknowns of life can cause a darkness within your soul that tempts you to believe that things will not work out ... that it's all going from bad to worse. The storm can cloud your vision like that. But Light will come. Your darkness will be filled with Light. In this moment, when all seems hopeless, you will need to choose to trust Me. You'll need to rely on Me for help and strength as you take each step of faith.

In darkness and in light, through times of hope and in moments of despair, I will give you the courage to trust Me. You don't need to know how it all works out. You don't need to have all the answers ... I am in control. Faith isn't always easy, but it's simple ... trusting in the Father who holds it all in place and holds you in His hands. It's relying upon His promises and trusting in His faithfulness that will see you through every storm of life.

His love for you is deeper than the flood waters that are pulling you under. There is nothing greater than His power within you to help you rise above the storm and look for the Light. I am here. There is always Light in the darkness. *Choose* to see it.

FAITH THOUGHTS

You will have to choose to believe that God sees everything that you cannot. There is nothing He can't do, no darkness where His Light cannot break through. God already knows what lies ahead and He holds your tomorrows wrapped in His love, mercy, and grace. Trust Him, even when you're not sure you can.

In Your Weakness

JANUARY 7

My life is consumed by anguish and my years by groaning; my strength fails because of my affliction, and my bones grow weak.
PSALM 31:10

I am not neglecting your pain or putting off your problems. I know you are losing hope, I know that your strength is nearly gone. I see your struggles and the emotions that cause a battle within you that threatens to destroy your faith. I want you to come to Me. I am with you and I am the source of your strength ... to give you the rest, refreshment, and revival that your soul so desperately needs.

I know you're tired. When you are past the point of exhaustion, follow My example in the boat, as I rest through the storm. I know, and so should you, that there is nothing to fear. I am with you, I am for you, and I am mighty to save. I have promised you that in this life you will have troubles. They should be no surprise. It is your faith in Me that keeps you from being overtaken by the storm ... it is in trusting in Me that the wind and the waves will be calmed. When all your strength is gone, I am your strength when you are weak, I will comfort you and consume you with grace.

Draw near to Me and I will draw near to you. I am not too weak to handle what you can't. My power and presence changes everything, especially the most hopeless of circumstances. All you need is Me. I am the lifter of your head, and I will give you the grace and strength to stand firm in faith and keep focused on sharing in My glory.

FAITH THOUGHTS

Find time to truly rest. Sit quietly in God's presence and listen for His voice as you pray. In what way do you need God to bless you in this moment? Let Him strengthen your faith through His promises as you eagerly wait for your prayers to be answered.

Assured Strength

*Surely God is my salvation; I will trust and not be afraid. The L*ORD*, the L*ORD *himself, is my strength and my defense; he has become my salvation.*
ISAIAH 12:2

You must *choose* to trust Me. You have a choice to be blessed. No matter what you're going through, I am not surprised. Your struggles are not about what they appear to be on the surface. They are about your spirit, your faith, your peace and your relationship with Me. Your confidence and hope will waver if it is not in Me. Your hope should grasp tight to God's promises to you and never let go. Your heavenly Father's faithfulness will calm your storm.

You are not perfect, but I am and you can trust Me. My mercy and kindness never change. I never change. My love for you remains through your mistakes and My love and grace embrace you at every moment. Even when you're not sure I'm with you, I'll remind you that I am. All your days, all your storms are before Me. And I am in the boat with you.

My mercies help you to see that I am faithful, and My love is displayed in My constant presence in your life. I never leave your side. The Spirit will help you in your weakness and your focus upon Me will give you the faith you need to pray the next prayer, to knock one more time and expect God's answer.

FAITH THOUGHTS

God is willing and ready to bless you, His faithfulness is beckoning your faith. If you feel as though you've been praying, waiting, and God is taking too long, know that His ways are perfect and so is His timing. Trust Him and trust His watch. He's never late – He is faithfully, exactly, right on time.

Heard and Held

JANUARY 9

*The righteous cry out, and the LORD hears them;
he delivers them from all their troubles.*
PSALM 34:17

Troubles will come, often without warning. Don't be surprised by your situation or give in to the doubt that keeps casting you into despair. Pray continually, but pray knowing that God hears you. He is not too deaf to hear you call and He is not too weak to save you. What is it that you think God cannot do? Know that there are miracles in your storm, greater miracles than just God calming it. His miracles, His blessings, are all around you. They are right in front of you … just as I am. His hand is on your life and you will see Him if you look for Him.

You've been blessed in so many ways in the past … what once were possibilities, hopes that seemed hopeless, are now predictable in your life. You so easily take for granted what you've been given, and yes, the hard times, the troubles in your life are blessings. You just can't see them through your pain. That's why I'm with you, so that whatever storm in life you face, whatever your fears, I will calm you in My arms and give you the assurance that God has plans for your future … to prosper you, not harm you, plans to give you hope.

I hold you and God hears you. Don't doubt what you know is truth, the lies cannot hold back God's power. Trust in His promises, regardless of what is threatening to overcome you. Though you sit in darkness, I will be your Light. Though you may have fallen into the despair of troubles, you will get up.

FAITH THOUGHTS

Pray that God will open your eyes to be aware of the blessings He's given you, even through your pain, in the midst of the storm. Let your heart be full of gratitude for what He's already done and look forward with faith to all that He's yet to do.

JANUARY 10

What Lies Ahead

*Yet what we suffer now is nothing compared
to the glory he will reveal to us later.*
ROMANS 8:18 (NLT)

I know that you feel as though the suffering you're going through is reflective of My lack of love and concern – you're certain that if I loved you, you would not be allowed to go through a tempest that casts your soul into the deepest despair. As you cry out "Where is God?" I am the one who is here beside you to assure you that the Father is in control and you can have peace because His grace will carry you and so will I.

Though you feel that you'll never make it … *you will*. Your heavenly Father has assured you a future of great glory for all eternity. Yet, I know that you need to experience His goodness now. His promises assure you that He mends the wounded, binds up the brokenhearted, and brings life out of things that are dead. You can have hope in His faithfulness. There is nothing that is too difficult for Him and although it feels like you'll never get through this storm … He will make a way.

Hold on to hope – stay focused on Me as the storm rages. And when there is disappointment and despair in your life, you can be assured that the Father is setting up your circumstances to display His powerful presence in your life. He will show up, at exactly the right time, in precisely the right way, and you will be assured what He has promised: His mercies never end and He is faithful. His Light will shine *in* your darkness and *through* the storm … there is wonderful joy ahead.

FAITH THOUGHTS

You can't see it right now, but one day you will see everything clearly, just as God does. Ask Him to reveal His plan to you, to give you peace, and strengthen you for the journey of faith through your storm.

Never Give Up

JANUARY 11

You wearied yourself by such going about, but you would not say, 'It is hopeless.' You found renewal of your strength, and so you did not faint.
ISAIAH 57:10

When you're consumed with circumstances that seem insurmountable even for Me, you tend to let go of your faith and walk by sight. My power is not limited by the severity of your situation and My strength will be enough to carry you through whatever it is that is leaving you feeling hopeless.

I walked on the earth and walked on the water to show you a life of faith. I set the example in showing you that you must endure and persevere through every circumstance of life. If you will trust in the heavenly Father's promises to you, that He is able to do immeasurably more than you could ever ask for or imagine, you will reflect My nature of trust and peace.

It's your endurance through the most difficult of circumstances where you will find the Father's grace strengthening you when you are at your weakest. You were never meant to walk this journey of faith alone … I am always with you. You have the same Spirit within you that empowered Me to rise from the dead. If death is defeated, can't you trust that anything that you face is too? The same power that has overcome the grave will overcome your storms of life. Keep holding on to faith. Never give up. Your miracle is only a prayer away.

FAITH THOUGHTS

Just because you're weary doesn't mean you're weak. You don't need to rely on your own strength, you have Jesus with you … to hold you, to carry you. The power of God is within you to accomplish more than you can dare to hope for or imagine. Take the dare.

January 12

Out of the Storm

Then the L<small>ORD</small> spoke to Job out of the storm.
JOB 38:1

Your heavenly Father hears you. He is in this moment. Whatever that moment is … joy, pain, or complete emptiness, He is fully in it and you can be sure He is a ready help in times of trouble.

I know it's easy to feel abandoned: like He has no clue what you're going through and certainly can't take the time to answer your prayer. I, too, cried out asking why the Father had forsaken Me, but regardless of the emptiness and loneliness I felt, His victory was sure. When what you're going through seems as though it is the worst possible situation, it is your heart separated from the Father that is worse. Your faith connects you to Him. And a heart devoted to His brings about a journey full of troubles *and* triumphs.

Don't ever lose sight of the goal: You are on this journey in life to be perfected – developing faith that prepares you to live with the Father, forever. Your problem with your faith is that you're not convinced He will do things the *way* He's supposed to or *when* He should. It's hard to understand that He has allowed the storm in your life, in an effort to increase your faith by threatening to destroy it. Know that even though My disciples had seen Me perform many miracles, they still doubted My ability to control their storm … you are not alone in your doubt and disbelief.

Out of the Father's desire to increase their faith, bringing them to the edge of their faith, I asked them to step into a boat and risk it. Faith isn't faith until it requires you to take a step into the unseen. And it's there that the Father will answer you.

FAITH THOUGHTS

You pray, but are you listening? God's voice doesn't always come in predictable ways. Listen with your ears, eyes and heart. If you seek Him, He's promised you'll find Him. Expect God's miracles when you're least expecting them.

Without Hesitation

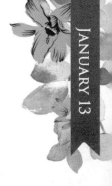

JANUARY 13

Let us then approach God's throne of grace with confidence, so that we may receive mercy and find grace to help us in our time of need.
HEBREWS 4:16

My grace is not earned … it's given. You don't need to do anything but come to Me, trust in Me, and rest in Me. I am perfect in compassion and love that comforts and heals your soul. You need Me. So, do not hesitate to call upon Me in your troubles, I am here to help you, to give you hope when all hope seems gone.

I am with you in the broken places, ready to pour out My mercy and grace upon you. In My presence you will experience My power through the peace you feel in being assured that I will overcome whatever is overcoming you. There is no reason to fear, no reason to hesitate in casting your burdens upon Me. You will find strength in your surrender.

Whatever has brought you to your knees has been allowed by your heavenly Father, the storms of your life are permitted with purpose and His hand is upon you. You will find Light in your darkness by walking with Me. Lift your hands up to where your help comes from … the Maker of heaven and earth – the One who remains faithful forever.

FAITH THOUGHTS

When you don't know what to do, you can be sure that God does. He wants you to come to Him, without hesitation. Don't seek Him as a last resort. God's grace waits for you, don't keep Him waiting.

HOPE WHEN HOPE SEEMS GONE

*"For I know the plans I have for you,"
declares the L*ORD*, "plans to prosper you and not to
harm you, plans to give you hope and a future."*
JEREMIAH 29:11

In a moment, in a single breath, life can bring a storm so fierce that hope seems completely gone. In a desperate final attempt to hold on to whatever hope you have left, you may even look for a lifeboat – some kind of quick escape to save your soul – but the relentless waves of emptiness, pain, and fear, instantly convince you that you're going under and nothing can save you. And faith … what you've so desperately held on to … which has somehow, ironically brought you to this point, seems to work against you. Your struggle to have faith seems endless when doubt's argument against it is so strong.

But you've missed something. You've forgotten. Jesus is with you. He's in the boat with you. He's never left you and never will. He knows every detail of the very storm you're in at this moment. He sees all and He knows all. And He's waiting for you to simply turn to Him. To stop trying and start trusting. To see His peace and enter into it. You can keep trying to bail water out of your boat, but all your efforts will be in vain. It's not about God testing your strength, the storm is about understanding your weakness and completely falling on the grace of Jesus' love for you.

Your journey of faith is about continually learning to let go of your own expectations for your life and simply embracing God's plan for you, even if that includes a raging storm. He's promised not to harm you, He's promised to prosper you, to give you a hope and a future. What part of that promise are you doubting? In this moment, stop looking for a way *out* and realize that Jesus, Himself, is about to take you *through*. What you see as the end is really just the beginning when your hope is in Him.

True Hope

JANUARY 14

*Therefore, since we have such a hope,
we are very bold.*
2 CORINTHIANS 3:12

There is nothing you are going through, no pain or suffering, that is outside of God's grace. So pray confidently, knowing that God's grace will answer you. I am with you to strengthen you as the waves of doubt come crashing in. Your faith changes everything.

It's easy to place your hope in someone or something rather than Me. When you must walk by faith instead of by sight, it seems more reasonable to believe in something you can see, rather than in something you can't see at all. But this world is not your home. Your hope lies in eternity with Me. Don't allow your circumstances to control your faith. My plans are never paused and I do not grow weary of being your ready help in times of trouble. My track record in performing miracles, in doing the impossible, is impeccable.

My love never fails. I will never forsake you. There is no problem too great that I am not greater still. So, when all hope seems gone, when there's nothing you can do, nowhere to go, realize that I am with you on this journey to give you a future and a hope … taking you from glory to glory.

FAITH THOUGHTS

Where have you placed your hope? Sit at the feet of Jesus and simply rest in His presence. Remember His faithfulness that carried Him to the Cross out of love for you and know that there is nothing good that He will withhold from you as you trust in Him.

Blessed To Be A Blessing

But joyful are those who have the God of Israel as their helper, whose hope is in the LORD their God.
PSALM 146:5 (NLT)

Blessings don't always appear that way. They can often seem like I've let you down, failed you in every way, and left you utterly alone and helpless, but I have not. There is never a moment that I am not with you … I have sent the Spirit to you to hold you and help you. I have always shown Myself to be faithful. I never change, even when your circumstances do.

My compassion and grace do not change. My blessings never run short or run out. When your confident trust is in Me, there is no good thing that I will withhold from you. Your faith in Me will never disappoint you.

My timing might be different from your own, but your blessings will always come at exactly the right moment. As you trust, do not allow your faith to waver, keep your eyes on Me, the author and finisher of your faith. Be determined to keep going, to fight the good fight, and never give up and never let go. Goodness and mercy will follow you all the days of your life and so will My blessings.

FAITH THOUGHTS

What are you praying for? What blessings are you waiting on and what blessings can you thank God for right now? Unleashing God's power in your life comes through your praise. Thank Him now, before your faith takes sight.

Don't Give Up!

*"But as for you, be strong and do not give up,
for your work will be rewarded."*
2 CHRONICLES 15:7

Life will always bring about circumstances that cause discouragement and despair. Don't be surprised by your troubles, I have promised that they will come. And yet I've also promised that I am with you always. I collect every tear you cry, I know the depths of your pain. I am fully aware of your breaking heart and I am constantly working to heal you, comfort you, give you joy and help you to rise up from the ashes in your life. I am all you need.

When you are filled with doubt, uncertain of the future, not sure if there is any hope at all, turn to Me and rest. Rely on My power and presence. Your worries will not bring about miracles, but your worship will. Focus on what blessings you've been given in the past and confidently expect greater ones than before. Though you can't always control your circumstances, I can. I only want what is best for you, what will strengthen your faith and prepare you for eternity.

The Father always has your best interest at heart, even when it doesn't seem like it. Trust in My love that has given you eternal life, there is no greater love.

FAITH THOUGHTS

Where have you placed your hope? Sit at the feet of Jesus and simply rest in His presence. Remember His faithfulness that carried Him to the Cross out of love for you and know that there is nothing good that He will withhold from you as you trust in Him.

JANUARY 17

Rest in Him

*Yes, my soul, find rest in God;
my hope comes from him.*
PSALM 62:5

I am with you to help you walk upon the water – trust My voice that calls you upon it. When the storm rages in your life, when uncertainties try to capsize your faith, look up … I am here … there is nothing to fear. Look directly into your fear and declare My peace. And look again, those are not waves of destruction, it is My grace, My consuming love pouring in on you. Choose to see your circumstances through My eyes instead of your own.

Most often, when you are fighting the battles of life, you should be resting. Resting in Me, resting in the Father's promises, learning to be still. You tend to believe your enemy is someone or something that it's not. Your focus needs to be on Me … it is My battle, let me handle the circumstances of your life as you remain in My peace. There is nothing that I am not aware of. I see your life from beginning to end. I am purposely with you at all times and in all ways. Nothing goes unnoticed, especially not your heartache and tears.

Storms will come, but so do My miracles when you're trusting Me in them. Don't be deceived by what you see, trust in what you know: I am with you, never will I leave you nor forsake you, and I'm taking you from glory to glory.

FAITH THOUGHTS

If you're tired, make time for rest. Do it purposely. Jesus was resting in the boat. He's shown you how this is done. And yes, He was resting in a raging, life-threatening storm … you can, too, when you're completely trusting in your heavenly Father.

Held in Hope

JANUARY 18

You will be secure, because there is hope; you will look about you and take your rest in safety.
JOB 11:18

When you feel as though you've lost control of life, when your soul is worried and weary, you are not alone. I am here. Your fears must face Me … and I have overcome the grave. Lay it all down at My feet. I can do the impossible. I am constantly with you, constantly speaking to you. Look for Me and listen to My voice. You will be surprised at how near I am to you.

I am your faithful friend. There is no greater love for you than the love I give. When you feel alone, pray in the Spirit and feel Me embracing you … holding you with My hope. It is the Spirit that will give you eyes of faith and help you to know My presence in every moment of your life.

Things may seem hopeless, it may feel like I've abandoned you, but I have not and there is always hope when your hope is placed in Me. Pray for the impossible and look expectantly for My miracles. Things may seem like they are falling apart when they are really falling into place. I work that way … mysteriously … miraculously. You are held in My hope and you are embraced with My grace.

FAITH THOUGHTS

What are you hoping for? Who or what are you placing your hope in? Turn to God. Give Him your heart and trust in His. He is your only true hope … worship and praise Him like He is!

JANUARY 19

Remembered

*Remember your word to your servant,
for you have given me hope.*
PSALM 119:49

You might wonder if I've forgotten you, left you in your struggle and simply walked away. And I will remind you to look at the Cross – the strength that carried me there is love and love keeps going until the end. There is no road in your journey that I will not travel down with you. There is no obstacle that I will not overcome. And when things seem hopeless, when you can't see a way ... know that I will make one. I give you My Word.

You will face the lies of the world more often than you'd like, and you'll be tempted to doubt and give in to fear. Don't. Turn to Me instead. Let the Spirit help you to remember the promises of God that will carry you and cover you. My faithfulness is not dependent on your own. I know that sometimes you falter and many times fail, but I'm a ready help in times of trouble, and My mercies never cease.

You so easily forget the times when I've turned to you and heard your cry, you've failed to see the times when I've run relentlessly after you, lifting you out of the slimy pit, out of the mud and mire. I am the One who gives your hope a firm place to stand. All you need to do is trust in every promise your heavenly Father has made and rest in the hope of His faithfulness.

FAITH THOUGHTS

You may see obstacles that seem unsurmountable. God doesn't. There is no miracle that He cannot perform. Think of one moment in your life where you felt all hope was gone and remember how God showed up and miraculously brought you to where you are.

To the End

January 20

We want each of you to show this same diligence to the very end, so that what you hope for may be fully realized.
HEBREWS 6:11

Hopelessness can drive you into a place of desperation that causes you to want to give up and give in. Don't. Don't give up right before the miracle. When you have placed your hope in Me, you must keep your eyes on Me. Your faith must focus upon the Word of God, in order that your faith would have the foundation it needs to keep going until the end.

The temptation to give up because a situation seems impossible can be overwhelming when you are experiencing pain that leaves you empty and alone. But I am with you and the Spirit is within you to help you and give you hope in the most hopeless of situations. Your faith makes all things possible. Your praise and worship move the hand of God. Don't walk by sight. Take your eyes off the storm and keep focused upon My peace.

Remember that I have given you My peace – not the peace that the world gives. You don't have to strive for peace in life … I give it to you and it does not rely on anything but My presence and power. Lean on Me, seek My direction, follow where I lead you … even if it's into a storm.

FAITH THOUGHTS

What situation in your life seems absolutely hopeless? What is causing you to feel as though you want to give up on God? Envision yourself at the throne of God, handing it over to Him, allowing His hands to take it, and then rest in peace and prayer, knowing that God is working on your miracle.

Set Your Hope

Therefore, with minds that are alert and fully sober, set your hope on the grace to be brought to you when Jesus Christ is revealed at his coming.
1 PETER 1:13

In every moment of life, we need hope. It's because of God's promises and His continued grace, that you have a sure and certain hope. The hope you've been given is not one that changes according to your circumstances but abides in His love and faithfulness. I have saved you. I have given you true hope. Set your hope on Me.

Your situations in life, the struggles that cause you to seemingly lose hope, are opportunities for you to choose faith, to choose to believe and draw closer to Me. They are not meant to destroy you but to draw you in. If you've found yourself in a place of doubting Me and looking for a way out instead of through, know that your heavenly Father is not surprised and He already has a plan to bring beauty from your ashes. There is no condemnation for where you are in your disbelief, there is only grace … there is only love and hope.

Don't be afraid to ask for My help. The disciples cried out to Me for help in the storm … you must do the same. There is always hope when your hope is set, placed firm in your foundation of faith and assured of God's faithfulness.

FAITH THOUGHTS

Right now, in this moment, you must choose to believe. Believe in what God's promised you, believe in His faithfulness and trust that He is watching over every situation in your life. He is not surprised by troubles, they give Him an opportunity to show you proof of what you believe.

Inspired Endurance

JANUARY 22

We remember before our God and Father your work produced by faith, your labor prompted by love, and your endurance inspired by hope in our Lord Jesus Christ.
1 THESSALONIANS 1:3

Your hope is what fuels your faith. It's your hope that inspires your endurance through the most difficult of times. But it's not a false hope, it is not one that trusts in others or life's circumstances to turn out in the way you think they should. It's hope in Me – hope of salvation – hope in glory. There is no miracle that is beyond My power, no situation that is without hope.

Each and every day you are called to walk with Me ... to do the work of the Father. You are given specific purposes on the earth to bring glory to the Father and inspire hope in others ... even when you are doubting through your faith. Do not allow the circumstances of your life which haven't lived up to your expectations to disappoint you in such a way that you question your purpose, question your hope and drown in despair. The best is just ahead.

Don't give up before the miracle, don't let go before your breakthrough. Be determined to stand firm in your faith. Keep your eyes on Me and take hold of My hand. I walk with you through each and every moment of your life. There is nothing to fear ... I am here.

FAITH THOUGHTS

Even in your doubt, with only momentary faith, you can keep believing, keep living your purposes that God has given to you and hold on to hope even though you feel like letting go. Rely on My strength, not your own and you will find all the hope you need.

The Eyes of Your Heart

January 23

I pray that the eyes of your heart may be enlightened in order that you may know the hope to which he has called you, the riches of his glorious inheritance in his holy people.
EPHESIANS 1:18

In a world that is filled with dire and desperate situations, when you are continually faced with discouragement and despair, I am with you to give you hope. I walk with you and call you to walk with me in order to encourage you to live in hope through your words and through your works. Each and every day, I want you to reflect on the hope of your calling, a hope of a world transformed by salvation – the hope of living for all eternity with your heavenly Father and leading others into that hope. My Spirit dwells in you to open the eyes of your heart.

You have been called to hope, to participate in the future kingdom of God. One day all things will be unified through Me. So, even through your storms of life, I walk with you, to strengthen you, and at times carry you. I will help you to live out your purpose with thoughts, relationships, and a soul that is shaped by the reality that lies ahead. I give you a hope that is made real to you through faith and through the work of the Holy Spirit. I give you a genuine hope that is about what I've done, it's in your receiving My grace.

My hope is not based on emotional enthusiasm, but a hope that is certain of the future. You are called to hope, live in the glory you've been given. Even though there may be troubles now, there is wonderful joy ahead.

FAITH THOUGHTS

Are you full of hope? Are you trusting in the promises God has made you or are you doubting His faithfulness because of the overwhelming circumstances in your life? Make the decision to live intentionally and consciously in light of God's glorious future He's promised you. Decide to hope and experience the joy that you are intended to live in.

Hold Unswervingly

*Let us hold unswervingly to the hope we profess,
for he who promised is faithful.*
HEBREWS 10:23

It may seem difficult at times to hold on to hope. But in My strength, with your heart set on My sacrifice for your salvation, unswerving hope is possible because your heavenly Father keeps His promises. It is not about your faithfulness, it's about His.

You're not hoping in what you accomplish, but in what I already have. So, you can cling to true hope. Life is not easy and your faith requires dedication and perseverance. You are called by your heavenly Father to be faithfully obedient and experience following Me every single moment of your life.

It's easy to get distracted by the troubles of life … by the storms, but I am with you. Keep your eyes on Me. Even when you stumble, I will keep you from falling. Don't get discouraged when you make mistakes and fall into doubt, just keep taking steps of faith, each step in the direction of your heavenly Father's will for you is good. No matter what lies ahead, you can trust that I am leading you into a future that is full of hope and glory. The best is yet to come.

Faith Thoughts

What is distracting you from keeping your eyes on Jesus? Ask the Spirit to help you to walk in faith, even through your doubt. When you're discouraged, lean on Jesus' strength that carried Him to the Cross. There is nothing you can't do in Him.

JANUARY 25

When You Hope

*Those who hope in the LORD will renew their strength.
They will soar on wings like eagles; they will run
and not grow weary, they will walk and not be faint.*
ISAIAH 40:31

When the weight of life's expectations are weighing in on you, I'm holding on to you. There is nothing to fear. You can rest. When you are resting in Me, allowing My peace to strengthen your faith, you will find yourself rising above the storms of life, soaring on wings like eagles. I am with you to carry you and the Spirit will keep you from growing weary. I will hold you up when you stumble in doubt … I will keep you from falling.

You need to have hope in what your heavenly Father has promised you. His promises are to give you hope, to strengthen your faith when doubt becomes too heavy to bear. It's the promises that will cut through the lies and reveal Truth.

It is the truth that will set you free from the doubt that is constantly trying to convince you that God won't show up. Pray for the Spirit to help you to trust in your heavenly Father's faithfulness. Look to Me as your guide through the storms of life. If I don't calm the storm in your life, I'll calm the storm in you and I will carry you with My grace.

FAITH THOUGHTS

What is it that you're facing in life that you're struggling to trust God with? God's faithfulness is not questionable. His Word is Truth and it is your choice to believe it. When you're consumed with doubt, find a promise that God has made and then believe Him for it.

Unfailing Love

JANUARY 26

*But the eyes of the LORD are on those who fear him,
on those whose hope is in his unfailing love.*
PSALM 33:18

In moments when you're feeling unloved and alone, know that I am with you. You may not always be able to "feel" My presence, but you can trust through the promises that your heavenly Father has made to you that you are truly loved. Your faith doesn't need to see to believe – it just knows and trusts in the promises. Ask the Spirit to help you pray, to lift you up, to comfort you.

Although you may have a battle within of what you know through Truth and what you're experiencing, and although you may be discouraged and depressed, there is hope. Stay focused on all the ways that you have experienced your heavenly Father's love for you in the past, remember My sacrificial love for you that carried Me to the Cross … that same love, that same power will carry, comfort and strengthen you.

Pray that the Spirit will move Truth from your head to your heart and be reminded that you are chosen to live with Me for all eternity … you are truly loved. Commit yourself, your daily thoughts and actions to drawing near to Me, to knowing Me more intimately through God's Word. Keep walking in faith even when you don't feel like it. Draw near to Me … to know Me is to love Me and to know Me is to fully experience true love and true hope.

FAITH THOUGHTS

When you feel empty and alone, it's drawing near to God that will keep you from allowing your feelings of doubt to drive you into disbelief. Set your mind on the things of God. Focus on what is true, noble, right, pure, lovely, admirable, excellent, and worthy of praise.

STRENGTH IN THE SPIRITUAL BATTLE

*But the Lord is faithful, and he will strengthen
you and protect you from the evil one.*
2 THESSALONIANS 3:3

It's when you find yourself lacking peace, consumed with clouds of confusion, facing storm after storm, struggling with temptation in ways you've never considered, and overwhelmed with despair, darkness, and fear, that you can be sure you're being spiritually attacked. See it for what it is. Otherwise, you'll try to fight your battles in ways you're not supposed to … giving into the flesh, instead of living life in the Spirit. And that's not the path of victory.

Spiritual battles are real *and* difficult – you can't see your attacker. And one of the goals of Satan is to keep you from recognizing him; even better, he wants you to think that he doesn't exist. You must be alert, always grounded in God's Word, because the Enemy will cunningly draw you further and further from God, one step at a time, and you won't even realize it's happening. You'll increasingly find your daily struggles intensified to a greater degree than normal. But don't think Jesus isn't aware. He may be resting in the boat, but that's because He knows His position of prayer and praise.

He knows the battle is already won and that's where your faith needs to be as well. You can't do this alone. You don't have this handled. You've got to remain in God's Word and completely rely on the guidance of the Holy Spirit. You'll win this battle because Jesus has overcome the grave and won the war, but you'll win it through only one way … on your knees.

Take Your Stand

JANUARY 27

Finally, be strong in the Lord and in his mighty power. Put on the full armor of God, so that you can take your stand against the devil's schemes.
EPHESIANS 6:10-11

Faith is not passive. Faith stands. And it stands firm in the faithfulness of your heavenly Father and His promises to you. When the attacks of discouragement and despair try to get the best of you, remember the battle you're in, the one that is unseen, so make sure you have every piece of the armor of God on so that you can adequately take your stand against the schemes of the devil.

The devil specifically seeks to destroy the good work of all believers. You are not the exception. So when it feels as though the world is coming against you, know that it is. But there is nothing to fear. I am with you and there is nothing that can come against you that is greater than My power. Your battle is to be upon your knees, praying and fully relying on the Father's resources so that you can stand firm.

Follow My example. It is in using the armor that your heavenly Father has given to you that you will find the key to surviving every spiritual battle. Know that you're not to conquer or lead a charge against your great Enemy, you are called to stand, holding a firm defense, allowing Me to win the ultimate victory. Always remember that you are engaged in a spiritual war, not an earthly one. Keep focused upon Me and I will lead you each step of the way, assuring you with My peace and strength that victory is just ahead.

FAITH THOUGHTS

What is your greatest struggle at this moment? If you look at it with spiritual eyes, can you see that there is a greater battle going on than what it appears? Have you used every piece of armor that God has given you? Remember your battle is to be fought upon your knees.

JANUARY 28

Divine Power

So he said to me, "This is the word of the L<small>ORD</small> to Zerubbabel: 'Not by might nor by power, but by my Spirit,'" says the L<small>ORD</small> Almighty.
ZECHARIAH 4:6

You're not expected to fight your spiritual battles in your own strength, but in Mine. Stop trying to do what only I can do. Most often the battle is in your mind. You become overwhelmed and try to wage war as the world does, but it is the Spirit within you that will remind you that the battle is not yours … it is Mine and you are to stand firm in faith, trusting in the divine power that has conquered the grave.

It is easy to get caught up in the lies of the world, believing what you know through the Word of God is not true. It's these thoughts of deceit, which are the Enemy's greatest tactic, that can create strongholds in your mind that can cause you to live spiritually defeated. The lies become recurring thought patterns and dominate your faith in ways that cause you to make decisions that drive you into deeper darkness.

Use the Word of God that you've been given as your greatest weapon. The Word has power … power to defeat the Enemy and win the war within you. Be aware of what you're thinking, focus on My thoughts. Stand firm in your faith and take every thought and make sure it is Truth. Outside of the truth, you cause Me to become less than what I should be and the Spirit's power in your life will be reduced to less than what it could be. Do not allow yourself to live in anything but the glory I have given you.

FAITH THOUGHTS

What are you thinking and believing? Ask the Holy Spirit to bring your thoughts into submission to Christ. You are fighting a spiritual battle. Remember to fight with prayer, the armor, the Holy Spirit, confession, and worship. Use the Word of God to replace the lies and live in victory.

Cast Down and Defeated

And no wonder, for Satan himself masquerades as an angel of light.
2 CORINTHIANS 11:14

JANUARY 29

You have an enemy. He will accuse and tempt you. He is out to destroy you and distract you from God's purposes for your life. At times you might feel as though the world is coming against you, and you're right, the ruler of this world, Satan, is continually at work, but he is not sovereign … only your heavenly Father is. So, you can rest in faith. You can look to Me for strength and you can be certain the victory is Mine.

The devil likes to remind you of your sin. He wants you to believe that you cannot possibly be loved by your heavenly Father. And it's when the Holy Spirit is convicting you of your sin and allows you to feel the pain of offending God that the devil will tempt you to believe you are separated from God … absent from His presence.

But the Holy Spirit's convicting wounds create the opportunity for Him to bring healing and restoration. The devil's work of accusation can paralyze you, preventing you from keeping your eyes on Me. It's the Spirit that will work within you to remind you of the grace brought about by My sacrifice. You need only to repent and turn to your heavenly Father … He forgives because you are saved by My blood. You can rejoice because the devil is cast down and defeated – simply trust in Me alone.

FAITH THOUGHTS

What is it that has you feeling down and defeated? What is it you think that God cannot do? Trust Him, right now, in this moment, to do it and then look expectantly for His miracles. The devil is defeated – choose to live in the victory that Jesus has given you!

January 30

On Your Knees

" … no weapon forged against you will prevail,
and you will refute every tongue that accuses you.
This is the heritage of the servants of the LORD,
and this is their vindication from me," declares the LORD.
ISAIAH 54:17

The things that are troubling you, the circumstances that are causing you to feel as though you can't go on are defeated by My blood. You have been given the victory. It's your faith in Me that will carry you through the most difficult times of life and help you to realize that there is nothing out of your heavenly Father's hands, nothing that He cannot do, and nothing that He will not do to protect you. There is no weapon used against you that will prevail. Believe what you've been promised.

As you walk with Me, growing stronger in your faith, the devil will do anything and everything in his power to drive you in another direction … to pull you away. Sometimes he'll use situations that seem appealing and sometimes he'll use people, even those you love. But if you will follow My example and use prayer as your weapon, you will never lose a battle. Every time you're tempted, pray. Every time you feel like giving up … pray. If you will remain in Me, I will remain in you and your heavenly Father will not allow the Enemy to have victory over you!

The Holy Spirit will give you the strength and courage you need to resist temptation. Stand firm, stay in God's Word, and praise your heavenly Father for the victory He's given you through My blood.

FAITH THOUGHTS

Your problems are meant to be defeated. Instead of praying for God to take your problems away, pray for Him to give you the strength to conquer them. Whatever problems you're facing, tell them that your God is bigger and then fight your battles upon your knees – God never loses a battle.

Redeemed Thinking

JANUARY 31

We demolish arguments and every pretension that sets itself up against the knowledge of God, and we take captive every thought to make it obedient to Christ.
2 CORINTHIANS 10:5

All too often, the struggles of your life are only taking place in your mind. You tend to rehearse scenarios in your thinking that have not and most likely will not take place. The Holy Spirit will convict you of your thoughts running wild, those thoughts that need to be repented over. And I will pray with you and help you to redeem your thinking, so that you can live in the victory I have given you.

Each and every day you'll be reminded that the greatest battles, many times, are in your mind. I want you to stay positive, thinking pure and lovely thoughts. And although it can be hard to do, the Spirit is within you to strengthen you.

It's your thoughts that lead to your beliefs and lead to your actions. Your thoughts have far too great of an impact on your life and you must guard them … keeping your mind on your heavenly Father's will for your life. You've been told to "destroy arguments and every lofty opinion raised against the knowledge of God and take every thought captive to obey" Me. Choose to believe Truth.

FAITH THOUGHTS

What is it you find yourself continually thinking about? What are those thoughts that do not agree with God's Word? Ask Jesus to take control of those and give you the strength to look at your life through His eyes instead of your own. Keep your mind on Him … His mind is always on you.

FEBRUARY 1

No Good Thing

For the LORD God is a sun and shield; the LORD will give grace and glory; no good thing will He withhold from those who walk uprightly.
PSALM 84:11 (NKJV)

It can be difficult to understand why your heavenly Father would allow pain and suffering. You might think that if you have faith you would be exempt from the troubles of your fallen world, but you are not. Yet through it all, I am with you. What you must understand is that many things will be broken until I return or call you home. Yet, through it all I pour out grace upon you. I paid the price and overcame the grave so that your heavenly Father would forgive your sins and give you grace, provision, and peace. He has given you the Holy Spirit to comfort you and guide you. I am your sun and shield, and I will protect you from the Enemy. I have never left your side and never will.

You may not always understand things in the ways that your heavenly Father does ... His ways are higher and better. My followers could not understand how My death was a part of God's plans for good yet through it, all are offered eternal life. The Holy Spirit will remind you of Truth during the times when you are doubting your faith most. Your troubles will come and go and your trials will eventually end, but My goodness and mercy will follow you all the days of your life. Choose to trust Me when you're not sure you can.

FAITH THOUGHTS

It's your faith that will carry you through your doubt. Call upon the Holy Spirit to fill you with Truth so that you can trust God for the impossible. God is only good – He will never fail you or forsake you. When a storm is raging in your life and in your soul, look to Jesus ... enter into His peace ... and be at rest with Him.

Fullness of Life

FEBRUARY 2

"The thief comes only to steal and kill and destroy; I have come that they may have life, and have it to the full."
JOHN 10:10

At times when you're experiencing struggles and suffering in ways that seem unfair, remember that you are in a spiritual battle. There is an Enemy, and he wants to steal your very life – since he can't separate you from Me, he works to make your life the opposite of abundant. He wants to steal your joy and peace, leaving you living a life that is less than abundant. He'll work to take your eyes off Me and lead you to continually focus on your circumstances so that you'll constantly feel discouraged and defeated.

But I have come to give you life, to the full … an abundant life. I will always give you more than enough. I am the only one that can provide you with a life that is abundant and full. I sacrificed Myself for you, to give you My peace.

Though the Enemy is a thief and a liar, clever and cunning, he comes from darkness and in walking with Me you will have Light. I give you purpose and it's the Holy Spirit that will lead and guide you into your heavenly Father's will. When you remain focused on Me, Truth will cut through the lies and you will live the abundant life you are meant to live.

FAITH THOUGHTS

What is the purpose God has given to you? Whatever it is, do not let the Enemy steal the abundant life you are meant to live through distraction, disappointment, and fear. Resist the devil and he will flee … look to Jesus, the giver of life to the full.

Greater

You, dear children, are from God and have overcome them, because the one who is in you is greater than the one who is in the world.

1 JOHN 4:4

Don't ever forget who I am and what I've done. Whatever you are going through may seem like the end. It may not look like your heavenly Father is in control. It may seem like nothing is getting better and it's getting increasingly worse. But nothing is over, nothing is finished, until I say it is. And when I finish one thing, I'm beginning another. I take you from glory to glory.

You are a child of God – bought by My blood. You are an overcomer, not by your own strength but in Mine … through My Spirit in you. Whatever obstacles you face, they are already overcome. Walk with Me, seek the Holy Spirit to give you strength and direction, keep focused on your faith, the victory has already been given to you!

Don't look back, don't look ahead, just look up and know that your heavenly Father is at work, making a way in the wilderness … your problems might be massive, but I am mighty. You have been made promises of victory and hope. And when you are trusting in the Word of God there is nothing greater.

 ## FAITH THOUGHTS

God holds you and your troubles in the palm of His hand. Your sorrows may be as vast as the heavens … God measures them … He knows. If your burdens are heavy, He will carry them for you. The power of His Spirit within you is greater than anything you are led to overcome.

Pushed Back

They swarmed around me like bees, but they were consumed as quickly as burning thorns; in the name of the Lord I cut them down. I was pushed back and about to fall, but the Lord helped me.
PSALM 118:12-13

Life has a way of throwing difficulties at you that you're not expecting. Each day there might be an obstacle that you face without warning, but it's not about how you will handle it, or what you will do, but how you will rely on Me to do what only I can do … Will you rely on the Holy Spirit to lead, guide, and direct you into your heavenly Father's will? You will never find greater confidence in facing your troubles than what you will find in Me.

My power overcomes any and all obstacles. There is nothing that surprises Me and nothing that I cannot do. All that you must do is trust. I am your ready help in times of trouble. You might get pushed back … but I will keep you from falling.

My Spirit within you will help you to fight your battles when life is hard. Refuse to give up and be determined to stand firm in your faith. I expect you to take control of your life and trust Me. I call you to walk upon the water, not merely drift in the boat. Faith requires action. It's your faith in action that will deepen your relationship with Me and lead you to greater joys that lie ahead.

FAITH THOUGHTS

Do you feel unprepared and ill-equipped for what you're facing … God is not. Ask the Holy Spirit to give you peace to trust God's power within you. You don't have to have all the answers … God does. Simply trust and rest and rely on His help.

February 5

More than Conquerors

No, in all these things we are more than conquerors through him who loved us.
ROMANS 8:37

You are more than your struggles and challenges. Your life of faith is more than just overcoming sin and the challenges in your life. Your heavenly Father has so much more for you than simply rescuing you out of difficult situations.

You are more than a conqueror. And because your heavenly Father loves you, and I sacrificed My life to take away your sins, nothing can separate you from that love. There is more to your faith than overcoming ... I want you to live in the fullness of the Spirit and walk in My love.

I want you to always walk in My love and I want you to always know that My love for you will never change. I am continually working in your life, drawing you nearer to Me, so that you might also walk in My joy.

Don't be surprised by what the Enemy throws at you. Be ready in faith and fight the battle upon your knees. Recognize your weakness and trust in My strength. I will give you mercy and grace to endure. There is nothing to fear. I am here.

FAITH THOUGHTS

What are you focused on? Is your vision centered around your problems and challenges or God's love for you? Seek His promises to you, find strength through His Spirit that lives in you and be determined to live in the joy and victory you've been given by Christ.

Expect to Win

The wicked plot against the righteous and gnash their teeth at them; but the LORD laughs at the wicked, for he knows their day is coming.
PSALM 37:12-13

I want you to start expecting your heavenly Father to provide for you in all the ways you need Him to. Live by My example, knowing that if He cares for the sparrows, He will care for you, too. You might only have a little, but it will be enough. You may stumble, but I will keep you from falling. You might struggle, but you will not fail. There will be times when you must lose things in order to make room for what your heavenly Father has for you. Ask the Holy Spirit to help you to be content.

There will be times in life, especially in raging storms, where you will believe that all is lost, that you've been wronged and there is no hope. But you have the promises to focus upon, to trust in, to overcome the doubt and renew your mind. It's in trusting in your heavenly Father's faithfulness to His word that shapes your thinking in every situation so that you can respond in a way that is righteous, even as you are wronged and treated unfairly.

I have shown you not to respond to evil with evil … instead to overcome evil with good. The battle is Mine, simply submit to My authority, be content and do what is right as you are led by the Spirit. Though it may seem that you are losing and others are winning, I have already secured your victory … live in that joy.

FAITH THOUGHTS

Does it feel like you're losing the battle in life? Does it appear like the Enemy has won? Know that those feelings and thoughts are lies. God has promised you the victory. He does not lie. It is up to you to choose to walk in His truth, knowing that what lies ahead is His justice … He has promised joy ahead!

FEBRUARY 7

Through the Fire

"When you pass through the waters, I will be with you; and when you pass through the rivers, they will not sweep over you. When you walk through the fire, you will not be burned; the flames will not set you ablaze."
ISAIAH 43:2

There is one thing you should never forget: I am with you. There is nothing to fear. This journey of life is more than what it appears to be on the surface. As I take you from glory to glory, there will be troubles that seem like nothing more than evidence for your doubt, but they will strengthen you. It's the Holy Spirit that is working in and through you to transform your heart and perfect your faith.

Know that there will be deep waters in which you will feel as though you're going under and rivers that will threaten to drown you … there will be fires that you must walk through … I am with you to keep you from being burned. You can walk confidently in faith through whatever it is you must face because I am with you to protect you.

Try to look at your troubles as challenges. Look at them as opportunities to draw near to Me and to grow your faith. You will still experience the fear, anger, and everything in between, but keep your eyes on Me … I will calm the storm within you.

FAITH THOUGHTS

There is nothing you are going through that God is not aware of. It might seem as though He is completely unaware, but He cares for every sparrow and He will care for you in every way that you need Him too. Look at your challenges in life right now as an opportunity to declare your trust and faith in Him.

On Guard

No temptation has overtaken you except what is common to mankind. And God is faithful; he will not let you be tempted beyond what you can bear. But when you are tempted, he will also provide a way out so that you can endure it.
1 CORINTHIANS 10:13

The Enemy can catch you unaware. He'll show up at times and in ways you never expected. In fact, it will be at times and in ways you *least* expected. Each and every moment you can fall into thinking you're stronger or better than temptations ... keep your guard. Pray your way through each day and realize that your heavenly Father is faithful and He will not allow any temptation to come your way that is too great for you to resist. I am with you, the Holy Spirit living in you, to give you the strength to bear up under the pull of sin.

Know that you will experience struggles that are far too much for you. And your heavenly Father knows that there will be trials, difficulties, grief and pain, that are more than you can bear.

It's all about learning to rely on My strength and power and not your own. I can do what you cannot. These difficulties are used for good to drive you to Me. You've never been promised that you will not have to endure trials and tribulations, I've promised you the opposite. In this world you will have troubles, but I hold out My hand and ask you to come with Me and walk upon the water.

FAITH THOUGHTS

What are you facing right now that you're just not sure you can handle? Are you trying too hard, instead of trusting with child-like faith? In this moment, Jesus is with you, the Holy Spirit is in you, to help you rise up in faith and live fully in the joy of standing your ground against the Enemy. God is faithful in all ways and at all times.

FEBRUARY 9

Nothing to Fear

Do not be afraid of them; the LORD your God himself will fight for you.
DEUTERONOMY 3:22

What you need to remember is that your heavenly Father has promised to defeat all the spiritual giants in your life. I have promised to be with you every step of your journey as you trust in your Father's Word. You must only obey His commands and learn to be content in your calling. I have sacrificed to give you the triumphant and fruitful life as you abide in Me and I in you. This journey of faith through life is about you learning to depend on Me and live humbly, dying to yourself and living for Me.

Though you will face obstacles in life, you must remember how deeply your heavenly Father cares for you. He hears your every cry for help and gives you the grace to stand firm in your faith. Look to Me, learn from Me, and depend on your heavenly Father's love and faithfulness towards you as you pass through deep waters.

It is in My strength that you are able to battle your Enemy. It is in Me alone that you can live a victorious life. There is no need for you to be shaken, your fear does not stand a chance against the love that has been poured out through My blood.

FAITH THOUGHTS

Instead of focusing on all the obstacles in your life, look to Jesus as your strength. It's His love for you that has brought you this far and will carry you until the day you see Him face to face. When you are tempted to fear, stand firm in faith and lean upon the grace that God continually pours out on you.

The Struggle

FEBRUARY 10

Our struggle is not against flesh and blood, but against the rulers, against the authorities, against the powers of this dark world and against the spiritual forces of evil in the heavenly realms.
EPHESIANS 6:12

Whether you realize it or not, you are in a personal battle with the forces of darkness every single day. The Enemy is after you, trying to cause you to doubt God's love and purposes for you. You should expect the attacks which push you toward pride, anger, lust, drunkenness and those things that are opposite of God's best for your life. Your struggle is supernatural, so your weapons must also be. Live by My example, stand fully clothed in the armor of God, so that you will be able to hold your ground against your adversary. There will be times when there is so much coming against you that standing your ground in faith is all you can do. And that's all you're told to do ... stand. Don't become so overwhelmed by the storms of life that you forget where you are ... in the boat with Me.

Ask the Holy Spirit to keep you focused on what God intends for you to be focused on. Don't get sidetracked or distracted by the Enemy. I am in you and you are in Me and I will not allow your faith to be shipwrecked. You will defeat the Enemy with the spiritual weapons you're given ... God's Word and prayer. I am your righteousness, I am your peace. I have given you victory through faith and triumphed over Satan through My death and resurrection. Stand firm in the battles, remain in My peace and watch what I will do.

FAITH THOUGHTS

Are you tempted to fight your battles in ways that are contrary to the way God has instructed you to? Are you trying to do it all on your own? You've already been assured the victory. Right now is the time to stand firm in your faith and remain in Jesus' peace. Don't be moved.

GOD'S PRESENCE WHEN YOU FEEL ALONE

Come near to God and he will come near to you.
JAMES 4:8

When waves of troubles come crashing in on you, it can seem as though God has completely abandoned you. You pray, but nothing happens. You look for a miracle and there are none. There is only silence and emptiness, and desperation. And it's your faith and doubt that collide in such a way that you're not sure you can keep believing through the pain and suffering. It's just too much. Besides, how could a God of love and mercy allow such emptiness. It's simple … so He can fill you.

God is always in the process of refining you, transforming your heart and molding you into the image of Christ. And there are growing pains. You will go through circumstances that you're not sure you can handle. You'll face the unthinkable and come through it all realizing that God is making your faith unbreakable.

Loneliness has its purposes. God uses it to get you alone so that you can hear Him speak to you more clearly. In loneliness, He has your undivided attention. Throughout the Gospels you'll find that Jesus went away to a quiet place to be alone with God. These were times when Jesus sought solitude so that He could seek the Father's will for His life. It's loneliness that can be of great benefit if you are driven closer to God in order to be given greater wisdom and strength. It's your loneliness that tests and increases your patience. And it's your deficiencies and insecurities that are revealed, so that the Spirit can go to work strengthening your character.

There's no reason to avoid being alone. Use those times of drawing nearer to God … but also realize the truth … you are never alone. Jesus has promised He is with you always.

With You

*"So do not fear, for I am with you; do not be dismayed,
for I am your God. I will strengthen you and help you;
I will uphold you with my righteous right hand."*
ISAIAH 41:10

As you face the daily struggles of life, I should be your source of strength. I am your anchor when the stormy seas are raging. Your heavenly Father has promised to provide you with strength, help, and protection. Meditate upon His promises, day and night. Your Enemy will try to distract you through subtle and successful traps. And he knows that fear will threaten your faith. He works diligently to make your trials and troubles your focus. It's once your attention is diverted from God that he knows your "humanness" will take over. You'll be tempted to give up on prayer and worship and give in to anxiety and doubt.

I know that as the storm rages, it's hard to keep focused on Me. You want to prevent your worst fears from coming true. And in times where the waves seem to be crashing in on you, you find yourself realizing how powerless and helpless you are, instead of becoming more confident and standing firm in the promises your heavenly Father has made to you. Now is the time to focus upon Me and the peace I give you and remain steady in your faith because I am with you … always.

FAITH THOUGHTS

What is it that is distracting you from praying, praising, and worshiping God? Whatever it is, ask the Holy Spirit to fill you with peace and strength through your overwhelming circumstances. There is nothing God won't do. No good thing will He withhold from you. Remember His faithfulness in the past and count on it now and in your future. He is with you.

FEBRUARY 12

Always There

Where can I go from your Spirit? Where can I flee from your presence? If I rise on the wings of the dawn, if I settle on the far side of the sea, even there your hand will guide me, your right hand will hold me fast.
PSALM 139:7-10

You may think that you're alone, but you are not. There is nowhere you can go where I am not there. You can try to be alone ... but you are not. Even Jonah thought he could hide from God ... in the bottom of a ship, in the midst of a huge storm, sound asleep, but God saw him. And just as the heavenly Father saw Jonah, He sees you. He knows where you are and where you're going. And He will take care of you through every storm of life.

Your heavenly Father does not sleep or slumber and I know what you are facing. I see you and I am with you. When you are in distress, when you can't sleep, when your heart is heavy and when you face troubles on every side, the Spirit is with you to comfort you. The Spirit prays for you in words that you cannot express.

Your heavenly Father hears your crying and bottles each tear. And His love heals all wounds. Each and every moment you should turn your heart over to your heavenly Father and know that I am your faithful friend. It is the Spirit that will strengthen and guide you, no matter how difficult the situation, there is nothing too difficult for Me. As you face each struggle, come before your heavenly Father's throne of grace and ask Him to filter your desires through His divine will.

FAITH THOUGHTS

When you need help, but your soul wants to hide in the hurt ... ask God to heal you, to replace your anger with forgiveness ... replace doubt with trust and fear with courage. Ask the Spirit to transform your mind and give you a heart like God's. Draw near to God and He will draw near to you. He's promised to.

Every Day

"As I was with Moses, so I will be with you; I will never leave you nor forsake you. Be strong and courageous, because you will lead these people to inherit the land I swore to their ancestors to give them."
JOSHUA 1:5-6

It may sometimes feel like there are days when I am with you and others when I'm not, but I am with you every day. In every moment of your life, in every area of your life, I am there. There will always be obstacles in life, but I'm with you to take you around them … or through them. Most often those obstacles will seem insurmountable and the weight of them will feel like they are too much to bear, but remember I am the one to carry your burdens, you were never meant to travel this journey of faith alone.

Don't try to push your way through or manipulate your way around your obstacles while giving in to hopelessness. Don't give up. Keep leaning on Me and trusting in Me to bring about the miracles in the moments you most need them. There is nothing you're facing that has not been approved by your heavenly Father. If He is allowing it, it is with good purpose. It's fear and worry that will reveal your doubts and you must decide to focus on Me instead of your problems.

Don't allow your disbelief to distract you from My power and presence. Don't walk away or give up and miss the blessings your heavenly Father has in store for you. My job is to remove whatever hinders you from following Me and your job is to follow Me and obey My commands and have faith in Me every single day.

FAITH THOUGHTS

Decide that today you will see Jesus with you in every moment. Whatever it is you're doing, allow your faith to show you that He is truly with you, beside you, helping you to have strength in the weakest of moments. Jesus is all you need … every day.

FEBRUARY 14

Strong

"Be strong and courageous. Do not be afraid or terrified because of them, for the LORD your God goes with you; he will never leave you nor forsake you."
DEUTERONOMY 31:6

Following God's plans for your life, trusting in His will, will mean stepping into the unknown. He will require you to trust Him in ways you never thought you could. It will always mean getting out of the boat and walking upon the water, being confident in My leading you and having faith even though you're unsure of what lies ahead.

There will be times in your life when you will realize that there is no other way out or through than with a miracle from Me. When I will receive all the glory, you can know with full certainty that you are living in your heavenly Father's will for you. It will cause you to feel uncertain, possibly afraid and overwhelmed, but the Spirit is within you to give you the strength and courage you need to take the very next step of faith in your weakest moment and darkest nights.

I will be your strength when you are weak. So, let go of trying to control what you can't and have courage in the face of your fears to trust that I go before you and will make a way. Listen to the still small voice inside of you and live joyfully in the hope I have given to you.

 FAITH THOUGHTS

If you are placing your hope in God, hope is never gone. There is nothing He can't do and there are no limits to His miracles. If you are uncertain of your future, fearful of what tomorrow holds, find your strength in God's promises to you ... they are full of His goodness and guaranteed by His faithfulness.

Never Forsaken

FEBRUARY 15

Though my father and mother forsake me,
the LORD will receive me.
PSALM 27:10

The world might abandon you, leave you to your struggles, without help and all alone, but I never will. Though others might reject you, even those that claim to love you, I never will. You are Mine and I am yours. Your name is written upon your heavenly Father's hands. You have been chosen to glorify the Father. And He has promised He will never leave you nor forsake you. Call upon Me in the day of trouble and I will rescue you.

When your faith is falling short, and your highest hopes and extravagantly bold expectations are trampled on by others, be secure in the hope and acceptance that you have in Me. Come to Me, the Living Stone, and remember when you are rejected by men you are chosen by Me and precious to Me in every way.

Rise up in the strength of the Spirit and set your faith on the foundation of your heavenly Father's promises to you. Ask the Spirit to open your heart and give you a vision of the beautiful gift of life you've been given and ask Him to reveal God's plans for you, step by step. Make the decision to follow the path that is set before you.

FAITH THOUGHTS

Are you feeling rejected, feeling as though you continually fall short of the expectations that others have of you? Maybe you're even feeling as though you're falling short of your own expectations and being consumed by the guilt of disappointing God ... come to Jesus. He's waiting for you to look to Him, to lean on Him, and to allow Him to lift you up on the wings of eagles.

FEBRUARY 16

Until the End

" ... teaching them to obey everything I have commanded you. And surely I am with you always, to the very end of the age."
MATTHEW 28:20

I've given you a mission, marching orders, until the end of time. There will be great joy in the saving of souls, the forgiveness of sins, and seeing the coldest heart opened to the message of My love and mercy. But, you will also endure rejection. The world will turn against you because you love Me. Yet, you must follow My example, in the midst of My suffering and death, showing others that the core of God's love shows us the power of forgiveness and the healing that it brings.

Through it all, through your journey of life and faith, I know your weaknesses, I know your doubt and fears, but I know your heart, too. I know what you need to fulfill your heavenly Father's purposes for your life.

Your mission, your Father's plan for you will never be easy, which is why I made the promise that I am with you to the end of time. You can believe and have hope in My promise. When you willingly follow Me, I am with you. You might stumble or fall, but I will never abandon you. I am faithfully by your side and always ready to enfold you in My grace and loving embrace.

FAITH THOUGHTS

In your most desperate times, Jesus is with you. Ask the Spirit to strengthen your faith. And in those times when you experience contentment and joy, know that it is a gift from God. Praise Him through the pain and worship Him in your worry, and run into the arms of Jesus.

Taken In

FEBRUARY 17

*A father to the fatherless, a defender of widows,
is God in his holy dwelling. God sets the lonely in families,
he leads out the prisoners with singing;
but the rebellious live in a sun-scorched land.*
PSALM 68:5-6

You may feel weak and forgotten, but you are not. When you're certain no one understands you, I do. I know that when you are feeling hopeless and depressed your first instinct might be to push Me away, but I am with you to teach you the greatest lessons of faith during the most difficult times. When your loneliness is telling you to give up and you reach out for Me instead, you will find that I am your closest friend and with you always.

Know that there is no barrier between you and your heavenly Father. I have made a way for you to be in right relationship with Him, and He is intimately concerned about every detail that concerns you. I have given you eternal hope and My extravagant love is made to consume you each and every moment of your life.

You can confidently look to your heavenly Father for all of your needs, and you can depend upon Him fully for protection and provision. Even if everyone else abandons you, I never will.

FAITH THOUGHTS

Are you feeling abandoned? Are you tempted to give up because you feel as though you have no support? Look to God, in this moment, and realize that not only is God with you, but He is for you and there is absolutely nothing that He can't do.

FEBRUARY 18

Never Forgotten

"Can a mother forget the baby at her breast and have no compassion on the child she has borne? Though she may forget, I will not forget you!"
ISAIAH 49:15

It's when you're hurting, lonely and afraid, overwhelmed by circumstances that are beyond your control, that you turn from Me and look for peace in all the ways and places you'll never find it. You need to run to Me and pour out your heart, instead of rushing to the phone to find help that will never provide you with what you truly need. No one knows the intricate plans that your heavenly Father has for your life, no one on earth can lead and guide you like I can into true joy. You're searching where you shouldn't. You need only look to Me.

You might feel like your heavenly Father is delaying His answers to your prayers and ignoring your cries for help, but He is not. As much as you try to escape the inner despair of your soul, there may be times when you are supposed to sit in the moment and experience the pain.

All of the answers to your questions, the help you so desperately need is found in the victory I've given you. You are not forgotten and are never abandoned, no matter how you feel. Do not carry the unnecessary burdens of guilt, fear, loneliness, anxiety and chaos simply because you're refusing to rest in Me and rely on Me. Turn to the precious promises your heavenly Father has given you.

FAITH THOUGHTS

You are carrying burdens you shouldn't be carrying. Jesus has asked you to lay your burdens down. You need rest. Your soul needs peace. Jesus is with you, the Spirit is within you and your heavenly Father is holding you.

The Promise

"I will not leave you as orphans; I will come to you."
JOHN 14:18

Regardless of the circumstances of your life, desperation or even death, you will never be left alone. I am with you always. Though I left this world, I sent the Spirit to dwell in you so that you would never be without Me. Day after day, moment after uncertain moment, regardless of what is happening in your life that is My promise to you … I will never leave you – you are never alone.

When I left this world and sent you the Holy Spirit, I sent you a Helper, to be with you forever. Even though I am no longer physically present, I would be with you through the presence of My Spirit. You have a leader, guide, teacher, and comforter. When you need direction, the Spirit will guide you with Truth. When you are hurting and sure that you will not make it through the pain, the Spirit will comfort you. When you feel abandoned, like no one cares and no one is there, the Spirit will fill you with My love and consume you with My peace. I am all you need … that is My promise.

FAITH THOUGHTS

God has made so many promises to you … are you relying on them and looking to Him for His faithfulness? No matter what you are facing, there is a promise He has made that will bring you peace and give you strength as you wait upon His miracles.

FEBRUARY 20

Not Alone

"Never will I leave you; never will I forsake you."
HEBREWS 13:5

When you're feeling heartbroken, worried about your circumstances, holding on to unknowns and unable to let go of your burdens, remember that I have promised that you do not need to fear. Your heavenly Father has assured you that He will protect you and save you. You are safe. There is nothing for you to fear. Nothing and no one in this world can harm you. Your worries are not worthy of your time. You were meant to live in love and peace and joy. Whatever troubles are holding you captive, lay them at My feet.

Always remember that you have been given eternal life and everything in the world is temporary. You have an inheritance in heaven that can never be taken from you. Though your present trials and tribulations can be overwhelming, and it can be difficult to remain hopeful, remember that you've been promised and given the victory.

Throughout your life, most of your misery will come from feeling unloved. And in the midst of adversity, you may feel as though your heavenly Father has withdrawn His love for you. But you have been promised that will never happen. Not even for a moment. When no one else stands by you, when everyone else walks away, I stand by your side … just as I stood for you at the Cross.

FAITH THOUGHTS

The presence of Jesus in your life far outweighs any need you have or suffering in this life. In moments when you simply can't breathe because of the burdens that are weighing down on you, remember that with Jesus, the worst place imaginable becomes the best place.

Precious Thoughts

FEBRUARY 21

How precious to me are your thoughts, God!
How vast is the sum of them!
PSALM 139:17

I know all about you. Be comforted that I am always thinking about you. You are the focus of My thoughts and attention. It will bring you joy and peace to continually focus your thoughts and attention on Me. Each and every moment, all that concerns you is flowing through My heart. I am constantly drawing you nearer through the good and the bad to build a personal relationship with you ... one in which you can continually rely and constantly trust.

You are never alone. And My plans to help you become all your heavenly Father has created you to be is My constant focus ... to prosper you and give you hope. Allow Me to do My work in you in order that you might reflect My image.

Your heavenly Father created you, numbered your days, and never stops thinking about you. They are not thoughts of condemnation and judgment, but thoughts of absolute love and adoration. His thoughts toward you are precious and they outnumber the grains of sand on the seashore.

So, when you're feeling alone, like no one cares, know that I do and your heavenly Father holds you in the palms of His hands. You are safe, you are loved and you are precious in His sight.

FAITH THOUGHTS

With every thought you have throughout your day, God is thinking thoughts about you that outnumber the grains of sand on the seashore. Focus on the truth that God loves you and is continually doing a work in and through you to not only accomplish His purposes, but also to give you a future and a hope.

His Own

FEBRUARY 22

For the sake of his great name the LORD will not reject his people, because the LORD was pleased to make you his own.
1 SAMUEL 12:22

You were created on purpose for a purpose, your heavenly Father's purpose. And I have redeemed you through My love, grace has saved you and you belong to Me. Each and every moment of your life, through the troubles and triumphs, the Spirit is working in you to take every thought captive, to teach your heart to live by Truth, and to draw you nearer to Me.

When you experience loneliness, when you're certain that no one cares, I do. I've promised to always be with you and your heavenly Father has promised you provision and protection.

When you're feeling abandoned, look to the promises made to you. Trust the eternal glories that have been prepared for you in heaven and rest in the love and grace that is continually poured out upon you.

And in your times of doubt, when you are faithless, remember that your heavenly Father remains faithful. You can completely trust that no eye has seen, nor ear heard, neither have entered into the heart of man, the things which God has prepared for them who love Him. My compassions never cease, My love never fails. I have ransomed you. You are Mine.

FAITH THOUGHTS

Don't allow your feelings to diminish your faith. Just because you feel alone doesn't mean you are. If Jesus is with you always and He has ransomed you, then you are never alone and you are His. No matter who you are or what you've done, you can always come to Jesus.

Just Call

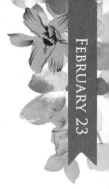

FEBRUARY 23

The LORD is near to all who call on him, to all who call on him in truth. He fulfills the desires of those who fear him; he hears their cry and saves them.
PSALM 145:18-19

You need to know that you are saved. There is nothing to fear. Nothing. Every cry for help is heard and every prayer is answered. Things may not always happen in the timing you would like or in the way you'd like, but your heavenly Father's plans are always better. Your prayers should reflect My character and they should always take into account your heavenly Father's will for you. Pray the promises that have been made to you. Draw near to Me and I will draw near to you.

It is in praying through the Word that you will find your prayers answered and always feel My presence more and more. I draw near to you as you meditate on the Word of God, allowing it to permeate your mind and heart. As you rely on the promises, you will grow in your relationship with Me and find yourself being refreshed and renewed by the Spirit.

Your heavenly Father is looking for you to worship Him in spirit and in truth. You can trust Him completely. There is no reason to doubt or despair. All you need to do is call My name … you'll always find I am right here with you, at all times and in all ways.

FAITH THOUGHTS

In this moment, praise God for always being with you. Ask Him to help you to lay aside selfish needs and desires and to pray in a way that reflects His nature and His will. Ask that He would teach you, correct you, guide you, and inspire you, as He continually draws you closer to Himself.

HELP WHEN YOU'RE HURTING

You will increase my honor and comfort me once more.
PSALM 71:21

Life is hard. And you will hurt. But you will also be comforted. When you're experiencing distress, remembering previous distresses filled with grief or regrets, you can become discouraged. When facing each new day's troubles and worries, and focusing too much on the future in which you haven't received grace for yet, you can suddenly find yourself in deep despair, unable to find your way out. God is with you to comfort you. In His mercy and love, He is eager to provide comfort in any and all circumstances. Whatever you're facing, He knows, and He wants to be your source of peace and happiness.

When you're hurting and you run to the temporary things of the world, they will only bring temporary comfort. But when you turn to God, there is healing from the inside out. It's through Jesus that you can receive true freedom from guilt and find true hope for your future. It's the Spirit within you that will strengthen your heart for the trials that will sanctify your soul. It's the Word of God that will cause you to be fearless in unexpected troubles.

No matter what you face, you can know that you will be delivered. It's through trusting in God's promises that you can have quiet confidence when troubles come. It's when you learn to be wholly satisfied in God, trusting in Him completely, relying on Him for His care and comfort that you will find your faith renewed and refreshed … when you seek the Lord, you will find Him a ready help in times of trouble.

Nothing But Grace

FEBRUARY 24

Turn to me and be gracious to me,
for I am lonely and afflicted.
PSALM 25:16

You might be surrounded by external and internal afflictions, but never forget that I am with you. My miracles are always waiting to be revealed in your life. Look for them. You may struggle with shame, loneliness, or a troubled heart … don't engage with your feelings, stay focused upon your faith in Me and the grace that is continually poured out into your life by your heavenly Father. And rely on Me. If you're relying on yourself or others to lead, guide, and direct you, depending on your own strength instead of Mine, you'll create more afflictions for yourself.

Put your trust in Me. It's by hoping in Me that you will find your heavenly Father's faithfulness to His promises to you and you'll experience the Spirit working within you to bring peace into your heart.

Whatever you're facing, face it in faith and resist the temptation to avoid it … refuse to lash out or try to fix it on your own. Don't allow bitterness to take root, or unforgiveness to rob you of your joy. This moment is the moment to break your cycle of suffering. It's time to lay down your pride, humble yourself at My feet and live in the victory I died to give you.

FAITH THOUGHTS

It's easy to just give in to feelings of despair when the weight of your world is on your shoulders, but you were never meant to live this life in your own strength. Seek God's guidance on how to handle your situations. Make the decision to put your hope in Him alone, to believe that He knows what He's doing.

FEBRUARY 25

Lifted Up

Humble yourselves, therefore, under God's mighty hand, that he may lift you up in due time.
1 PETER 5:6

Each and every day you have a choice: the choice to humble yourself. It may seem like you're giving in and giving up, surrendering in the battle, and you are. You're turning the battle over to Me, the One who gives you the victory. Things won't always make sense, especially in the moment, but right now you need to submit to Me and put all of your anxieties into My hands.

Every single day, I carry you through the day. But all too often, you insist on carrying your troubles in life instead of laying them down at the foot of My cross. Your humility is essential to your faith and it is what ultimately draws you nearer to Me and brings about the miracles in your life.

When you lay it down, you will be lifted up. Let go of what you're holding on to … what was, what expectations you have and embrace what's next. Whenever your heart begins to feel anxious about the future, speak Truth into it by asking what exactly can nullify your heavenly Father's promises to you. If He's promised to prosper you and give you a future and a hope, do not lift your anxiety above Truth. Continually humble yourself in peace and joy and trust in the love that has been poured out through My blood.

FAITH THOUGHTS

Choose right now to surrender. Don't allow your despair to tempt you to lift your problems above the promises God has made to you. If there is nothing He can't do, then lay the very thing you think He can't do at His feet … and then wait expectantly for His miracle. It's coming … in due time.

Always Listening

FEBRUARY 26

For he has not despised or scorned the suffering of the afflicted one; he has not hidden his face from him but has listened to his cry for help.
PSALM 22:24

Your prayers are heard – every single one of them – the ones whispered in praise, adoration, and joy, and the ones shouted in anger, pain, and despair. Not a tear goes unnoticed, all of them are collected in your heavenly Father's bottle. Nothing is wasted and your heavenly Father uses it all. You have the Spirit who prays on your behalf, sitting at the throne of God … interceding for you in ways you know you need Him to and in ways that you do not. Your heavenly Father has written your life from beginning to end and I am the author and perfecter of your faith.

You have been given a confidence in knowing that I truly understand your suffering and grief because I, too, have experienced it. I am the only one you can truly come to for help. For a moment, I experienced the total abandonment of God, so that you will never have to know the depths of that pain and loneliness.

It is because of My sacrifice that you are blessed with the Spirit's constant presence. Pray that you will have faith to trust Me regardless of your circumstances, knowing that I understand your suffering and the Spirit is always interceding for you.

FAITH THOUGHTS

Is there something you've been praying about and it seems as though God is ignoring you? The truth is that He listens continually and He is already at work in your circumstances. It's when you feel He is being silent that He is trusting you more than you're trusting Him … He knows the faith He's given you and He is strengthening it in your weakness.

FEBRUARY 27

Through the Suffering

For no one is cast off by the Lord forever.
Though he brings grief, he will show compassion,
so great is his unfailing love.
LAMENTATIONS 3:31-32

There is hope … even in your suffering. You may not be able to see it or sense it in any way, but when your hope is in Me, there is always hope because I am eternal. It is through the Word, the promises, that you are assured of that hope and have the evidence that your heavenly Father's faithfulness to fulfill His promises has never failed. He will never fail you. His love for you is abundant and faithful at all times, bringing joy from your pain.

There will be times when you are going through painful emotions and you are in the valley of suffering that feels as though it will never end. Rely on Me and the promises made to you to give you the strength to have faith even when your suffering continues for months or even years.

I am with you through it all. Though you may feel you can't go on, you can in My strength. You have hope in Me. You have been accepted and saved by My sacrifice and it's My life, death, and resurrection that is to remind you that you may endure pain and suffering on this earth, but it will not last forever.

Be with Me, in the back of the boat, and rest. Rest in the hope that your suffering and troubles will not last forever. Rest in the truth that the steadfast love of your heavenly Father endures and He will deliver you.

FAITH THOUGHTS

In what ways are you desperate for God? If you need reassurance of His love and faithfulness, turn to His promises. Rely on the hope of Jesus and seek the Spirit to strengthen your faith through your questions that remain unanswered and your suffering that seems endless. There is truly wonderful joy ahead – that is God's promise to you.

Tears in a Bottle

FEBRUARY 28

*Record my misery; list my tears on your scroll –
are they not in your record?*
PSALM 56:8

My love and mercy are all consuming and never failing. I am with you and your heavenly Father not only knows your sadness and pain, your weariness and wanderings, but He collects every tear that falls. Every single teardrop that you have cried, He holds in the palms of His hands, they are recorded in His book for all eternity. And one day, every one of your tears will be wiped away, there will be no more pain and suffering, no more crying, and the joys to come will last forever.

Sometimes there are no words, and the Spirit will communicate your heart to the Father. My gift to you, the Spirit, is a gift that will carry you through until you see Me face to face. The Spirit is your guide on this journey, to lead you in the way that you should go … into paths of righteousness. And know this: following Me will not be easy, but you will have all you need and more.

You were created to love and worship your heavenly Father with all your heart, mind, soul, and strength. Your emotions are a part of your intense devotion to Me. You were created to be emotional, so in your most intense moments, whether despair or great joy, tears will come. I, too, wept. I understand. Know that your heavenly Father's bottle of your tears also holds the promise of His blessings.

FAITH THOUGHTS

When you're crying out to God, know that He holds every tear. No one else may acknowledge or understand your pain, but God does. Accept His love and compassion and allow yourself to feel His warm embrace. You can trust your tears to God.

MARCH 1

All Things

And we know that in all things God works for the good of those who love him, who have been called according to his purpose.
ROMANS 8:28

When you've been promised that your heavenly Father works all things for good, it may be easy to allow doubt to question your faith because it is clear that all things are not good. I've promised you that in this world you will have trouble because all have sinned and fallen short of God's glory. But in His greatness, through My resurrection, all things can be made new. In your heavenly Father's wisdom and love, anything that has fallen apart in your life can be put back together and used for good.

You can have peace in Me. I am your reminder that God always has a redemptive plan and purpose. Every situation in your life is being used for good, to bring about your heavenly Father's glory. Because of Me you are free of God's judgment and condemnation. You have been ransomed from death and destruction. I have won the victory by grace through your faith in Me.

You may have to face difficulties and dangers, and you might have pain, suffering, and disappointments, but I have reminded you that you have the unfailing love of your heavenly Father through My blood that has overcome sin, the world, the Enemy, and every single circumstance that tries to defeat you. And through it all, you are being transformed, conformed to My image and there is nothing that can compare to the glory that will come from that good work.

FAITH THOUGHTS

Whatever it is you're struggling with at this moment, thank God that He is in the process of using it all for good. Ask the Spirit to open your eyes to what God is doing in your life and to fill you with hope and strength as you are transformed into the image of Christ.

What Comes

MARCH 2

*... weeping may stay for the night,
but rejoicing comes in the morning.*
PSALM 30:5

Whatever happens in this life is only a shadow of the life to come ... heaven ... where there will be no more weeping and rejoicing will be complete. If you are in a place in life where you're consumed with despair, let Me illuminate your darkness with My Light. I am with you in the storm, throughout the darkest night. Know that life will not be perfect or free of pain and struggle, but in the midst of any pain, suffering, uncertainty and fear, I am always with you and your heavenly Father is preparing a miracle that will make all of the troubles of this earth grow strangely dim, in the Light of My glory and grace.

In this moment, you may not be able to see light through the hopelessness, discouragement, and afflictions, but My Light will come from within, through the Spirit. And your heavenly Father has promised that you will be blessed if you will trust in Him and make Him your hope and confidence.

If you will trust, you will be like a tree planted along a riverbank with roots that reach into deep water ... not bothered by heat or worried by any drought. You will stay green and never stop producing fruit. And as your faith strengthens through your times of trusting, when nothing is happening, when prayers go seemingly unanswered, your heavenly Father is working to turn your mourning into dancing, your sorrows into joy.

Faith Thoughts

When troubles seem to never end, it's easy to allow doubt to get the best of you. You can grow weary in the waiting and unable to find the strength to take even just one more step of faith. But your focus should be on the face of Jesus – on His glory and grace. Don't take your eyes off Him. You're assured through God's promises that joy is coming.

MARCH 3

In A Little While

"So with you: Now is your time of grief, but I will see you again and you will rejoice, and no one will take away your joy."
JOHN 16:22

I came so that you might have peace, so that you would be full of joy, even in the midst of troubles. You can live with joy by keeping your confident hope in Me and not looking to the world to fulfill you ... when only I truly can.

I want you to have an eternal perspective – keeping your eyes off earthly things and staying focused upon heaven. Your real joy will come from pointing others to Me. As long as you are following Me, as long as you are on this earth, you will have troubles. You will still face hardships and disappointments and keeping your joy will not always be easy, but true joy comes from trusting in Me and that joy can never truly be taken from you.

You've been given resurrection hope. I have risen and so will you. There is great joy in knowing that you are saved and will live for all eternity. I have chosen you. If you will find your joy in Me, you will be freed to live for Me. When your joy and satisfaction are in Me then nothing will be able to stop you and you will lack nothing. I'm calling you to lay down your life, to follow Me and lead others to Me. Let them come to know Me through your joy that can only be found in Me.

FAITH THOUGHTS

As you struggle through your doubts and fear, know that if you are trusting in Jesus, no one or nothing can take away your joy. It's still within you, even in the darkest days and hardest nights. Call on the Spirit when you feel alone and unloved, He will help you when you're hurting ... He will be your comfort and strength.

Constant Comfort

MARCH 4

Praise be to the God and Father of our Lord Jesus Christ, the Father of compassion and the God of all comfort, who comforts us in all our troubles, so that we can comfort those in any trouble with the comfort we ourselves receive from God.
2 CORINTHIANS 1:3-4

I have given you the gift of the Spirit to be with you through difficult times, to encourage you when you're discouraged and to strengthen you in times of weakness and suffering. Suffering is a part of living, but the Spirit will constantly comfort you through every moment when your pain goes deeper than you ever thought it could or should.

Your faith in Me does not take away your problems … it takes you through them. And know that there is nothing too difficult for God. Nothing. So, whatever storm you're facing, whatever circumstances are causing you to doubt your heavenly Father's ability to perform a miracle, that's where He will show up – unexpectedly, suddenly, right when you're sure He won't.

It's the Spirit that will enable you to press on, when you're sure you can't. There's no limit to the power of God, so don't allow your doubt to convince your faith that there is. In your weakness, dwell in the shelter of the Most High and rest in the shadow of the Almighty. You have a refuge and a fortress, a heavenly Father in whom you must trust … He is faithful.

FAITH THOUGHTS

Whether you realize it or not, God's arms are wrapped around you. He's always holding you. You are never alone. You might feel alone, but the Spirit is within you to comfort you … to give you the strength to believe in the victory you've been given.

MARCH 5

The Darkest Valley

Even though I walk through the darkest valley,
I will fear no evil, for you are with me;
your rod and your staff, they comfort me.
PSALM 23:4

You have nothing to fear. In your moments of distress, I am closer to you than ever. I am in the dark with you, leading you towards My goodness and mercy. It's through the darkest valleys that I grow your faith. Remember, we just came from quiet streams, and green pastures and I restored your soul ... for a time such as this ... for times of trouble. Walking with Me, trusting Me, means that your circumstances will change but your faith remains. You must trust Me in the good times *and* the bad, or not at all. Faith and trust require that there will be moments when you doubt.

It's in the darkest valleys of your life, when it's hard to see, when your vision is distorted by pain and suffering, that you must rely on the Spirit to keep your focus on the joy set before you. And always remember ... I led you there. You didn't get to this impossible place alone and I did not bring you here without purpose.

I lead you through circumstances that will transform you into My likeness. At times, I will have you walk with Me beside still waters, at other times you will follow Me into the shadows. But know that in all the different paths, you are being taken from glory to glory. Trust in Me, hope in Me, and be found in Me.

FAITH THOUGHTS

Life is hard. And when you find yourself in a valley, you may have more questions than answers, wondering if God really cares. God knows your heart. He has given you faith and He's aware of your doubt. Now is the time to draw near to Him, the moment where you're not sure if He's even there, and when you do, get ready to see His hand and His face. He's never left you.

Day by Day

MARCH 6

Therefore we do not lose heart. Though outwardly we are wasting away, yet inwardly we are being renewed day by day.
2 CORINTHIANS 4:16

I am telling you not to lose heart. I set the Cross before Me and I've given you the saving grace that has come from My sacrifice. It is because of My living hope that you can believe without a doubt that even the most excruciating trials of life are minor in comparison to the glory that will last forever. Trust in Me. Have faith. Do not give up. Miracles will not always happen how or when you think they should. And even though you feel as if you're being consumed by the wind and the waves of the storm, your faith in Me is giving you new strength for what lies ahead.

I know that suffering and difficulties that never seem to end can tempt you to lose faith, to walk away and reject the life I've called you to. Do not allow your heart to be hardened. Stay in constant prayer and allow the Spirit to freely flow in and through you.

Always remember that no matter what difficulties you face in life, you always have hope in Me. You are continually given grace and in your suffering the Spirit will strengthen and empower you. Though your paths in faith may be difficult, you have been promised they lead to glory.

FAITH THOUGHTS

Are you staying focused upon God's grace or the disappointment and discouragement that has brought you to a place of doubt and despair? If you continually lift God up in your life, staying focused on Him, you will find that you will have all you need and more.

MARCH 7

Purpose in the Pain

*Son though he was, he learned obedience
from what he suffered.*
HEBREWS 5:8

I lived My life as an example. I know what it is like to be hungry and thirsty, despised and rejected, hated and betrayed. I lived to show you what an obedient servant, dependent on God, must endure. With the heavenly Father as Provider and Protector, following Me means resisting temptations and trusting in His plan when you're not sure you can. It means that although you don't understand the plan and you must endure suffering for a time, you trust that His plans are for good … to give you a future and hope.

It is in obeying the Father's Word and walking according to His will that you will find the blessings He has stored up for you. You will find victory in every circumstance of your life, if you will trust in the Father's wisdom, refusing to blame Him.

It's in fighting the good fight of faith, casting yourself upon your heavenly Father's loving care that will sustain you in the most difficult times. No matter how deep your pain, or how great your suffering, you can draw near to the throne of grace with confidence. What you believe is the end may truly be the beginning in the hands and plans of your heavenly Father.

FAITH THOUGHTS

It's vital that you continually pray God's will be done and not your own. He knows what is best, there's no possible way you can know everything. It's in trusting Him completely that you will experience His greatest blessings fully. Let go of your expectations for perfection in your life's circumstances and know that if you're suffering, you will soon experience great joy.

Closer

MARCH 8

*It was good for me to be afflicted
so that I might learn your decrees.*
PSALM 119:71

You need to know with all certainty that your heavenly Father loves you and I have poured out My blood for you ... to save you ... to live with you for all eternity. I have promised you that in this world there will be troubles ... and that also means suffering. Though your struggles and suffering can cause you to experience bitterness and rob you of your joy, they can also bring you closer to your heavenly Father.

I have shown you that you must live in a trusting dependence on the Father. With each step I took closer to the Cross, I stepped closer to the Father. My afflictions drove Me to depend on the promises and find strength in My weakness. Know that at times it is your afflictions that will help you turn from sins and bring you back to your Father.

Troubles can reveal things that need to be revealed that are keeping you from walking in the will of the Father. At times life's greatest lessons can only be learned through pain and suffering. But I am with you. Your purpose on earth is to be refined, conformed into My likeness. So, when troubles come, be reminded to look up. Afflictions are meant to draw your attention to the Father. They force you to depend, trust, hope and have faith. Don't be tempted to give up and give in. Keep your eyes on the Cross and the joy and glory that has been promised to you through it.

FAITH THOUGHTS

How do you handle times of uncertainty when you're enduring pain and suffering? Faith is not easy, but you have the Spirit to strengthen you and guide you through all of life's obstacles. Look to the promises of God as your assurance that He is with you and will always take care of you. Use the times of affliction to draw closer to Him.

GOD'S GUIDANCE THROUGH UNCERTAINTY

The Lord is my shepherd, I lack nothing.
PSALM 23:1

You are meant to face challenges, even difficulties, where you must make important decisions, so that you can grow and develop in your relationship with God. It's during these trying times that the Spirit gives you a sustaining power of faith. It's times of uncertainty that allow you to exercise your faith in new ways so that you will be strengthened for the journey ahead.

It's through the times where you're not sure what to do and you can't understand that you are to seek God with all that you are. And He is your shepherd, leading you, loving you, throughout your journey of life. But, it's in the wilderness moments, when you feel absolutely, utterly alone that you will learn to trust in Him more and learn of His willingness to provide help when you're in need, no matter how challenging your circumstances.

He'll use this time when your faith is fighting through doubt to bring you into His quietness and help you to learn to listen to the Holy Spirit leading you. If you will continue to seek God's help, you'll develop a faith that is sure and unshakable, powerful and uplifting … a divine force in your life.

And in sincere faith, you must have strength and understanding in accepting the will of the Father when it is different than your own. The times of testing your faith are for building your character. And it's the building of your character that will enable you to fully exercise the power of faith to bring about the peace and contentment you so desperately need … no matter what lies ahead.

Straight Paths

MARCH 9

Trust in the LORD with all your heart and lean not on your own understanding; in all your ways submit to him, and he will make your paths straight.
PROVERBS 3:5-6

Your heavenly Father has poured out His grace on you by giving you a plan and purpose for your life. As you follow Me, He will reveal that plan, that pathway that He's designed specifically for you. Your faith walk will require you to trust in the Father, just as I did with each step I took to the Cross. You must have confidence that the promises are for you and that the Father is faithful to His Word as you follow His plan.

You'll be tempted to rely on your own understanding, trying to figure out things on your own ... looking for a quick fix for your problems, but you must have faith that the Father is always gracious, merciful, and trustworthy. You can rest in His sovereignty over every detail of your life. Rely on the Spirit to help you through your uncertainty, instead of relying on your own knowledge and reasoning. Faith is when you don't understand what's happening, but you continue to move forward in the Father's ways and what He's asked you to ... looking for His grace with confident expectation. It's when you acknowledge Him having authority over your life, you must surrender to Him fully ... and I have set the example. I followed His path straight to the Cross, leading to the saving of many lives and the redemption of yours. His paths won't always be easy, but they are always best.

FAITH THOUGHTS

In what areas of your life are you having the most difficulty trusting God? Why do you think it's hard to trust Him sometimes? Is it because of your fear of the unknown or the pain and suffering you're enduring by walking in His path? When you begin to question and doubt, turn to His promises and decide to trust without hesitation.

MARCH 10

The Right Path

"I will instruct you and teach you in the way you should go; I will counsel you with my loving eye on you."
PSALM 32:8

Surrender. And wait for Me. I will lead you. I want you to follow Me. You do not need to be afraid or worried about what lies ahead ... I've gone before you. I will instruct you, teach you in the way you should go and keep My eyes upon you ... at every moment of every day. It's your submission and obedience to the Word and the authority of your heavenly Father that will lead to the greatest blessings of your life.

I have shown you humility, holiness, and faithfulness that seeks to obey the Father. Always keep your eyes on Me, not the storm, not your circumstances. I did not sacrifice My life to save you just for you to live in the way you desire to. I died so that you might live for Me. But the decision is yours ... which path will you take? The one that leads to true life, or the path of destruction?

I call you to live life abundantly, settling for nothing but the Father's best. And you need direction, you need Me to lead you, because you may find yourself lost in life. And although I know where you are, you will need to find your way back to Me. You must turn to Me. Seek Me and you will find Me. Be guided by My eyes, not by your eyes in the world, following its ways. It is the Spirit who will give you understanding through the Word and help you to see the Lamp for your feet and the Light for your path. And know that I will never leave you to yourself. I am always watching you, like a shepherd with his sheep, I will care for you and leave the ninety-nine to find you when you go astray.

FAITH THOUGHTS

Do you need direction in your life right now? Now is the time to get into the Word of God and pray and seek the Lord's face. He promised to teach, instruct, and keep watch over you and your life ... believe in His promise.

Seeking Help

*If any of you lacks wisdom, you should
ask God, who gives generously to all without
finding fault, and it will be given to you.*
JAMES 1:5

There will be times in your life when you do not know what to do or which way to turn. I am with you. As you seek Me, embrace your faith and ask the Spirit to give you insight. Know that I already know all of your fears. Your heavenly Father will always provide all that you need … you will lack nothing.

I use your faith to test and strengthen your faith in Me … producing patient endurance that is needed for your spiritual growth. Relying on the Spirit will enable you to stand strong in your faith without wavering. Continually remain in Me and I will remain in you. You desperately need My wisdom through life's disappointments and difficulties. With all of the choices you have to make, you continually need My guidance along with a willingness to surrender to the Father's will.

Ask the Spirit to make you eager to admit your faults and to learn the lessons that you are meant to through your journey of faith. I have given you a position at the throne of your heavenly Father, so that you might receive His mercy and grace … when you feel faint of heart and you need wisdom and understanding, you will be given what you need. When your faith is being tested, the Spirit will help you to maintain a steady heart and an unwavering, uncompromised faith in Me.

FAITH THOUGHTS

God knows when you're weary and He's told you to seek Him and you will find Him. But when you ask, make sure you listen to His voice and obey His Word. It's when the pressures of life are pressing down on you that the Spirit will miraculously give you the strength to patiently endure and help you to grow in grace as you rest in Him.

A Lamp and Light

Your word is a lamp for my feet, a light on my path.
PSALM 119:105

I have promised that in this world you will have troubles. And at times you will lose your way. You need the Light of the Word, given to you by the Father, to make things clear and visible. My sacrifice has given you the Spirit to lead you down paths of righteousness. I am your guiding Light and your eternal hope of glory. Keep your eyes on Me.

Each and every day you must search the Word and the promises within it to help you stand firm in your faith. Without the Word, you will stumble in the dark, unable to see your way out. It is the Light of the Word that will illuminate your path. Walking in the Light involves continually making choices to listen and obey the heavenly Father's Word. It's His Word that has the power to lead to salvation, bringing all those who are in darkness into His marvelous Light.

You will find yourself wanting to see exactly where you're going in life, knowing your life from start to finish, but I only lead you one step at a time. My guidance, giving you grace for the moment, will enable you to refuse to worry about tomorrow, trusting Me for this day ... for this moment. You will always find the grace and guidance you need for every circumstance that you face. There is nothing to doubt or fear. You don't need to see beyond what I will reveal to you. There will always be enough light for each step you take along the path the Father has set before you.

FAITH THOUGHTS

If you're walking in darkness, if you're consumed with doubt and worry, the Word of God will be your guiding Light. Are you being led by it or are you stumbling? Don't get caught up in the details, trust Jesus and follow Him step by step with the confident assurance that God will provide all you need.

The Way

MARCH 13

*Whether you turn to the right or to the left,
your ears will hear a voice behind you, saying,
"This is the way; walk in it."*
ISAIAH 30:21

There are many "ways", but only one leads to Life. I care about you deeply and personally. You can trust Me to lead you and the Spirit to comfort and guide you. You can trust your heavenly Father's path for you and you can look to Me for your example, asking the Spirit to strengthen you for each step of faith.

You don't have to be afraid. You don't have the burden of having to direct your own steps. You can depend on your heavenly Father's plans for you and look to Me to lead you into them. And I walk with you every step of the way. There is never a moment when I leave you. I am with you to help you with the day-to-day choices that form your character, to wisely make decisions that impact your influence on those around you.

I am with you, and the promises in the Father's Word are given to you to help and guide you through the unexpected twists and turns of life. I know the right path, I know how to keep you on it, but you must trust in Me and walk with Me. Lean on Me when you're too weak to carry on, keep going even when you think you can't. You can do all things in My strength ... don't try to do it on your own. Keep your eyes on Me, rest in Me, live in My victory.

Faith Thoughts

You can walk in God's will with confidence and strength because you trust in Him, not concerned about the details, only believing in God's goodness. Ask the Spirit to turn your thoughts to Him and His Word continually so that you might receive His constant instruction, support, and encouragement for every step of faith you take.

MARCH 14

Blind Faith

Show me your ways, LORD, teach me your paths.
Guide me in your truth and teach me, for you are
God my Savior, and my hope is in you all day long.
PSALM 25:4-5

You don't need to see it all, you don't need to know it all. I am your guide. Let Me lead you. Rely on the Spirit to strengthen you through the promises, helping you to trust completely, without doubting. Faith requires you not knowing what lies ahead, but trusting that I do. Don't try to go your own way ... you need Me, you need the Spirit's help. Stay firmly attached to Me, turning your eyes upon Me at every moment.

I do not want you to be anxious. I want you to let Me carry your burdens. Hold on to Me tightly in your struggles and rest in knowing that I am preparing a way out or through whatever your circumstances. Faith will not always make things easy, but you can have peace in Me, knowing that I'm with you every step of the way and that the Father's plans for you are for good ... to give you a future and a hope.

Stay close to Me so that I might show you My ways, guiding you in Truth and teaching you through grace. No matter what you face, put your hope in Me all day long. There is nothing I can't do. Trust that the same power that raised Me from the dead lives in you and can work miracles in and through you to bring about the greatest blessings in your life.

FAITH THOUGHTS

Pray continually that you will keep your eyes on Jesus, even through the most treacherous storms of life. Ask the Spirit to strengthen you so you do not lose your grip on faith. And when you're tempted to doubt, cry out to Jesus and ask Him to help your unbelief ... then thank Him for the hope that He continually gives.

A Gentle Reminder

"But the Advocate, the Holy Spirit, whom the Father will send in my name, will teach you all things and will remind you of everything I have said to you."
JOHN 14:26

Do you really believe that you have My power, the wisdom of your heavenly Father living inside of you? Then why do you worry? I'm right here, the Spirit within you, there is nothing to fear. Don't downplay the Spirit's influence on your life … there is nothing greater. Not even death. I have won the victory … nothing more needs to be done than for you to walk in it.

When you're struggling, in need of help and direction, the Spirit will teach you and remind you of My words. I lived to set a living example and to speak Truth that will convict you of your sin, provide insight and bring glory to God. And it's in your times of doubt that you can have comfort in knowing that no matter how things "feel", I am with you, and because of the Spirit, I am closer to you than ever before.

Through My words, actions, and miracles, you can have the confidence to trust in the heavenly Father's faithfulness. I will lead you into true peace and contentment when all other ways cannot. Focus on the value and dignity you have because you were created by the heavenly Father and see yourself in the Light of God's authority over your life. Find joy in learning to do things His way, the way that leads to His blessings, and not your own. I am with you every step of the way. I will carry you when you're too weak to carry on.

FAITH THOUGHTS

When you're wondering how to deal with the brokenness in your life, how to survive the never-ending struggles and challenges, turn to the promises of God. He is faithful and will keep every single one of His promises. He'll never give up on you or fail you.

MARCH 16

Held Up

*The LORD makes firm the steps of the one who
delights in him; though he may stumble,
he will not fall, for the LORD upholds him with his hand.*
PSALM 37:23-24

Your pathway has been ordered by your heavenly Father, but you can choose your own way. Each and every moment you need to stay surrendered – confessing and repenting, keeping your eyes on Me as I lead you into the Father's path for you, watching your steps, providing and protecting you.

There will be times in life when you fail to follow the Father's will and you'll be tempted to give into guilt and give up your walk of faith. But, that is why you need Me. If you confess your sins, your heavenly Father is faithful and He will forgive you and cleanse you from all unrighteousness. In the world where there are troubles, there will be unexpected circumstances that can overwhelm you, but I will provide a way out of temptations – temptations to doubt, to lie, to try to escape.

There is nothing that I cannot and will not do for you. I will provide for you and protect you. All I ask is that you continue to follow Me through the pain and suffering ... I promised you that there is wonderful joy ahead. Though you can't see it, right beyond your troubles is your triumph. Keep walking forward in faith, even when you don't think you can take another step. I will hold you up. I am holding your hand in this moment and every moment to come.

FAITH THOUGHTS

In this moment, are you fully aware that Jesus is not only with you but holding you? Life is hard and challenges are great, but God is greater still. Don't rely on your own strength, trust in the Spirit to carry you and comfort you as you walk through God's will and into His blessings that He's prepared for you.

The Way Things Appear

MARCH 17

There is a way that appears to be right,
but in the end it leads to death.
PROVERBS 14:12

It can be difficult to understand what is right and what is true in your fallen world. You might perceive something as good based upon what others around you tell you. You might forget that it is the Word that is to determine right from wrong, good from bad. You will need the help of the Spirit to help you see your circumstances from My perspective. And sometimes things aren't always what they appear to be.

You must be careful not to exclude Me from the areas of your life that you want to control. I need to be in control of every part of your life, in order for you to fully live the life you're called to. And you might feel like you're doing right things and making right choices, but I examine your heart – the things that are hidden. You will need to make Me and obedience to Me your goal in life, so that the Spirit will dwell in you.

In following Me you have the assurance that I am working in and through you to work all things together for good. Whatever it is you're struggling with at this moment, lay it down at My feet. Once and for all, allow Me to be your Savior in every part of your life. Allow My grace to consume you, so that you can live in the peace I died to give you. See yourself as I see you and walk with Me to your eternal destination. I love you with an everlasting love.

FAITH THOUGHTS

Don't try and rely on your own wisdom to navigate through the decisions of your life. You were never meant to walk through this life alone. You have been given the Spirit to lead and guide you and strengthen your faith. Keep laying down your life for Jesus, just as He did for you. Surrender leads to God's best and you deserve the fullness of His love.

MARCH 18

Even to the End

For this God is our God for ever and ever;
he will be our guide even to the end.
PSALM 48:14

You can rejoice, and find peace in this moment and every moment for the rest of your life on earth. Your heavenly Father has not abandoned you. You were never meant to travel this path of faith on your own. You are guided … to the end. Your faithful Father whose steadfast love endures forever will be with you and guide you through every circumstance of life. There is nothing to fear. There is hope.

I have called you to follow Me so that I can lead you down paths of righteousness. You have no better guide. There is no one in the world that knows your life from beginning to end. Your heavenly Father created all things, is sovereign at all times and in all ways, directing and governing all events, planning your life down to the finest detail.

He has promised that all things work together for good and has assured you that light afflictions, that are for a moment, work within you to bring about your exceeding and eternal weight of glory. There are no accidents, there are no chances, and I know at times that makes faith really hard for you. All things take place according to God's determinate purposes. You can look to Me through it all, seeing the glory of My life on earth and its purposes and finding peace in the importance of My death and resurrection. You are saved. In every way.

FAITH THOUGHTS

Do you feel all alone, like there is no one who can help you and your faith is fading? God never changes. He is always with you, even when you don't "feel" that He is. He never lets go. He is watching over you, and He knows your doubt. Lay your burdens at His feet and then "get up" … it's time to keep walking.

Increasing Faith

The apostles said to the Lord, "Increase our faith!"
LUKE 17:5

I know that at times you doubt. Faith is built upon doubt. Through the storms, through every struggle, you must walk by faith, trusting in My presence that is real and calming. You need to find peace and strength day to day by walking with Me and learning to rely on Me and My promises every step of the way. And when you don't believe, I will help your unbelief. The Spirit will convince you of hope through the promises made to you and you'll be calmed with My presence.

When you come to Me, I will rid your mind of the doubts and fears of your troubles and build your faith by providing you the assurance of My peace by the power of the Spirit. Complete assurance and rest will fill your heart by trusting in Me. Trust in My resurrection power. Know that nothing is impossible, no matter what your circumstances, whatever you're facing or trying to overcome. Your faith in Me will strengthen and grow through every struggle.

My love for you has no bounds, and I have compassion on your doubts and troubled heart by reminding you that I am alive. I am ever present, in the middle of your confusion … I will never leave you or forsake you. Right now in this moment, with each breath you take, I want you to receive My assurance, standing firm in confident faith because you trust in My promises, power, and presence. Rest in Me and know that I am able to do exceedingly, abundantly above all that you ask or think.

FAITH THOUGHTS

You may not realize that your doubts drive you deeper into your faith. Don't be afraid to doubt, but when you do, run to God. Don't allow your mind to distort what your heart knows and is trusting in – promises of God Almighty, faithful and full of grace. He waits for you a ready help.

MARCH 20

Ordered Steps

A person's steps are directed by the LORD.
How then can anyone understand their own way?
PROVERBS 20:24

You may have plans for your life, even determining the finest details, but when you follow Me, I order your steps of life. I know the way. I am the Way, the Truth, and the Life. I am in control, whether you believe I am or not.

If you allow Me to be Lord of your life, leading and directing you in every way, you will find that My power and My timing are far more important than anything you can accomplish in your own strength, wisdom, and understanding. You don't know what lies ahead ... but I do. If you need wisdom and direction, submit to the heavenly Father's will for your life and allow Me to lead you in the path He sets before you.

Live each moment in humility and obedience as I did. Give praise to the Father, knowing that all things are His sovereign gifts to you. Trust that He holds your future in His hands, enveloped in His mercy, love, and grace – you have no reason to do anything other than hope. There is never a step that you take that is independent of Me, if you go to the left or right, it is determined by Me ... I allow it ... I oversee it. All of it.

All things are directed as the Father has purposed. And everything that happens, does so to accomplish the goals of glory. Don't try to understand it all, just trust ... and watch what I will do.

FAITH THOUGHTS

Are you trying too hard to understand the circumstances of your life, trying desperately to devise a plan for a way out instead of trusting Jesus to take you through? Trying to control what you can't will drain your faith and drown you in despair. Whatever you're struggling with, turn it over to God right now, and don't take it back. Rest in His promises of comfort and hope.

Light of Life

MARCH 21

*When Jesus spoke again to the people, he said,
"I am the light of the world. Whoever follows me
will never walk in darkness, but will have the light of life."*
JOHN 8:12

You were never meant to walk in darkness. I came to destroy the devil's work, to set you free, to give you a new life, following Me and walking in the Light. I came to give you peace and freedom from the chains of sin that held you in the darkness. If you will continually trust in Me, you can walk in My Light in every area of your life. No matter what you're facing, even in your doubt, you can come to Me and walk with Me in My Light.

You've been given a path in life, and I will light your way. Each step in faith is not grounded in blind faith, but in the hope I have given you through My resurrection. You can have true hope, real peace, when you continually walk with Me. You don't need to have fear, you don't need to give in to doubt, you can seek the promises of the Word and stand confidently firm in your faith that your heavenly Father is faithful at all times and in all ways.

I'm with you in the middle of every mess, when you're questioning the Father's ways and struggling to move forward in faith … I love you the same. In moments of despair, call upon the Spirit, find your strength in Him. He is your helper in every way, a comforter when you're crumbling beneath the weight of pain and suffering. In the darkest moments, My Light comes to show you the way and give you hope.

FAITH THOUGHTS

If you find yourself in a dark place, you are not alone. Jesus never leaves you and He will bring you into His Light. You might have times of momentary despair, but God is in control and has promised to bring you into His glory. Keep trusting Him, even in the dark … you will soon see the Light.

MARCH 22

Everything Good

... equip you with everything good for doing his will, and may he work in us what is pleasing to him, through Jesus Christ, to whom be glory for ever and ever. Amen.
HEBREWS 13:21

If you're discouraged, focus on Me. Take your eyes off the storm and be confident of the heavenly Father's plan for your life. You've been chosen to accomplish the Father's will, and I am with you to walk with you through all of the doubt and fear. Don't live by what you feel, walk confidently in your faith.

Your faith is not only about you, it's about your obedience to the Father's will and relying on Him to provide whatever you need in order to accomplish His will, even when you don't understand. There is always work being done in and through you, a transformation in process, to make you into My likeness.

Although at times you may feel as though you're being led into circumstances that are more than you can handle, the Spirit is within you and every difficult situation is a part of growing your faith. Amid all the chaos in the world, you can have peace, you can live full of hope because of grace. Things may not always look good, it may look like you're losing the battle, but you can fully trust that the war is won.

Remember to daily surrender, to place yourself at My feet throughout your day, to keep the Cross ever before you. Let nothing move you, but stand firm in the promises that the Father has made to you. Rely on My power, rest in My presence, pray the promises, and trust in the Father's faithfulness.

FAITH THOUGHTS

Refuse to be an obstacle to God in your life – He needs a surrendered heart, enthusiastic to do His will, no matter the cost, in order to accomplish His purposes. It's on that path of obedience that you'll find His greatest blessings in your life. Lay everything at His feet and then follow Him.

Whatever You Do

*Commit to the L*ORD *whatever you do,*
and he will establish your plans.
PROVERBS 16:3

Trust is the key to a relationship with Me. If you are going to follow Me, to accomplish the purposes of the Father, you're going to have to trust, especially when you don't understand and things simply don't make sense. I know that you become exhausted at times, certain that you simply can't continue the journey of faith. You can find shelter in the Almighty. He will cover you with His wings, you can find refuge and His faithfulness will be your shield and rampart. Whatever you do, trust in the promises.

It's when you focus too much on your circumstances instead of listening to My voice, that you become an obstacle to My work in and through you. But, if you choose to trust, to listen to Me, and follow My instructions, life will become easier because I will only guide you down paths of righteousness. You will need to commit yourself to Me in the face of conflict so that I can build godly character in you.

You will need to face the unthinkable, at times, to realize that the Father's ways are higher and also better. When you depend on Me, trusting in the Father's love and grace, you can expect Him to bring about blessings that are unexpected in your life. Seek Me, at all times and in all ways. If you align your will with the Father's, you will find true success in whatever you do and goodness and mercy will follow you all the days of your life.

FAITH THOUGHTS

You might not know what this day will bring, but you must know that God wants you to commit it, and the opportunities it brings, to Him. Pray that the Spirit will open your eyes to the situations that allow you to do God's will. Even when it's hard, know that God will use your struggles to strengthen your faith ... and trust that His blessings will follow.

WINNING OVER WORRY AND FEAR

"Therefore I tell you, do not worry about your life ... "
Matthew 6:25

When you are consumed with worry and fear, when uncertainties cause you to question everything about your faith, you can be sure God is still on His throne. It's easy to forget that God is in control when nothing seems as though it is. So when you forget, God calls you to remember. Remember the things He's done in the past. Those times previously when you were overwhelmed with the fear that God was not with you or for you and He showed up unexpectedly. Focus your faith.

Submersing yourself in the Word and remembering who God is will put your fears in perspective. He has answered prayers before in your life. Recall those. Remember those times of desperation when you were sure you were at the end and you were out of faith. He was there then, and He is here now. He has delivered you from destruction before, and He will do it again.

You will continually experience fear, but you must choose how to respond to it. It's where you worry and fear that Satan will attack you the most, so don't be surprised when he pours gasoline on them all. Doubt is your faith being distorted. Keep your eyes on Jesus and refuse to doubt who God is, who He created you to be, and all that He's promised ... if you do, you'll miss out on the miracle that's just on the other side of your fear.

Cast It All

Cast all your anxiety on him because he cares for you.
1 PETER 5:7

You worry when you shouldn't. It's your anxiety that keeps you from moving forward in your faith, creating an obstacle to the Father's work in you and causing you to stumble as you follow Me. You've been told to cast your anxiety on Me, I can handle it, but you must humble yourself, realizing you can't do this on your own. You need Me. It's your confident humility that will change everything. It's in surrendering your life into My hands that miracles happen.

Just because you can't do what only I can, is not a sign of weakness, your strength is shown by your humility, being confident and walking in peace, knowing that I will care for you in every way. The battle within you, the worry and the weariness, comes from you not resting. Only I can truly give you rest for your soul and the peace that surpasses all understanding.

So, whatever is a burden to you, whatever is troubling you, weighing you down and causing you to worry must be surrendered. If you could handle it, you wouldn't need to worry. You worry because you're holding on to what you need to let go of. Although things may not make sense now, they will in due time. Things may not seem to be working out right now, but they will. The Father knows what He's doing and everything He does is out of His love for you. Trust Him to work all things together for good just as He has promised.

FAITH THOUGHTS

What are you holding on to that you need to let go of? In this moment, surrender whatever is troubling you and make the decision not to take it back from God's hands. With a humble heart, ask the Spirit to fill your heart with peace as you expectantly wait for God to work all things together for good.

March 25

Delivered

*I sought the L*ORD*, and he answered me;*
he delivered me from all my fears.
PSALM 34:4

Though there are many things in the world that cause you to fear, and you continually feel surrounded by troubles, I have overcome the world. Your fear and worry comes from holding things in your own hands instead of surrendering them into Mine. Know that whatever you try to accomplish on your own will be futile. Seek refuge in Me ... the only one who can deliver you from your fears and save you out of your troubles.

The Father has shown His great love for you by reaching down in His mercy and becoming like you, giving Me life on earth, to bear your burdens and allow you to share in His glory. Fearing the Father will end all of your fears. In humble submission, in praise and worship, the Spirit will assure you that you rest in the arms of the Father's love. And when you seek Him, He hears you, and He will deliver you from all of your fears.

In moments of despair, seek Him, look to Me, and cry out with the fear that ends all fears. You need only fear the Father. In following Me, you should faithfully and fervently seek to understand through the Word and learn to fear the consequences of disobedience.

Ask the Spirit to search your heart and convict you of anything that separates you from Me. Your heart must be continually cleansed, I must right the wrongs. And the result of that cleansing brings about joy and radiance. Know that as I work to lead you in the way you should go, you will be delivered, you are saved.

FAITH THOUGHTS

Are you seeking God continually? Is He the focus of your thoughts throughout your day? Ask the Spirit to rid you of your worry and fear and give you a humble heart to bring before God's throne of grace ... there you will always find His help when you need it the most.

Doing What Is Right

MARCH 26

But even if you should suffer for what is right, you are blessed. "Do not fear their threats; do not be frightened."
1 PETER 3:14

At times, you will suffer for doing what is right. The Father knows, He sees all, and if He is for you, who dares to be against you? Know that your suffering will not be in vain. It will not be wasted. Every tear is collected and every situation, good and bad, will be used for God's glory and to bring about blessings in your life. Trust Him for it.

If you go through persecution and sufferings, they cannot truly hurt you because they will always result in greater spiritual blessings in the hands of the Father. If you are devoted to Me and are always ready to give others the explanation for your faith in Me, you won't fear those that come against you. I am the perfect example of going through suffering for doing good.

I was perfect and died for all sinners, to bring them back to the Father. I suffered the penalty for all of those sins in the way of death. But I triumphed and you can now walk in that victory. In your suffering, you are living and sharing My love. You aren't meant to walk alone, I walk with you … just follow Me.

The works you're called to is not something you need to make happen on your own. I will make the difference in you and others will notice that difference. I will give you reason after reason for the hope that you have, so that others will be drawn to Me through you when you do what is right.

FAITH THOUGHTS

Do you feel like you're enduring suffering because you're doing what is right? Ask God to assure you of His blessings in the middle of your despair. Look to Jesus and every step He took to the Cross to strengthen you through whatever you face, knowing that one day you will see Him.

MARCH 27

Don't Worry

Then Jesus said to his disciples: "Therefore I tell you, do not worry about your life, what you will eat; or about your body, what you will wear."
LUKE 12:22

I will help you through the troubles of life ... the big ones and the small ones. Nothing is too difficult for Me. Worry will never change your situation ... I will. Worry simply gives you the illusion that you're in control, when the truth is that you are not – never were, never will be. Everything is under My feet. Let go of what is holding you back from fully trusting Me.

I spent My entire life on earth trusting the Father. I have shown you how to walk in faith, and I'm walking with you ... the Spirit is within you. When you feel worried and alone, come to Me and let Me teach you to cast all your cares upon Me. Day by day, moment by moment, with each worry that forms in your mind, pray that you will take every thought captive and make it obedient to Me. Ask for My help and give Me your anxious thoughts, and allow the Spirit to fill you with promises of hope and security in the faithfulness of the Father.

I will carry you through all of life's difficulties and the Father will watch over you, providing all that you need. You can find peace in My goodness and grace, you can walk confidently with joy in your heart because I am handling all of your worries. Realize that everything is out of your hands anyway ... the weight of your fears belongs in the hands of the Father, the one who keeps the world in motion ... including yours.

FAITH THOUGHTS

What do you continually worry about? What would happen if you turned that over to God and refused to worry any longer? Whatever you're going through, there is a promise of God that will strengthen and comfort you. Everything is under His control and He will always take care of you.

Help

*You are my help and my deliverer;
you are my God, do not delay.*
PSALM 40:17

It might be difficult to believe that the heavenly Father is always watching over you, always caring for you, when life is continuously difficult. But you should know that in all His majesty and glory, He is concerned about you … He is faithfully watching over every detail of your life. He is never too busy for you. I am with you always, and I walk with you every day. The Spirit is living in and through you … you have all that you need.

You might sometimes feel the Father's absence or abandonment when your pain and suffering tells you that if He were real He wouldn't let bad things happen … He wouldn't allow you to suffer. But, you must always live by Truth – the truth that His ways are higher, secured in His love, mercy, and grace. You are exactly where you need to be.

Right here in this emptiness and pain, all things are being worked together for good. There is nothing you are lacking. You have what you need for this moment. Ask the Spirit to give you the assurance that you have been provided with exactly what you need for the season you're in.

Look to Me for your peace in the chaos. I am always here, I never leave your side. I know you're tired and weary … but hold on … I'm holding on to you.

FAITH THOUGHTS

Try to focus on all that you have. All the good things have been given to you by God. There were times in the past when you were in despair and you were sure God had abandoned you and wasn't going to show up … but He did. He's full of surprises, expect one now, when you desperately need His miracles.

Consider It

*"Consider how the wild flowers grow.
They do not labor or spin."*
LUKE 12:27

Your heavenly Father loves you more than all creation. Just follow Me, you will have everything you need and more. You don't need to worry, you don't need to be afraid of tomorrow ... the Father's grace awaits you there. Live with Me, in this moment, trusting in the Father's love. When life gets difficult and troubles come, and they will, you will need to trust then, too. You will need to have faith through your doubt.

I know that at times you feel as though things could not get worse. I know you're barely holding on. Everything you've hoped for seems gone and you simply don't have any faith left to believe through your pain and sorrow. But pray. In the middle of it, in the darkest night. I am your hope, I am with you. Everything is going to be more than alright because your heavenly Father cares for you and has only good things planned for your future.

It may look different from your viewpoint. The Cross looked like anything but redemption and eternal life. I know it's hard to see right now. I know you question and I know you doubt. But the truth is that I have overcome, the grave does not hold you or Me and it does not hold your hope. You can live in the joy I've given you ... let nothing stop you.

FAITH THOUGHTS

When life is difficult, when things aren't turning out the way you thought they would and you're fearful of the future, keep your eyes on Jesus. Ask the Spirit to assure you, through the promises of God, that everything is going to be okay. God knows what you need and He will faithfully care for you in every way.

Weighed Down

MARCH 30

*Anxiety weighs down the heart,
but a kind word cheers it up.*
PROVERBS 12:25

It's easy to lose sight of Me when the world continually causes your vision to be blurred by the weight of the troubles of life. I know it seems like your pain and suffering will never end. It appears there is no hope of things getting better. When anxiety creeps in, it can make your heart heavy, weighed down by doubt and despair. Know that when life seems out of control, it's not … the Father is always in complete control.

Your thoughts and actions, whether good or bad, color your life in reflective ways, until you turn to the Father and trust Him with the outcome. When you're weighed down, it is usually because you're experiencing feelings of insecurity about the situation you're in. You see no solution, no way out, and your faith crumbles beneath the weight of it.

Sometimes, a simple word of praise will break through the darkness and give way to light. I am the true source of peace and prayer is the best way to deal with any of your problems. If your heart is heavy, come to Me for a Word of hope, strength and joy. If you see that someone else's heart is heavy, point them to Me through your praise, in the middle of it all.

FAITH THOUGHTS

There will be times when your heart seems too heavy, so broken, that it seems like it will never be the same. But, the God of miracles has a miracle just for you … one that will heal your heart and bring about greater peace and joy than ever before. Will you trust Him for it?

MARCH 31

Never Shaken

Cast your cares on the LORD and he will sustain you;
he will never let the righteous be shaken.
PSALM 55:22

I ask you to follow Me, I ask you to call upon Me for help because I will hold you, I will sustain you. I will never allow you to slip or fall ... I will hold you with My powerful nail-scarred hands. Though the struggles of life are unavoidable, the burdens of them are not meant for you to carry. I will carry your burdens because I care for you.

It's your burdens that can make you weak and weary, but if you allow Me to carry them, having faith, trusting Me and taking Me at My word, you will find your heart strengthened and you will experience the peace and joy of letting go and letting Me do what only I can do. Moving the immovable. Breaking through the impossible. Regardless of the situation and circumstances you face, you must know My love for you. I died for you. What is it that I can't do?

I overcame the grave. When things become so overwhelming you lose sight of Me, but I am with you, beside you, in the flames and through the fire, and the Spirit within you. Yet, the Father has promised that if you trust, you will not be shaken. He's assured you that in My strength, you can do all things. When you question, when you feel as though you're crumbling beneath the weight of your burdens, lay them at My feet. I will take them, I will carry them, and I will walk forward with you in your faith.

FAITH THOUGHTS

What burden are you carrying right now that you know you shouldn't be? Are you convinced that it's something that is even too big for God, or you're not sure He'll do what you think He should? Call upon Jesus. Ask Him to carry that very thing you're not sure you can trust Him with and watch what He does. He's taking you from glory to glory, trust Him.

All the Power

*For the Spirit God gave us does not make us timid,
but gives us power, love and self-discipline.*
2 TIMOTHY 1:7

I have told you not to fear because it's a choice. You can allow My Spirit to live in and through you or you can be an obstacle to the power and plans of the Father. In the face of hostility, you can walk in My strength. I am your confidence, I am your stronghold in times of trouble.

Though the battle rages, I am still winning. Be still. Through whatever you must face, you can walk boldly and confidently knowing that I am with you through it all and there is nothing I can't do. The same power that lives in Me is in you. If you fear the Father, acknowledging His supremacy, His sovereignty, then you will clearly see that you don't have to be afraid of anything else.

You've been given a boldness, a humble confidence and power to walk forward in faith, filled with love, and having self-control when you realize you can't control the things around you. I will help you. The Spirit will help you to trust.

Trust in the promises and know that you don't have to worry because the Father cares for you. You don't have to be anxious when I am your peace. Do not find confidence in yourself or your circumstances. You have not been given a spirit of fear … so you don't have to live in it. Live confidently in the power I've given you – power that raises the dead, makes the blind see, and the lame walk. Live in that power.

Faith Thoughts

What causes you fear, anxiety or worry? Pray over those things. Ask God to work specifically in those situations. Trust Him with it all and trust in His will for you. Allow Him to use the adversity to strengthen your faith, not weaken it. Keep turning to Him for help and don't stop.

April 2

No Fear

There is no fear in love. But perfect love drives out fear, because fear has to do with punishment.
1 JOHN 4:18

In your fallen world, it is fear that motivates much of what you do. You have fear of the future, fear of consequences, and fear of being judged through it all. At times, you can be tempted to believe that the Father wants you to live in fear. But He is only love and love cannot exist with fear. I do not want you to fear … I am with you. It is My love that replaces the fear in your heart.

You need My power to continually be unleashed on your fears, to cast out all doubt. Everything the Father does in your life is influenced by His love. My love is always available to you as you trust that I hold you in My hand and I promise to never let you go. It's divine love that takes away your fears. The key to overcoming all of your fears is your total and complete trust in Me.

Refuse to fear. Through deep waters, through the fires. Even in the darkest times, you can trust the Father to make things right … to work all things together for good. Find strength in His promises and hope in Me. When you continually learn to trust in Me, you will no longer be afraid of the things that come against you. If you always take refuge in Me, you can have confidence in the future and live in the joy I give to you.

Faith Thoughts

You can face anything because Jesus is with you. There is no circumstance that is a surprise to God and nothing too difficult for Him. Worship through your worry. Know that you are not alone, and at this very moment, when you feel God has abandoned you, His promises tell you that He is at work in your circumstances.

A Stronghold

*The LORD is my light and my salvation –
whom shall I fear? The LORD is the stronghold
of my life – of whom shall I be afraid?*
PSALM 27:1

It's in the sorrow and difficulties that bring you to the end of yourself, that fear and worry can take hold and bring you to your knees. You are right where you need to be. At My feet. It's often in these times of despair that the Father's purposes are hidden and you feel like just because there are troubles, you are moving in the wrong direction in life. I know you want relief. I know you want out. But I'm with you to take you through so that your faith can strengthen. I am your stronghold.

Your pain and suffering will come to an end. Ask the Spirit to help you to become patient and keep you from being angry and trying to take things into your own hands. You can have strength in Me, even in times of uncertainty and brokenness. I am always with You and the Father's faithfulness to His promises are always unwavering.

Wait upon My direction, wait for the Spirit to move you, find your peace in the promises that have been made to you. If you are patiently waiting, you are relying on Me, trusting that the Father will supply all you need. Patiently waiting, means moving in faith, walking in the Father's will, trusting in His timing and believing in His goodness. The Father knows all, is above all and can do all things. There is nothing to fear. I am your Light and Salvation. Hope in Me.

FAITH THOUGHTS

Jesus is always with you and the Spirit is within you. Pray that God would bring Light into your darkness and hope in the midst of all your troubles. Surrender your life in obedience to Him each and every moment, and trust that He can handle all that you need Him to.

April 4

Be Strong

... say to those with fearful hearts, "Be strong, do not fear; your God will come, he will come with vengeance; with divine retribution he will come to save you."
ISAIAH 35:4

I have the power that has saved you. My power raises the dead, makes the lame walk, and enables the blind to see. Live in My hope. I know that it is easy to become overwhelmed, to be anxious and fearful as the crashing waves of your storms seem sure to take you under. But I am with you so that you can be strong, relying on the Father's divine perspective instead of relying on your own. The Father's viewpoint is of the certainty in hope that has come from My death and resurrection.

The Father's promise in your persecution, in your suffering, in your doubt and fear, is that I am with you. Your pain and suffering is not a sign that I have abandoned you, but a reminder of the promise the Father has made to redeem a fallen world, to end suffering and death, and to redeem and reconcile you to Himself forever.

You can make the choice not to fear because I am your strength and hope. You can be strong, you can have hope because your eyes are always upon Me. There is nothing I am not aware of, there is no road that I lead you down that is a dead end, all things are used by the Father for good purposes. Along the way, when you are discouraged, be still and know that what you see before you is momentary ... the joys to come will last forever.

FAITH THOUGHTS

In the middle of your struggles, thank God for His promises and His faithfulness. Even when you're not sure He'll show up when you need Him to, trust that He will. Ask the Spirit to give you an eternal perspective that trusts in the promises of God and faces suffering with hope.

Fix Your Focus

APRIL 5

*The LORD is with me; I will not be afraid.
What can mere mortals do to me? The LORD is with me;
he is my helper. I look in triumph on my enemies.*
PSALM 118:6-7

No matter what happens in life, I am with you. It's because of My death and resurrection that you are assured that if you trust in Me, your sins will be forgiven, your life renewed and a place will be reserved for you in heaven. You will face times in your life when you need to be reminded that My love endures forever. When things go from bad to worse, I know you question the Father's love for you. Most of the time you won't know the answers to your questions, but you can know that in the Father's faithfulness to His promises, everything you go through is to prepare you to live with the Father forever.

Trials are a part of life and necessary in your spiritual growth, transforming you into My image. But remember that no matter how bad things seem, how treacherous the storm, how desperate and alone you might feel, I am with you to the end. I will never leave or forsake you. And when your burdens are too heavy to bear, I will carry them for you.

The Spirit is always alive within you, making sure that you are not tempted beyond what you are able to bear, assuming that you will always rely on My strength in your journey of faith. When you feel afraid, cry out to Me. In Me you are more than a conqueror and I have given you the ultimate victory.

FAITH THOUGHTS

When the darkness closes in on you, thank God for His unfailing, enduring love. Pray that when you fall short of His glory, doubting when you should trust, He will renew your strength when you come to Him. Ask to continually be filled with the Spirit so that you can have joy, peace, and contentment no matter what your circumstances are.

SECTION 2

"Don't You Care?"

Jesus was sleeping at the back of the boat with his head on a cushion. The disciples woke him up, shouting, "Teacher, don't you care that we're going to drown?"

Mark 4:38 (NLT)

Your faith assured you that God was with you. You stood firm in believing that He was with you always ... but now, when life is falling apart and your expectations of life are shattered, you feel abandoned ... especially by God.

When you're overcome with troubles, when the storms of your life are raging, you look to God in faith, only to find Him "asleep". And you wonder if the faith you've been clinging to has been in vain because not only does it seem that God doesn't care, but He also seems completely unaware of what is going on.

Life can unravel within moments, through circumstances that are out of your control, and you truly want to believe that they are within God's control. But in times of desperation, when God is not showing up as you expect Him to, it feels like He's failing you.

What you fail to realize is that it's the storm that will show us God's presence and power like never before. You want a way out and God is determined to take your faith through. You're certain you won't make it ... *He knows you will*. Trusting God doesn't make faith easy, it makes *all things* possible.

FINDING FAITH THROUGH YOUR DOUBT

*Now faith is confidence in what we hope
for and assurance about what we do not see.*
HEBREWS 11:1

There will be countless times throughout your life where you'll be grasping at what little faith you have left to keep you afloat in your sea of doubt. You can evaluate and reevaluate your faith all you want – faith will always present itself beyond evidence. Let your doubt and darkness have its place, just as your faith does. Allow it to have its argument and then let God's Truth settle it all.

It's in embracing your doubt that your faith will go through a process of being strengthened. Don't be fooled, it's harder to believe than it is not to. So, continually pray that God will help your unbelief, and yet, don't have expectations of how He'll do that. He may take you into a raging storm. He may bring more doubt to the surface. You need to understand and recognize that it's the times of doubt in your life that play the most significant role in strengthening your faith.

Walk through the doubt and draw closer to God. Your doubts don't define you, so don't let them – when they are overpowering and overwhelming, God is greater still. He is not challenged by your doubt. He'll use them for good just like He uses everything else. Life will not be easy. Don't look for it to be. Just know that Jesus is with you and when you face the storms of life, when you trust Him, keeping your eyes on Him, you will know Him better … as a person, an advocate, as Savior. The One who is with you every moment of your life … the One who gives your faith sight.

Known

APRIL 6

*"Are not five sparrows sold for two pennies?
Yet not one of them is forgotten by God."*
LUKE 12:6

You need to remember that you have a Father in heaven and you are His child. He knows your life from beginning to end and knows every detail in between. You are fully known. Nothing that you go through, nothing that you face has not already been faced by Me. Everything is under My feet. Everything is under My authority. You are saved.

Know that My eyes are always fixed on you. I know everything about you. I have seen you at your very best, and I have seen you at your very worst. My love for you never changes. There is not a thought that you have that I am not aware of. I am fully aware. And it's in your brokenness that My love has embraced you with grace. Nothing can separate you from Me.

When nothing is happening, when you've been praying and you're not getting answers, I have not forgotten you. I am with you in the storm. I know the fear you feel and face and I will strengthen you. You are valuable to the Father, you have purposes that He needs you to fulfill, and there is nothing that He will allow to come against you.

FAITH THOUGHTS

Always remember that you are a child of God Almighty. You are entitled to those benefits. You can have rest and peace, at all times and in all ways. You don't have to live as the world lives, you have a higher calling and you are loved beyond human understanding. Remain in that divine love.

APRIL 7

Confident Trust

*"But blessed is the one who trusts in the LORD,
whose confidence is in him. They will be like a tree planted
by the water that sends out its roots by the stream. It does not
fear when heat comes; its leaves are always green. It has
no worries in a year of drought and never fails to bear fruit."*
JEREMIAH 17:7-8

You are called to be faithful, although I know at times you doubt. Yet, when troubles come, if you are grounded in the Word, trusting in the promises, instead of focusing on your problems, you will grow stronger in your faith, deeper in your relationship with Me and not be tossed about by the wind and the waves of doubt.

As you struggle for solutions to your problems and continually seek answers to your questions, pray that the Spirit will fill you with peace and contentment. Be reminded that the Father is in control and you can place your hope firmly in Him. Know that the greatest enemy of your peace is having expectations of perfection, having your will be done instead of the Father's.

It's when you find yourself in the middle of something you didn't expect that you must find Truth in the Word and refuse to give into the disbelief that is constantly looming. Whatever you're facing is not the end. I'm taking you somewhere in this, the Father is going to do something good with all of it. If you're feeling lost, overwhelmed, and uncertain about the future, that's what faith is for … to believe in My power that is greater than it all. A power to instantly calm the storm … I will do it, trust Me for the miracle you desperately need.

FAITH THOUGHTS

Whatever it is you're going through, know that you can victoriously walk through it all if you are planting your hope deep in the roots of God … His Word and His promises. It is your source of life, and you are going deeper spiritually each time your faith is tested and you keep trusting.

Faith Without Doubt

APRIL 8

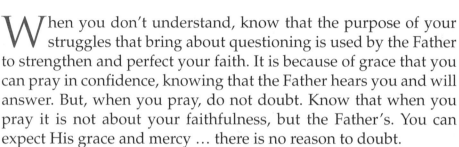

But when you ask, you must believe and not doubt, because the one who doubts is like a wave of the sea, blown and tossed by the wind.

JAMES 1:6

When you don't understand, know that the purpose of your struggles that bring about questioning is used by the Father to strengthen and perfect your faith. It is because of grace that you can pray in confidence, knowing that the Father hears you and will answer. But, when you pray, do not doubt. Know that when you pray it is not about your faithfulness, but the Father's. You can expect His grace and mercy … there is no reason to doubt.

You must have faith in Me, believing that even when prayers remain unanswered, I have a miracle that is being designed just for you. If you try to do things on your own, if you fail to come to the throne of grace, your troubles will certainly go beyond your own ability to handle them, and you will find yourself tossed and driven by the circumstances of your life … whether good or bad.

I have given you salvation for this life and the next. The Father has proven Himself since the beginning of time that He will fulfill every one of His promises … cling to them. Meditate on the Word, day and night. Seek Me when you need Me *and* when you think you *don't*. Be aware of My presence in your life at all times. Talk to Me, walk with Me, have faith and do not doubt.

FAITH THOUGHTS

In which areas of your life are you finding it difficult to trust God? What is it that you think He can't do? Is your doubt based on any truth? Because the evidence in the continual faithfulness of God and His fulfillment of every one of His promises is where your focus must be. Seek Him and find the promise He has for you today.

April 9

Moving Mountains

Jesus replied, "Truly I tell you, if you have faith and do not doubt ... you can say to this mountain, 'Go, throw yourself into the sea,' and it will be done.'"
MATTHEW 21:21

Moving mountains is impossible for anyone but Me. Nothing is impossible for Me. If you rely on Me, trust in the Father's faithfulness, and cast out all doubt, you can expect miracles. It may not always be the miracle you've asked for, but it is what the Father sees as best. You can't always understand His ways, but you can trust them because of His proven love, mercy, and grace through My sacrifice.

All miracles are about the Father's sovereign purposes. When miracles happen, the focus is always on the One who brings about the miracle, not the miracle itself. You can trust that the Spirit will work in and through you to do whatever is necessary and good in the fulfillment of His will and plans and purposes for your life.

It's about more than just moving the mountains in your life. But you must believe. If you continue to trust Me, to rely on My strength, even those obstacles in your path that are obviously unsurmountable will suddenly seem insignificant. Your doubt is truly about doubting Me, My character, and the Father's promises, it's the Father's ability you question.

You are being tested when you doubt. Recognize it for what it is. Know that without mountains in your way, your faith would never be tested in the ways it needs to be, in order to refine and grow it. Trust in My strength and rely on My power. Have faith and do not doubt. Walk by faith and not by sight.

FAITH THOUGHTS

Do you find yourself doubting God's presence and power? Is it because you're focusing on the difficulties instead of the divine? You will be tempted to doubt, but refuse to give into the temptation. Always trust God.

Losing Sight

APRIL 10

*Be strong and take heart,
all you who hope in the Lord.*
PSALM 31:24

No matter how long you've believed in Me, no matter how long our journey together, you will always have spiritual battles, temptations to doubt. When you waver, hope is not gone. Hope in Me, trust in Me and rest in the promises. Through every battle, keep your eyes on Me so that you do not lose sight of the eternal hope you have been given. Pray that the Spirit would strengthen your heart to have faith and not doubt.

Your trials and troubles are more than what they appear to be. Do not focus on your burdens, simply hand them over to Me and do not give the Enemy a foothold. I will not allow you to remain in darkness, I've called you into My marvelous Light. If you live by faith and not by sight, you can rest and rejoice every day.

If you continue to come to Me, continue to love Me, you will rise above the fog of doubt and find that your faith is richer for having been refined. Through it all, always remember that the Father is faithful. Don't lose yourself in those desperate moments and fall into fear. Fear clouds your judgment and keeps you from recovering from failures and disappointments. You need to be strong and take heart so that you can hear My voice and make the decisions that are right and good. And above all, put your hope in Me alone.

FAITH THOUGHTS

When troubles come, when desperation overwhelms your soul, do not panic. Jesus is in the boat with you. Pray that the Spirit will still your mind and fill you with the transcendent peace of God to calm your soul. Above all else, keep focused on the hope you have in God and praise Him for it. Ask that He will continually show you the wonders of His love.

APRIL 11

Believing and Not Seeing

*Then he said to Thomas, "Put your finger here;
see my hands. Reach out your hand and
put it into my side. Stop doubting and believe."*
JOHN 20:27

Even though My disciples had walked with Me, had seen Me work miracles beyond comprehension, they still doubted. Doubt is a part of faith. Don't allow despair to overwhelm you. Sometimes you will hear My voice, sometimes you won't. Don't rely on a supernatural sign or personal revelation to secure your trust in Me. Live by faith, not by sight. You will be blessed because you believe and have not seen.

Trust in Me, trust in the Word of truth and believe. Don't allow your life and your faith to be controlled by your senses or situation. Live by trusting in your heavenly Father who has proven Himself trustworthy. Blessings come to you when you believe that I am risen, ascended, and glorified, without actually seeing it with your own eyes.

If you're in a challenging and difficult season in life, where you can't see Me, where you don't see the evidence of the Father's work in your life, stay the course and keep believing. It's okay that you struggle with faith and doubt. You can come to Me with your doubt – the Spirit will comfort you, assure you, and strengthen you. When you continually seek Me, when you follow Me, your doubt will be turned to belief.

FAITH THOUGHTS

Ask God to help you trust, even through your doubts, and not to rely on your senses and emotions. Ask the Spirit to fill you with the promises of the Word and to strengthen and comfort you as you follow Jesus through situations where you're tempted to give in to unbelief.

Don't Forget

He said to his disciples, "Why are you so afraid?
Do you still have no faith?"
MARK 4:40

Faith will put an end to your doubt, worry, and anxiety. I control the things you cannot, so it's your faith in Me that brings about the power to calm your storms in life. Don't forget I am the One who can calm the storm. Don't forget how I've calmed your storms in the past. With just one word, I can stop the winds, I can calm the waves and the rain will cease. Your storms obey My voice when you put your faith in Me.

What you need to know is that you don't need to fear. You don't need to doubt. It's your choice to have faith in Me. Through every storm you must make that choice. I will protect you and take you through the storm safely, if the Father's will is that we must go through it instead of it ceasing.

There is no reason to fear the circumstances you face and over which you have no control. Your faith assures you that the Father is always in control, even when life is not. You might not understand the Father's ways, you cannot see life from beginning to end, but you can trust in His love for you. His timing is perfect and so are His plans. Faith won't always make things easy, but don't forget it makes all things possible.

FAITH THOUGHTS

Don't forget that Jesus is with you always. The Spirit is living in you. Don't go through your storms of life afraid simply because you forget about Jesus' presence and power. Ask the Spirit to encourage you when you're struggling in your faith and simply trust God for the blessings He's preparing for you.

APRIL 13

The Struggle

*When they saw him, they worshiped him;
but some doubted.*
MATTHEW 28:17

When you're facing the struggles of life, don't struggle with your faith. Your confidence and hope should be in the assurance of what you do not see. Lay down your burden of doubt. Let the Spirit remind you of the promises made to you, so that the struggle is not within you, and your soul can rest in My hope.

Don't be surprised when you struggle with doubt and disbelief. Faith that is unquestioned and untested is not faith at all. Even at times in My ministry when faith should have come easiest to those who witnessed My miracles, they still doubted. Genuine faith must come from trusting in Me and relying on the Father to care for every detail of your everyday life. I want you to be honest about your doubts. Nothing is hidden from Me. I know your heart.

Let Me help you. Just because you doubt doesn't mean your faith is defeated. Don't allow yourself to ask questions that cannot be answered here and now. Surrender to the Father's sovereignty. Rely on the Spirit to teach you to have peace when you can't understand, assured that God has a plan and a purpose for everything He allows and does.

FAITH THOUGHTS

It's your faith that will disarm your doubt. Don't give up one moment before the miracle. Don't be surprised by doubt and expect Jesus to show up in the middle of it. With all the struggles you face in life, don't allow the struggle within ... trust and pray your way through your day.

Only Believe

APRIL 14

> *"'If you can'?" said Jesus.*
> *"Everything is possible for one who believes."*
> MARK 9:23

It's your faith in Me that will give you the assurance that all things are possible. It's by believing in Me that you are given the Holy Spirit, living within you, with the same resurrection power that lifted Me out of the grave. So, what is it in your life that My power is not greater than? I am able to do *all* things.

Regardless of your circumstances, no matter how difficult the obstacle, I am greater still. You will have moments of unbelief and you will need to be willing to surrender it all. To overcome your unbelief, you will need to acknowledge that you can't do it all on your own. You must have a desire to live for Me and not yourself, yielding to the Father's will in every area of your life instead of living according to your own desires. And with every situation, with every choice, you must turn to Me for help.

I have given the Spirit to you to comfort you, teach you, strengthen you and fill you with My love. It is the Spirit that will give you eyes to see and a willingness to lay down your pride. I need you to trust in My infinite wisdom, love, mercy, grace, and power, knowing that where you end is where I begin.

 ## FAITH THOUGHTS

You are going to face situations that are so desperate, so difficult that you are tempted to believe that they are difficult for even God. But the truth is that nothing is impossible for Him, He can do all things.

APRIL 15

Without Faith

And without faith it is impossible to please God, because anyone who comes to him must believe that he exists and that he rewards those who earnestly seek him.
HEBREWS 11:6

The only way to have a relationship with Me is to have faith. You must believe. And in your belief, you must continually seek Me, trusting in Me, following Me. It's the timing of the Father's will for your life that can cause you to doubt, but faith overcomes all doubt. Even though I appear to be leading you in the wrong direction, you can be certain that I always walk in the Father's perfect will and there is no reason to doubt His good plans no matter how painful and confusing your situations or circumstances.

The reality of the heavenly Father's sovereign love for you is that you can be sure that whatever you face in this life is preparing you for eternity. He works all things together for good. Don't allow your discouragement to drive you into doubt. Keep trusting and obeying even through all of your questions. I am with you in the middle of it all. If you continue to walk with Me, your confidence will grow and your faith will be unwavering. It always comes down to faith. Either you believe or you don't.

There is no in-between in order to walk with Me. Without faith, you will only experience hopelessness and despair. Without faith you cannot please the Father. Even when life seems out of control, He is still on His throne. The peace you need can only be found in a relationship with Me, trusting in the Father's love for you and confidently assured that He will do what He's promised.

FAITH THOUGHTS

Do you find yourself doubting, even though you know you must believe? Faith is a daily decision. It means trusting God at His Word no matter what your circumstances look like. God is worthy of your trust.

Before Dawn

APRIL 16

*I rise before dawn and cry for help;
I have put my hope in your word.*
PSALM 119:147

With your hurried, busy life, it's easy to get distracted. Start your day in strength by meditating on the Father's promises to you. It is your offensive weapon in the spiritual battles that you face … and there are many. Your prayer must feed upon the Word and your hope must rest in Me.

Pray that the Spirit would lead you, that you would hear the Father's voice according to His love and kindness. It's the Father's gentle and unchanging love, along with His grace, that overlooks your sins through My blood, that will bless you with an unwavering hope that is anchored in His Word. The evidence of His goodness, the evidence of His love is all over your life … ask the Spirit to help you see it.

I know that at times you are uncertain whether you want to keep following Me, since it doesn't seem to be getting you anywhere. Pray with your whole heart that even in your struggles you will stay focused on Me and devoted to Me. Meditate on the Word, on the promises fulfilled and those that are yet to be. It's in committing your time to having a relationship with Me and learning to rely on and trust in the Word that you will find the peace you need and the joy of knowing there truly is hope.

FAITH THOUGHTS

How do you start your day? Do you immediately seek God and ask the Spirit to lead and guide you throughout your day? You need God's help. You were never meant to go through your day alone. Make sure you are making time to continually praise God and give thanks for all He has done and all He is yet to do.

April 17

Hold On

"I am with you and will watch over you wherever you go. I will not leave you until I have done what I have promised you."
GENESIS 28:15

Before you have a problem, the Father has a solution. I am with you, I have saved you, and you have been given eternal life. It's the promises of the Word that lead and guide you until you see the Father face-to-face. It is up to you; you must make the daily decision to read the Word and allow the Spirit to use it to work within you. You have the Word to inspire you and instruct you. And you've been given the gift of the Spirit to fill you with strength and hope as you walk out your faith.

When you're tempted to doubt and give up the fight of faith ... hold on. It may not seem like your prayers are being answered, but the Father is at work in your life at every moment in ways that go unseen, unnoticed, and are often taken for granted. When difficulties arise you're tempted to believe that I am not with you and that's when you must walk by faith, relying on what I promised you and not living according to how things seem or appear.

When you doubt, run back to the promises, knowing that anything you face in life, the uncertainties, the unexpected overwhelming situations, are held in the loving, faithful hands of the Father.

Many times, His blessings are in disguise. His power brings the dead to life, He brings light out of darkness, and His power will be with you wherever you go ... He's watching over you and I am walking with you.

FAITH THOUGHTS

You'll continually face overwhelming situations and you'll be tempted to give up on God right before the miracle happens. Trust Him for what you think you can't and find peace in knowing that He is always with you, watching over you, preparing blessings for you before you need them.

To the Finish

*Finishing is better than starting.
Patience is better than pride.*
ECCLESIASTES 7:8 (NLT)

You will experience the weariness of life weighing you down from time to time and worry can convince your faith that you should doubt. That's why you need My strength. Whatever stands before you, whatever obstacle you are certain can't be moved, be sure that faith in Me makes all things possible. There will always be circumstances that are out of your control and when there is nothing you can do, wait on Me.

When you wait upon the Father, when you walk with Me, when you rely on the Spirit to lead and guide you, you'll learn to rest and trust. You'll find that you no longer need to be weary from the burden of all your troubles. Faith is simple. Pray and wait. I know it's easy to focus on your problems to the point that you're ready to give up. Keep your eyes on Me. It's in placing your trust in Me and the Spirit to lead you into the Father's will, that you will have the strength and hope you need to face each day with joy.

You need times of refreshment and renewal. I am your unending source of strength. Continually meditate on the Word, devote time to focus upon the Father's faithfulness. Come to Me when you are empty and I will renew your strength.

FAITH THOUGHTS

Are you tired and weary? Are you feeling empty and in need of renewed strength and faith? Jesus is always the answer. If you come to Him, He will show you ways to find rest, to refocus and live in joy even when your circumstances are far from joyful.

SEEKING GOD IN YOUR STRUGGLES

I love those who love me, and those who seek me find me.
PROVERBS 8:17

You'll no longer have a sense of God's absence once you enter into His presence. It's where you find yourself most vulnerable, empty and facing the endless unexpected uncertainties, that you'll find God most powerfully present. When you're faced with circumstances that tempt you to go in a direction that your spirit knows it shouldn't, faith gives you another way.

Know this: your heart will be restless until it rests in God. Your struggles will often be less about your circumstances and more about your expectations for your life that seem in complete opposition with God's.

It's through your faith in Jesus that your difficulties in life take on new meaning. If you're struggling, God is working. He's developing your character. Bringing about patience and hope. And it's when your problems and pressures are too big for you, that God has your attention. He'll make you stop and reevaluate your life, forcing you to look to Him for wisdom ... driving you to His Word. Whatever you do, don't give up. There will be a heaviness in your heart that will tempt you to.

Your struggles invite you to experience the power of God ... to witness miracles. Your struggles are not the end. They are simply a dying to self. It's where blessings are brought from brokenness. It's that place where God's grace shows up and gives you strength in your weakness. It's when you think you're completely lost and you can't find God that He finds you.

One Thing

APRIL 19

*One thing I ask from the LORD, this only do I seek:
that I may dwell in the house of the LORD
all the days of my life, to gaze on the beauty
of the LORD and to seek him in his temple.*
PSALM 27:4

Faith requires action. It requires actively seeking the Father and continually trusting in Me while relying on the Spirit. Sometimes your challenges in life are to teach you to seek Me, so that the Spirit can transform your perspective and give you eyes to see things as I do. The hope I've given you gives you the ability to persevere through trying times, the ability to grow spiritually in godly character and the ability to hold on to hope in the most trying times.

Pray that your heart's desire would simply be to be with Me. To know My heart and not only seek My hands. Those things you seek other than Me will never truly satisfy you. Temporary pleasures only lead your heart astray.

You were created to love the Father, to experience the ultimate fulfillment of living in His peace and dwelling with Him and I in you. Make it your greatest desire to enjoy more and more of My presence. I am your shelter and when you dwell with Me you can feel safe and secure, full of peace and joy. Allow Me to lift you above your circumstances … turn your eyes upon Me.

FAITH THOUGHTS

Instead of continually looking at the troubles in your life, turn your eyes upon Jesus. Seek Him and meditate on the promises, so that you can hear His voice and experience the fullness of His presence in your life. Don't miss out on the one thing that changes everything … Jesus.

Always

*Look to the LORD and his strength;
seek his face always.*
PSALM 105:4

My desire is to bring healing and wholeness to every broken aspect of your life. When you experience confusion or pain, come to Me, and allow Me to embrace you with grace through your confession. As you rely on Truth and trust in My hope, you can walk in faith, confident that wonderful blessings lie ahead.

Instead of relying on your own strength or looking for things in the world for your hope, stay focused upon Me. The Father has proven that He has the power to do anything … He raised Me from the dead. There is no greater power than overcoming death as I did. Every moment of every day you need to follow Me and seek the Father's will. Rely on the Spirit to direct you in the paths that you are to follow and let Me carry your burdens along the way.

I will never leave you … I will always be with you. You must believe in what is true and what has been promised to you. It is in living your life for Me that you are able to accomplish My work in the world. All the power that is Mine is yours. I will bless you with the assurance of My presence and provide all that you need to bring the Father glory.

FAITH THOUGHTS

When your troubles are too difficult, where do you go for strength? Are you relying on the resurrection power of Jesus, or limiting your possibilities by doing things on your own? You are not meant to walk in faith alone … Jesus is with you. Don't forget to ask the Spirit to help you draw near to God every day and to rely on Him in every way.

Completely Committed

APRIL 21

*Blessed are those who keep his statutes
and seek him with all their heart.*
PSALM 119:2

I am the Way, the Truth, and the Life … there is no other way. Blessings lie within the hands of the Father, given to a heart that is completely committed to Him. There is no other easier road, you can't have it your way and the Father's. It's His way or nothing at all. Obeying Him is not an option, it's a necessity if you want joy and happiness in your life. And seeking Him means that He is first in your life. It means that you value Him more than anything or anyone. It's living a life totally committed to Him, making Me Lord of your life.

It's in following the Father's instructions, trusting in His sovereign love that you will find joy in your heart. Although your life may be filled with troubles, you can know that His love and compassion is unfailing. You can trust Me to walk with you through affliction and persecution when it is a part of the Father's plans.

And although you may not understand why He allows your sufferings, you can be sure, with Me by your side and the Spirit within you, that you will be blessed in some way by it all. Hope might seem gone, but it is not. I am alive. I have risen. So, just when you think that things can't get worse, keep walking in faith, keep obeying the Father, and keep seeking Him with all of your heart.

FAITH THOUGHTS

Is your heart completely committed to God? Is He at the forefront of your thoughts and the focus of all your actions? If you're falling short, longing for His blessings in your life, keep seeking Him, continually, and allow the Spirit to fill you with His Word. Listen carefully and obey and look expectantly for His blessings in your life.

Heart and Soul

Now devote your heart and soul to seeking the L<small>ORD</small> your God.
1 C<small>HRONICLES</small> 22:19

You are called to more than just existing. You may think that food, water, and shelter are your vital necessities in life, but you cannot really live unless your heart, soul, and mind is set on seeking Me. You can exist, but without seeking Me, you cannot truly live. You are called to live an abundant life, seeking Me, serving Me, and bringing glory to the Father.

When you seek Me, when you are devoted, at all times and in all ways, in every situation, both good and bad, you will be blessed. In everything you do, seek Me and the Kingdom first. Fix and focus your mind's attention and your heart's affection on Me. I am not lost, but there is always something getting in the way of you seeking Me … because of all the distractions, I can seem hidden.

All the obstacles can cause you to stumble in your faith and get in the way of you enjoying the continual consciousness of dwelling with Me. Seeking Me takes a conscious effort to get to Me … to constantly set your mind on Me and allow the Spirit to direct you into the Father's plans and purposes for your life. Don't let anything get in the way of My presence and the fullness of your joy.

F<small>AITH</small> T<small>HOUGHTS</small>

Pray that you will set your mind on God, living according to His Word in all you do and say. Ask the Spirit to show you the Father's faithfulness and assure you that hope is alive. Ask Jesus to show you the way so that you can walk in righteousness and receive the fullness of joy that comes from following Him.

Reaching Out

APRIL 23

*God did this so that they would seek him
and perhaps reach out for him and find him,
though he is not far from any one of us.*
ACTS 17:27

Everything the Father does is so that you will seek Him. He will never force Himself on you. Everything, all creation, is continually pointing you to Him. Embrace His love as He pours out His grace on you – He is closer than you think. He has done everything necessary for you to have a relationship with Him. His fingerprints are everywhere and He sent Me into the world to provide evidence of His love and mercy.

Don't allow your pride to keep you from turning to Him. You are created in the Father's image. You are loved, sinful, and redeemed. Nothing can separate your heart from Him. You are His child ... even in the middle of your mess. And He is always near ... present everywhere, at all times.

There is no place you can go where He is not already. Even in death, financial ruin, and breakups of relationships, the Father uses all things to teach you that you cannot make it without Him. Everything in all creation, in some way or another, is meant to draw you to the Father and His saving grace. When you're struggling in your faith, reach out and take My hand. Walk with Me in the Father's will and find rest for your soul.

FAITH THOUGHTS

Do you feel close to God? Are you wondering if He's left you? Know that it's not that God has moved away from you, but possibly that you have moved away from Him. Is there an obstacle that is keeping you from feeling like you're in right relationship with Him? Whatever it is ... give it to Jesus.

April 24

Pray, Seek, and Turn

" ... if my people, who are called by my name,
will humble themselves and pray and seek my face and
turn from their wicked ways, then I will hear from heaven,
and I will forgive their sin and will heal their land."

2 Chronicles 7:14

Your obedience to the Father will call you to humble yourself, lay down your pride and stop trying to control what you cannot. It's the Spirit that will lead you to reflect, repent, and realign your will to the Father's, so that you can rejoice in sharing in His glory.

Your life of faith in Me will always require humility, prayer, devotion, and repentance. Everything in your life must be in submission to the Father. You must live a life of surrender. There is no greater blessing than being used by the Father and allowing the Spirit to work within you to mold you to His will. Always remember that the way to the Father is prayer. It's when you pray that you bring your life to meet Him in the moment and it's in that moment that He pours Himself into your life. It's the foundation of growing a relationship with Him and having a deeper connection to His heart. Each and every day you make the decision to grow closer to Him or remain right where you are.

If you will follow Me, you will see that the path to His greatest blessings in your life requires refinement, growth, and a longing to know Him better. Now is the time for revival in your soul. Pray, seek the Father, and turn from anything that is keeping you from Him.

Faith Thoughts

When life's troubles get suddenly overwhelming, you can easily forget to simply pray. When you can't understand, when you're not sure what to do, simply pray. Call out to God and when you're not sure what to say, allow the Spirit to speak for you. Ask God to align your will with His and draw your heart closer to His own.

Thirsty

APRIL 25

*You, God, are my God, earnestly I seek you;
I thirst for you, my whole being longs for you,
in a dry and parched land where there is no water.*
PSALM 63:1

Are you troubled? Praise the Father. It can be easy to focus on the negative things in life, instead of the positive, and worry instead of worship. Along your journey of faith, you can find yourself moving through spiritual dry places. But know that it's your wilderness moments that are meant for you to learn to rely more on Me for strength and the Spirit for direction. Now, in the middle of your overwhelming circumstances, is the time to focus your heart on worship and praise.

Don't wallow in your woes. It leads to nowhere. It's in your worship that you are given power to overcome whatever you're facing. Your soul is supposed to long for Me, do not be surprised when you feel unsatisfied in your struggles and desperate for Me to hear you and answer you. And I will come to you. I will listen. It is in Me, through Me, and by Me that you will have everything your heart and soul desires. I am all you need.

When you are thirsty, come to Me and drink of the Living Water I will give you … you will never thirst again. Embrace your difficulties and see them as the Father refining you in the fire just as silver. All of the impurities will rise to the surface and you will be conformed more into My image, reflecting My love to the world around you. There is purpose for your pain when you surrender it all into the loving hands of the Father.

FAITH THOUGHTS

Do you feel as though at times something is missing? Like you need more? Turn to Jesus … He is all you need to be filled to the full. He alone is what will satisfy the deepest longings of your soul.

APRIL 26

Seek and Find

*"You will seek me and find me
when you seek me with all your heart."*
JEREMIAH 29:13

Hope is never lost. There is still an empty grave. So, when hope seems gone, you are commanded to seek the Father … with all your heart. An undivided heart seeks for a moment and is distracted … prioritizing worldly desires above Me. I lived My life continually seeking the Father, in constant prayer. I exemplified longing for His presence, seeking fellowship and intimacy with Him. My only desire was to live My life according to His will and continuously seek His guidance every step of the way.

Know that the Father is always waiting to hear from you. Always waiting at His throne of grace. He never changes, He never moves. He is the same yesterday, today, and forever. Never let anything get in the way of you seeking the Father with your whole heart. He doesn't need well-polished prayers – He needs your sincerity, your surrender. And it's your prayers of submission to His will that will allow the Spirit to work within you, to sanctify you and take you from glory to glory.

Don't question His ways – you cannot possibly understand them. His perspective encompasses your past, present, and future. Only He knows what lies ahead and I will walk with you through it all.

FAITH THOUGHTS

Are you looking for God … continually? Are you seeking Him constantly for the help that you desperately need? What are you facing that requires His help … His miracle? What is it that is keeping you from giving it all to Him completely and trusting Him entirely? Keep seeking Him and don't be surprised when you find Him.

Never Forsaken

APRIL 27

Those who know your name trust in you, for you,
Lord, have never forsaken those who seek you.
PSALM 9:10

You will always experience heartbreak and disappointment. Your pain, your frustration is your longing for heaven … your home. And although the troubles in your life can leave you feeling abandoned and alone, making heaven seem so far away, I am right here with you. I am your stronghold.

I alone am your protection and your strength. When your pain is crushing, when you're not sure you can keep going, I will lift your head. I am your shelter in the storm. You might feel depleted and defeated from the struggles of life, but I am full of abundance … I am everything you could ever need. The Father is full of grace for every moment of your life. His love never fails or runs out.

Your doubts and your brokenness are not too much for Him. Your weakness does not deter Him from blessing you. When you are weak, I am strong. The Father is the source of life and you were meant to seek Him, find Him and be filled. Ask the Spirit to comfort you in your trials and troubles and make room for grace to empower you to walk forward in faith, full of joy in trusting in the promises you've been made. Allow Me to carry your burdens, let Me lift the heaviness you've been carrying. You can't keep moving in the direction you've been going … you cannot do this alone. Come to the Father and be filled with the peace that gives true rest to your soul.

FAITH THOUGHTS

If you're feeling disappointment, your frustration is most likely coming from expectations you had for your life that aren't being met. It's not easy to trust God when everything is uncertain and falling apart, but that's exactly what you must do. He has never forsaken you – you are still here, Jesus is still with you, and the grave is still empty.

April 28

Any Who Seek

The LORD looks down from heaven on all mankind to see if there are any who understand, any who seek God.
PSALM 14:2

The Father cares deeply about you and all of His creation, and He continually looks for those seeking Him. He searches the earth for those who are faithful, not too busy or preoccupied to call upon Him and seek His kingdom. He is looking for a willing heart, surrendered to His love.

Wherever you are in your struggles, you have not reached the end of your hope, even though it may seem like you have. You are still alive and the grave is still empty … there is hope. Your story is not finished. It's easy to get caught up in your past, the failures and disappointments, and find it difficult to move forward. I know that you struggle to believe in My redeeming power that can assure you of the hope in your future.

If you make the Kingdom your primary concern, heaven will come to earth and your hopes will be fulfilled. Let Me be the one you're running after in this life, knowing that the Spirit is within you.

I am with you at all times. Look to Me for everything you need and look expectantly for My miracles in your life. Trust in Me to do what only I can do in your life … above all you can hope for or imagine.

FAITH THOUGHTS

When God looks down from heaven, what does He see when He looks at you? Does He see you seeking wisdom and insight? Does He see you seeking Him at all? Are you seeking Him for transformation of your heart by yearning for His? Call upon the Spirit and be driven to seek God at all times and in all ways. Strive to bring a smile to His face.

Turn Back

APRIL 29

Seek the LORD, all you humble of the land, you who do what he commands. Seek righteousness, seek humility; perhaps you will be sheltered on the day of the LORD's anger.
ZEPHANIAH 2:3

I know you lose your way from time to time. But don't get lost and refuse to seek help. You may have realized you were wandering, or maybe you have found yourself lost unexpectedly. Know that when you're lost, I will find you. And when you've gone astray, turn to Me, repent, and walk forward with Me in faith.

In order to walk in faith you must always humble yourself, ridding yourself of your idols and allowing your kingdoms to crumble. Let it all go. When you end up in a place where you shouldn't be, refuse to give in to pride. Admit your sin and allow My forgiveness of sins to cover you. At all times, seek the Father's righteousness.

If you'll turn to Him, He will always respond with grace and cleanse your heart. Without Me, you will walk in fear. I give you the peace and assurance in the promises. No matter what, no matter how difficult your circumstances are, My power is greater. It is only in going through the impossible that you will see My miracles. I am the way when there seems to be no way.

Always remember the Father has the final say in everything you face in life. Trust in His love and mercy, rest in His grace and find strength through trusting in Him completely.

FAITH THOUGHTS

Ask the Spirit to humble your heart, to keep you from wandering off God's path and getting lost. If you are facing times of confusion, ask for comfort and peace as you wait on God's voice and direction in your life. In the middle of your struggles, your solution is simply to surrender.

APRIL 30

Just Ask

I love those who love me, and those who seek me find me.
PROVERBS 8:17

When you're facing overwhelming circumstances, your cry to the Father is the same as Mine, "Why?" It's in these most troubling moments when sufferings are simply too much to bear that you must trust what the Father is doing, not basing your faith on what you feel or on your own understanding, but in the assurance you have in God's promises. In the midst of your troubles, regardless of what they are, you need the Father's wisdom and guidance so that you do not try to take things into your own hands and lean on your own understanding.

It is the Father's desire that through your trials you will learn to rely on Him more and more and cling to Him. There is nothing more vital to your faith and life than knowing His promises when you must go through tests of faith that go beyond your ability to understand. It's when you go to Him, truly trusting, that His Word will give you the wisdom you need to continue to walk in faith.

You cannot say you're trusting and then be filled with fear and doubt. You must make the decision to trust Him and His wisdom, believing fully in His unfailing love for you. When you're in need, the answer is simple, even before you pray … just ask and it will be given to you.

FAITH THOUGHTS

So often, when you're facing overwhelming circumstances, struggles that never seem to end, and prayers that seem to go unanswered, you forget to just ask God for what you want and need. He holds all of your yesterdays, todays, and tomorrows. He alone is able to do the impossible, just trust that He will do what He's promised.

Right Now

MAY 1

*Seek the L*ORD *while he may be found; call on him while he is near. Let the wicked forsake their ways and the unrighteous their thoughts. Let them turn to the L*ORD*, and he will have mercy on them, and to our God, for he will freely pardon.*
ISAIAH 55:6-7

You are invited to rely on the Father's presence and help, the choice is yours. Whatever your challenges in life, whether financial, relational, physical, or spiritual, you can't waste any time in bringing it to Me. I am to carry your burdens. Know that the Father always hears your prayers and your cries for help. He has promised to be a ready help in times of trouble … you can count on Him.

The Word must be the foundation of your prayers, knowing that the Father is still sovereign and powerful and has proven Himself faithful to every one of His promises. Don't underestimate the Father's concern about every detail of your life. Don't exclude Him from the small stuff because all things are small to Him. There is nothing in your life that is unimportant to Him. Whatever concerns you concerns Him. You can rely on the Spirit to strengthen you, you can count on Me to lead you and always be with you. No matter how great your challenges are, the Father is greater. Turn to Him, seek Him, and find His mercy waiting for you.

FAITH THOUGHTS

There is nothing too difficult for God. Whatever it is you think He can't do, He can do more. Sometimes you just need to turn to Him. Sometimes you just need to let go and let God. And all the time you need to pray and seek Him in every area of your life.

FACING YOUR ANGER IN ANXIETY

He says, "Be still, and know that I am God."
PSALM 46:10

Your challenging circumstances can cause you to feel injustice and betrayal. You may be angry at yourself for making wrong choices in your life. You may be angry that the actions of others have brought you to this destructive place, or you may be angry at God. It's in the moments that you feel a complete lack of control over the circumstances in your life that anger sets in and bitterness and wrath rule. But you don't have to react in despair. Remember? You have hope. You have Jesus. You can simply repent, reject your anger, and walk away from it.

When your anxiety and anger arise, it's because there is something in your life that is being denied, delayed, or disrupted. In these moments it's time to call upon the Spirit to work within you to retrain yourself in righteousness. Life won't usually go according to your plans. And when they don't, your anger can come from worry and anxiety, believing that you're supposed to fix everything and control the chaos in your life. But God has told you to rid yourself of your restlessness, fretfulness, and self-centeredness. It's about being God-centered. It's about realizing that there is no panic going on in heaven.

You are commanded not to despair, acting as if God is no longer on His throne. You're not supposed to control every aspect of your life. Ask that the Spirit will give you the grace to stand empty before God, relying on Him, casting your fears and worries upon Him, and trusting Him with all that you think you can't.

Let It Go

*Refrain from anger and turn from wrath;
do not fret – it leads only to evil.*
PSALM 37:8

Don't be weighed down by anger. Ask the Spirit to search your heart and reveal the truths about your feelings and the root cause of the anger you're feeling. Ask Me to carry the burdens that are causing your anger and then let it go. Even though you can't control your circumstances, you can control your anger over them, in My strength … with the Spirit's help.

Your anger is only the tip of the iceberg. Anger is the sum of every other negative emotion. It is your sadness, loneliness, grief, disappointment, depression, shame, anxiety, regrets, jealousy, and the exhaustion that leads to it. Anger is when things have gone too far. When you have not come to Me and given Me the burdens, one by one, sooner. You thought you could do it on your own. You thought you held the resources and the ability to walk through the fire on your own. And anger is the result.

When you are faced with troubles, there is grace in the face of every one of them. You don't have to be strong. You don't have to be right. You don't have to depend on others for the blessings in your life. The Father will make sure there is justice. Vengeance is His. Lay it all in His hands. Rest in My peace and let Me handle the things that you're crumbling beneath the weight of.

FAITH THOUGHTS

What is it that you continually feel angry about? Is it truly something you can control? Have you handed it over to Jesus, or are you afraid to trust Him with it because you're afraid justice will not be served how and when you want it to be? You need peace … you need Jesus. Make it a priority to give Him your anger.

MAY 3

Don't Be A Fool

*Whoever is patient has great understanding,
but one who is quick-tempered displays folly.*
PROVERBS 14:29

Your anger will never help you when it causes overreaction, misreading circumstances, misjudging motives, and taking action without the Father's wisdom and insight. When you respond more severely than you need to, speaking with harshness and without love, you are walking outside of the Father's will. If you are wise, in daily devotion with Me, relying on the Spirit, you will be slow in letting your anger develop because you will be giving Me the burdens that are causing the emotion.

If you're angry, whatever you're trying to accomplish will fail because you have no influence over your circumstances when you are angry. It causes unnecessary troubles and leads quickly to many sins. Since it begins in the heart, you must be diligent at addressing it because the heart is deceitful above all things. When you feel anger rise up, focus on grace, longsuffering, and patience. You must hate sin. You must hate anger. So, take time to submit yourself to the Holy Spirit continually. Allow the Spirit to take you deeper in understanding your anger so that you can look at your heart's condition.

The Spirit will walk you through and help you to understand why you are struggling with it all. In the searching, in the sanctifying, the Spirit will give comfort and grace, healing you and helping you to become all the Father has called you to be … giving you a heart that has patient love and understanding … just like Mine.

FAITH THOUGHTS

It is vital that you call upon the Spirit to search your heart each day. Emotions can creep up quickly when you're facing continual overwhelming circumstances. You aren't supposed to walk through the fiery furnace alone. Let Jesus help you. He can handle anything.

Calm Down

MAY 4

*Do not be quickly provoked in your spirit,
for anger resides in the lap of fools.*
ECCLESIASTES 7:9

Listen, you're not supposed to have it all figured out and have life perfectly put together. Let go of expectations for your life that can only lead to disappointment and anger. Your resentment and bitterness should be a warning sign of the anger and rage within you to come. You have not been given that Spirit. Your heart needs healing. You can bring it all to the foot of the Cross and lay it down. Whatever it is that is hurting you, let Me heal you.

There are so many pressures in life that it is not surprising that you often feel crushed under the weight of them. That pressure can cause fear, disappointment and a loss of self-control. But if you will remain quiet before the Father, you can free yourself from the things of the world that cause your heart to be unrestrained. Yearn for the Father.

Pay attention to fellowshipping with the Spirit and thirst for the Father's truth. It's the Word that shows you how to live, leading to the blessing of peace. Regardless of your circumstances, you can live in accordance with the Father's Word and will, entrusting your difficulties to Him and allowing Him to heal your heart.

If you continually surrender your heart to Him, you won't be tossed around by your circumstances. You'll realize that you can calm down and ignore the Enemy's deceit that is sure to make you think and do foolish things. Keep seeking, keep knocking. Seek the Father's heart, so that He might comfort yours.

FAITH THOUGHTS

Pray that the Spirit will keep you from holding on to foolish anger in your heart. Ask Him to fill you with godly wisdom and a gracious spirit, so that you can reflect the love of Jesus in your life. Ask to be an example of His goodness and grace as you walk in ways that reflect God's glory.

MAY 5

Before Sunset

*"Be angry, and do not sin": do not let
the sun go down on your wrath.*
EPHESIANS 4:26 (NKJV)

You can't allow anger to grip you and provoke you to act contradictory to the Father's will. It's when you're stirred up in anger that you are unable to think straight and you will find it more difficult to hear the Spirit's voice. You must always take immediate steps to deal with all of the situations that stir up emotions that lead to anger. Don't allow anger to seep in and settle. Come to Me, your spirit does not have to be a reflection of your situation.

Know that your response to what you can't control is your decision, and your anger is the devil's playground. When your heart is unsettled and your emotions are out of control, you should go to the Father in prayer, expressing your hurt and anger, asking Him to bring justice, to quiet your heart and give you peace to be still. Being still causes the anger within you to slowly quiet and subside so that your heart does not give a place to the devil.

It's when you are angry and have lost self-control that you are living under the authority of the devil instead of the Father. It's your unresolved anger that leads to resentment, bitterness, gossip, slander, envy, fights, and an endless list of destructive behaviors.

I have already won this battle you're fighting. The devil does not have a place in your life, so don't give him one. Before the sun goes down, bring your anger to Me ... I will take care of it and give you peace.

FAITH THOUGHTS

Understand that anger is a part of living in our fallen world. You can't deny your anger, but because you belong to Jesus, you can't let it lead to sin. You need to make it a priority to deal with the feelings that lead to anger, and always remember during these times that you're in a spiritual battle ... fight them on your knees.

Changed

*My dear brothers and sisters, take note of this:
Everyone should be quick to listen,
slow to speak and slow to become angry.*
JAMES 1:19

There is a freedom and peace that comes when you respond the right way to the pressures of life. Begin by being quick to listen, slow to speak, and slow to be angry. Walk in submission to the Father and His perfect will. Let everything you do and say demonstrate the Father's love.

I know that you cannot prevent yourself from ever getting angry because there are some things that *should* anger you. You will get angry from time to time. If you experience righteous anger, it will fuel you into taking right actions to do the will of the Father. But your anger driven by other emotions will surely lead to unrighteousness. Know that I didn't come and ask you to follow Me to make you a *better* person, I came to make you a *new* person. You need Me living in you to be able to accomplish what you're called to. You are changed. If you believe that I am in you, then see the truth about who you are. You are My fullness, My grace, My mercy and kindness and holiness.

Continually ask the Spirit to rid you of anything that is not of Me. Be aware of your lust, impatience, unbelief, and anger that holds you back from following Me and living a life that is completely changed … I make all things new.

FAITH THOUGHTS

Do you take your responsibility seriously that you are to lead others to Jesus? Do you struggle with feeling like you should be an example but also dealing with failures in your life? Don't give up. Ask the Spirit to give you the power of God to do all that you're called to do and live a life that is changed by Jesus' saving grace.

MAY 7

The Choice

Get rid of all bitterness, rage and anger, brawling and slander, along with every form of malice.
EPHESIANS 4:31

You will never be able to avoid getting hurt in this life. There is sin in the world and people hurt others intentionally and often unintentionally. Don't hide your hurt. Don't avoid the pain. Bring it all to Me, letting go of your bitterness and anger and desire to seek revenge. Do not act like everything is alright when it's not. It's time to walk in love and in order to do this you must learn to forgive others as well as yourself.

Letting go of your anger and unforgiveness is more for you than it is your offender. As you set them free, you are set free from the weight of the hatred and unforgiveness in your heart. My forgiveness allows the heavy burden and weight in your heart to be lifted. When you are treated poorly and disregarded, I want you to respond with peace and love, so that you are not chained by bitterness and rage.

Don't expect to overcome the evil in your heart on your own, do it in My strength and with the help of the Spirit. You are no longer an unbeliever, you believe, therefore you must turn from your old ways of responding to offenses and respond with a righteous heart. You have a choice. Always.

Bitterness, malice, and hatred toward others are the attitudes that fail to edify and encourage. They only tear down the Kingdom. Make the daily choice to do everything you can to live in peace and live as I did, with a tender heart, fully forgiving.

FAITH THOUGHTS

What unforgiveness are you holding in your heart right now? It can be difficult to forgive when you are enduring ongoing pain and suffering. Bitterness tends to take root quickly if you aren't carefully paying attention. Ask the Spirit to help you to always respond in love.

Refuge and Strength

*God is our refuge and strength,
an ever-present help in trouble.*
PSALM 46:1

From time to time you will face overwhelming circumstances in which you will not find refuge or hope anywhere other than through Me. Even as you follow Me, you will face troubles of all kinds. When the weight of it all is too much to bear, allow your fear and anxiety to draw you to Me … seek Me more and more. Your ability to stand steadfast in your faith will depend on whether you're depending upon your own strength or Mine.

When you can't run from the storms of life, find shelter in the Father through them. Struggles in life will leave you feeling empty, and you'll need the Father's wisdom to navigate through it all. Call upon Me, call upon the Spirit, help is right here … ever-present.

If you continually look at your present circumstances, you will be tossed around by doubt and despair, but if you are grounded in the Father's Word and His promise of eternity, you can stand firm in your faith, being courageous and strong. You can know that no matter how overwhelming your circumstances, no matter how frightening, the Father is your refuge and strength, and His love and grace is unchanging. Pray for strong faith to continue to trust the Father so that you can experience the peace of His presence.

FAITH THOUGHTS

Hold on to the hope you've been given in Christ. Whatever you're facing, He has already overcome. Each and every day realize that you need God. Whatever your circumstances, the Spirit can lead you to the solution. Don't try and walk in faith in your own strength, rely on the resurrection power of Jesus.

Choosing Grace

*Because human anger does not produce
the righteousness that God desires.*
JAMES 1:20

There is always hope to renew your spirit. It's submission to the Word, in humility, that makes you moldable to My image. Pray that the Spirit will continually show you how to respond to situations that might cause you to fall into bitterness and rage. Ask to be reminded how negative feelings are detrimental to your body, soul, and spirit. I came so that you might live an abundant life, not one that is chained by anger.

It will not always be easy to choose grace and you can't do it in your own strength. It will take confessing your sins, continually, and asking the Spirit to search your heart and reveal those things which keep you from walking in the Father's will. Ask to be shown the reason for your anger. It is when you feel as though you're treated unfairly, and you are overtaken by impatience and despair, that you will find yourself falling into anger. It's the Spirit that can calm you and help you to be slow to anger.

Keep the Cross always before you. Don't allow your reactions of anger to get the best of you, causing irrational thinking, and pushing you in a direction where you are likely to sin. Be willing to face your problems courageously with a prayerful spirit. When life is hard, accept it, deal with it, and choose grace. Walk with Me in forgiveness, kindness, and tenderheartedness.

Faith Thoughts

Is there something that is continually making you angry? Have you asked the Spirit to reveal to you why you are angry? Seeing the true condition of your heart will never be easy, but it is vital to living righteously. When you're angry, take time to breathe and ask the Spirit to help you respond in a godly manner instead of reacting in a way that falls short of God's glory.

In Distress

*Tremble and do not sin; when you are on
your beds, search your hearts and be silent.*
PSALM 4:4

You are redeemed, but still human. You will feel the entire spectrum of emotions given to you by the Father: fear and anger, sorrow and happiness, discontent and peace. You are set apart from the sinful patterns of the world. And you are set apart for more than just yourself and the benefits you will gain from walking rightly, you are set apart for the Father … for His kingdom.

There will be countless situations that you will face that will cause you to feel anger. Ask the Spirit to continually search your heart and then quietly wait and listen. When the Spirit searches your heart, He will make sure that your heart is properly aligned with the Father. Your faith must believe that things will get better, but even if they do not, you must walk forward, trusting in the Father.

Know that when you're questioning the Father and His ways Truth tells you that He loves you and He is your joy even when your situation is not joyful. You can trust Him, even as all others fail you … He never will. Do not allow the situations of your life to control you, come to Me. Allow the Spirit to support and strengthen you. The Father's grace is not dependent on your feelings. Keep trusting in His goodness and look for His faithfulness in your life.

FAITH THOUGHTS

Where in your life do you need more of Jesus? Ask the Spirit to help you in your distress, when you feel like you just can't take anymore. You can't go through life's storms on your own, you need Jesus in the boat with you. And you need to recognize that He is in the middle of it all with you. Look to Him … He's resting because He knows the Father is working … you can rest, too.

May 11

Glory Be

A person's wisdom yields patience;
it is to one's glory to overlook an offense.
PROVERBS 19:11

You can show God's glory today when someone offends you. If you will look to Me and rely on the wisdom of the Father, you can defer your anger and forgive. Your heart needs to be free, not chained by evil in the world. I'm asking you to choose mercy over wrath, but you can only do so with the help of the Holy Spirit.

You can choose to put off, delay and postpone your anger at offenses and allow the Father to handle it. Your self-control, given to you through the Spirit is faith in action, exemplifying a gracious and gentle spirit. It is proof that you are following Me. I know that your human nature, your initial reaction to your pain and suffering, is hostility, revenge, bitterness and rage. Do not allow your feelings to rule your heart. Do not allow yourself to live contrary to the wisdom and grace of the Father.

Your anger causes misjudgments and retaliations that lead to greater troubles. Once you allow your feelings of anger to control you, the offense turns into ongoing conflict and strife and you find yourself in a war that is not easily ended. Fight your battles upon your knees, defer your anger … the battle belongs to Me and the victory is Mine. Choose to walk in the Spirit, forgiving those who hurt you, choosing wisdom, peace, and love. Your enemy thrives on your quick retaliation and retribution. You must reject and despise it. If you are walking with Me, you will not see the wrongs in others … you will choose peace. Do not be provoked, do not be irritated, do not compromise your faith.

Faith Thoughts

How will you respond when others offend you? Through God's wisdom, grace, and glory? Pray that the world around you would see your good works of mercy and forgiveness and glorify God.

Not the Same

MAY 12

Therefore, as God's chosen people, holy and dearly loved, clothe yourselves with compassion, kindness, humility, gentleness and patience. Bear with each other and forgive one another if any of you has a grievance against someone. Forgive as the Lord forgave you.
COLOSSIANS 3:12-13

You are chosen and you are called. If you are following Me, if you've made the decision to walk in faith, you're not the same person. You are redeemed, you are changed, and you have a renewing of mind, a change of heart that seeks transformation through the Word. When you are seeking the Father, obeying Him and following the leading of the Holy Spirit that I have given to you, your process of desiring and seeking after the kingdom of God becomes who you are.

Walking with Me will mean searching your heart and asking the Spirit to do so as well. You will need to recognize the ways in which you are living that are falling short of the Father's best for your life. It's the Word that reveals what is beneath the surface, the things that must be confessed.

The place where you will find new strength is when you imitate Me, My personality. Your responsibility is to follow Me in My ways, living in the new nature that I have created for you. It is a process, a transformation. With each step of obedience, My peace will increase within you and the desires of the flesh will diminish. Embrace the new you – you are set apart for holiness.

FAITH THOUGHTS

Are you still trying to live life the way you used to instead of how God has told you to? You can confess the things that are weighing you down. God is not surprised, He can handle it. Acknowledge your struggle, then embrace God's process of transforming your heart into the likeness of His.

Faithful and Just

*If we confess our sins, he is faithful
and just and will forgive us our sins and
purify us from all unrighteousness.*
1 JOHN 1:9

When emotions take over, it's your anger that can cause you to sin. At times, when life is relentless and troubles never seem to cease, your response to it all can fall short of the Father's glory ... but there is forgiveness. There can be a renewal of your spirit. The Father is faithful and just to forgive all sins.

Through Me you have a promise of hope, comfort and deliverance that is always available to you when you're carrying the burden of guilt ... if you're willing to confess. Acknowledge that your difficult circumstances have weighed you down, worn you out and caused you to wearily react in a way that is contrary to the Holy Spirit.

When you believe in Me for eternal life, the Father begins to work within you, by the Spirit, to conform you into who He created you to be. You are to grow and mature, understanding more of the truth and walking in obedience through your faith. Do not deny your sin, do not exclude your bitterness and anger from that which separates you from the Father. Acknowledge those feelings that are not fruit of the Spirit as sinful and ask for the forgiveness that is always waiting for you at the throne of grace.

FAITH THOUGHTS

Do you recognize your bitterness and anger as sin? Anger may seem irrelevant, but it is dangerous to your faith. It can cause you to walk down paths you were never supposed to, causing more pain and suffering than that which caused your anger in the first place. Run to Jesus in your disappointment, let Him give you His peace and assure you that the Father is faithful and just.

The Purpose

MAY 14

For those God foreknew he also predestined to be conformed to the image of his Son, that he might be the firstborn among many brothers and sisters.
ROMANS 8:29

The Father has loved you since before the beginning of time. He sent Me to save you and to conform you into My image. Everything is designed for the Father's glory. So, when you're frustrated, struggling to see purpose in your pain, wrestling with anger and distress, hold on to the hope you've been given and look to Me for your peace.

Your present sufferings will end in glorification. Don't doubt what you've been promised. I call you to keep the faith, not blindly, but trusting in the Father's promises and in His faithfulness. The Father knows your life from beginning to end. There is nothing that comes as a surprise to Him. And though He allows you to walk through fires and deep waters, I am with you. It is My strength and power that will carry you through the most trying times and places of hopelessness.

When you are weak, I will carry you. There is nothing too difficult for Me and your feelings of doubt and despair do not diminish My love for you. Fight your battles upon your knees, surrendering to the Father's will, and looking to His promises to strengthen you as you wait patiently upon His miracles.

FAITH THOUGHTS

It's difficult at best to understand that God loves you even when He allows bad things to happen. When you're in the middle of deep pain and suffering, it seems that God not only doesn't care, but you're not sure He is even there. No matter what you feel, keep believing. Keep seeking Him and trust that He has purposes that are for good. Let Him hold you in His grace and give you peace.

WALKING IN GOD'S WILL

Observe the commands of the Lord your God, walking in obedience to him and revering him.
DEUTERONOMY 8:6

Too often you focus on what God wants you to do instead of realizing He's more concerned about who you are and your journey of faith that forms godly character. Walking in God's will is not to be done in your own strength, but in His, and you must first have a humble heart, so that the Spirit can guide you and teach you the path for your life. If you will always look to God's Word, you find His will, if you'll acknowledge your need for His strength and wisdom.

God's will won't usually agree with your own. He calls you to live a life that is above your circumstances, giving thanks through the good and the bad. He calls you to a place of contentment, to live according to the Spirit with a mind that is controlled, full of life and peace. Yet, all too often, life gets the best of you and you struggle to believe that God is going to help you or that He has any plans at all ... much less good ones.

When life feels anything but good, it's easy to strive to direct your circumstances instead of relying on God to. Walking in His will is going to continue to challenge your faith and you must be willing to step out in faith, believing that He can do the impossible and that He will reward you if you will earnestly seek Him.

Faith is going to take you into the unknown, and you'll often find that God is going to ask you to follow Him without disclosing a full understanding of His plans, provisions, or purposes. And you're going to need to persevere so that you can receive what He's promised. Don't miss out on the good part.

What's Required

*He has shown you, O mortal, what is good.
And what does the LORD require of you? To act justly
and to love mercy and to walk humbly with your God.*
MICAH 6:8

I know that you struggle to know what the Father expects from you, always feeling like you're falling short, but often unsure of where you're failing. Know this: just three things are required as you walk with Me and in the Father's will – justice, mercy, and humility. And you can't do this without the Spirit.

What the Father requires of you is not to be done in your own strength and power, but Mine. And each action of faith that is required starts with a soft and loving heart. You can't act in love if you are harboring resentment or hate. You can't show kindness and mercy if you are making yourself and not the kingdom of heaven your priority.

Don't allow your heart to be filled with pride and walk ahead of Me. I'm to lead you in the way that you should go … down paths of righteousness. And I need you to walk closely to Me, submitting your will to the Father each and every day. The Father is continually pursuing your heart and the Spirit is working to transform you into My image. Though troubles may come, and you're tempted to give up and give in, not knowing what you're supposed to do and which direction to take, you can walk with Me and know that I will show you the way.

FAITH THOUGHTS

You might struggle on a daily basis to understand exactly what God wants you to do and instead of being confused, you need to stick to the three simple things He requires of you: justice, mercy, and humility. When life is chaotic, and you're desperate for God, focus on these three things and He will give you peace.

MAY 16

Walking Worthy

... that you may walk worthy of the Lord, fully pleasing Him, being fruitful in every good work and increasing in the knowledge of God; strengthened with all might, according to His glorious power, for all patience and longsuffering with joy.
COLOSSIANS 1:10-11 (NKJV)

You are earthen vessels that the Father has designed to be filled with the knowledge of Me. It's your faith in Me that will result in the transformation of your life, giving you a life that manifests My power. You are called to walk in a way that is worthy of Me, consistent with who I am, what I have done, and am yet to do. Your walk of faith should be one that brings attention to the grace of the Father, filled with the wisdom and knowledge of the Father. And as you seek to live the worthy life, in the Father's grace, it's important to always keep eternity in mind.

Whatever you do, always give thanks to the Father ... being thankful for the awesome and countless blessings that you have through My sacrifice, making you in right relationship with the Father, able to approach His throne of grace with confidence.

I want to heal your hurts and remove your scar tissue, bringing comfort to all of your pain and suffering. In doing so, I want you to be filled with My love, so that you can go out into the world, accomplishing all that you're meant to. Everything that you are must be surrendered to Me, willing to follow Me wherever I lead. When you are weak, I will be your strength. When you are anxious, I will calm your soul and fill you with hope.

FAITH THOUGHTS

You may struggle in feeling that you're not doing what God wants you to do in your life. Either you've gone your own direction, or you just can't seem to hear God's voice or understand the Spirit's direction. In looking to please God and live according to His will for your life, start with surrender ... every single day.

Following

Whoever claims to live in him must live as Jesus did.
1 JOHN 2:6

If you are following Me, you are living as I have – you are walking according to the Word and you're obeying and repenting when you don't. If you love Me, if you believe in Me and what I've done, you will continually walk with Me to the Cross … where your sins die, where your sinful nature dies, where you die to self and live for Me.

You can walk to the Cross by faith, not in your own strength or power, but in Mine. The Cross is where you should always be driven. I earned forgiveness and everlasting life for you and I advocate for you until the end of time. I present My righteousness to the Father as your righteousness which opens the door for you so that you can live in fellowship with Him. I made it clear that all that I accomplished and the way that I lived was done by the Father living in Me. And now I live in you, enabling you to live in the way I did, accomplishing even greater miracles.

You need a quiet, unrelenting dependence on Me dwelling in you, always at work within you. Your profession of faith cannot be genuine if it does not result in your life being transformed. You can't claim to know Me and walk with Me and then deny Me by your actions. You cannot walk with Me without keeping the Father's commandments. You cannot say that you have received My saving grace and not become like Me, as a result.

Faith Thoughts

You need to continually ask yourself where you stand with God. Ask the Spirit to give you a fresh outpouring of love and rely on His strength to live in God's mercy as you humble yourself to walk in the way that Jesus did. Pay attention to the ways God is trying to transform your heart.

MAY 18

Prepared

For we are God's handiwork, created in Christ Jesus to do good works, which God prepared in advance for us to do.
EPHESIANS 2:10

The Father, rich in mercy, through His gracious loving-kindness, has offered the faith in My death and resurrection as forgiveness for your sinful condition. Once separated from Him, your belief in Me has redeemed you and brought you back into right relationship with the Father. When I died, you died. When I was raised from the dead, so were you. You cannot live in the newness of life and be used by the Father to do good works, which He prepared in advance for you to do.

You cannot do what you're called to do without My power. Never forget that it is only by the Father's grace that you have been saved. It is through Me that you have been given salvation. You are the Father's masterpiece in Me, able to live out the unique plan for your life that will bring glory to His name. It's your action and works that can only be carried out through your new abundant life in Me, controlled and guided by the Holy Spirit working in and through you.

Ask the Spirit to lead and guide you, opening your eyes to the opportunities around you to serve Me. Your primary purpose is to live for Me, continuing what I began, walking in love, motivated by compassion, speaking Truth, forgiving, prayerful, and committed to the Father's plan. When you're not sure what to do, just simply follow Me.

FAITH THOUGHTS

Are you continually looking for the opportunities God puts before you to be the hands and feet of Jesus? You were created on purpose for purposes that go far beyond your understanding. Don't be distracted by the world around you, set your eyes on Jesus, follow Him, and live for Him.

Faithfully

MAY 19

"As for you, if you walk before me faithfully as David your father did, and do all I command, and observe my decrees and laws, I will establish your royal throne, as I covenanted with David your father when I said, 'You shall never fail to have a successor to rule over Israel.'"
2 CHRONICLES 7:17-18

You are called to live a life of submission to the Father, one that follows Me and does the Father's will. His laws are not to keep you from experiencing good things in life, they are to enable you to reap the very best things ... eternal blessings. It's your choice to walk in the Father's will, but you should know that when you walk outside of it you will experience the consequences of those actions. If you simply follow Me, I will lead you down paths of righteousness and from glory to glory.

You won't be able to follow the law in your own strength, you've been given the Spirit. You have resurrection power living inside of you. The Father longs for you to be successful and He has given you supernatural power to transform you. The ultimate goal for your life is to transform you into My image. Your faith is meant to radically transform you, opening your eyes to see the incredible journey you are taking as you long for eternity.

As you walk according to the Law, you will find yourself increasing in My character and nature, being compassionate and gracious, slow to anger, abounding in love and faithfulness, forgiving others and living devoted to the Father. In Me is where joy and blessings are found.

FAITH THOUGHTS

In what ways does it appear that God is trying to transform you into the likeness of Christ? Take a look at your struggles, which part of your character do you think God might be working on? Ask the Spirit to search your heart and strengthen it as you are continually sanctified.

In the Light

*Come, descendants of Jacob,
let us walk in the light of the Lord.*
ISAIAH 2:5

Though darkness surrounds you, you no longer have to walk in it. When you're always trying to manage your life on your own, giving in to pride and arrogance, you'll put distance between us and challenges will continue to find you. I am here to walk with you, so that you can walk in the Light and live in the hope you've been given and promised in the middle of your struggles.

You are meant to follow Me, to learn My ways and to walk in the Father's path for you. Too often, you allow yourself to get preoccupied with your worries and emptiness soon consumes your life. Your soul will hunger for an inner peace that can't be found anywhere other than in Me. I have given you the Spirit to lead you, teach you, and show you the way, setting you free to walk in the Light. It's through My victory that you can have the confidence to seek Me and then walk with Me.

If you come to Me, I will give you rest. Walking in the Light requires that you put your hope in Me alone. It means looking for ways in which the Spirit leads you to live for Me. It is about taking those opportunities, given to you as a blessing from the Father, that helps others to see the Light.

Faith Thoughts

Are you tempted to stumble around in the darkness instead of seeking Jesus, the Light of the world? What worries are you focusing on that are causing you to feel empty? If you are longing for inner peace, lay your burdens at the foot of the Cross and let the Spirit comfort you in your distress. Be determined to walk in Light and not take a single step ahead of God.

Until That Day

*Being confident of this, that he who began
a good work in you will carry it on to
completion until the day of Christ Jesus.*
PHILIPPIANS 1:6

You've been called by name and the Father had a plan for your life before you were born. Your redemption, being made new, through Me will bring the Father glory and what He began in you He will finish. You've been chosen and your life is not complete until the day of My return.

You are made in the image of the Father and it is in His design for you that you would reflect His beauty. There is nothing good that can be displayed in our lives if we are disconnected from Him. It's the love, grace, patience, kindness, and mercy in your life which reveals that you belong to Me.

You are uniquely created to fulfill specific purposes in the world and for the Kingdom. The work being done in and through you, your sanctification, is ongoing. And I never leave you in the process. Even when you've messed everything up, the Father is continuing to work in you. Rest in the hope that the Father has always had a plan for you, is at work on that plan at this moment and that He will continue to work until I see you face-to-face.

FAITH THOUGHTS

Do you recognize that God has always had a plan for your life? If you're not sure of His plan, ask the Spirit to reveal it to you through your belief in Jesus. Don't let a day go by without realizing the responsibility and blessing you've been given to live life to further the kingdom of God.

MAY 22

Faith to Faith

For in it the righteousness of God is revealed from faith to faith; as it is written, "The just shall live by faith."
ROMANS 1:17 (NKJV)

My sinless life is the only payment for your sins. It is the Father's righteous judgment on sin that was secured at the Cross, and now salvation is offered to all who believe in Me. And it's all based on faith. It's all grace through faith.

The first step of faith is to believe in Me. But the Father's righteousness is revealed from faith to faith. Your life is a work in progress, every situation in your life, good and bad, being used to prepare you to live for eternity with the Father. It's as you continue to walk through life, growing in grace that you move from one degree of faith to another.

You are saved by your faith alone and you're called to live by that faith – instructed to keep on living by that faith, knowing that the Father who began His work in you will be faithful to complete it until that day that I return. You are justified, sanctified, and will one day be glorified by your faith, when you see Me face-to-face. It's in that moment that your faith will be rewarded by sight.

FAITH THOUGHTS

Sometimes it's easy to think that things will never get better. Troubles keep coming and God isn't helping. But, God is always at work. He's promised that He is. The situations you face, good and bad, are used in the hands of God to grow and perfect your faith. And He promises to do it all through His goodness and mercy. Hold on to your faith and don't let go.

The Claim

MAY 23

*But if we walk in the light, as he is in the light,
we have fellowship with one another, and the blood
of Jesus, his Son, purifies us from all sin.*
1 JOHN 1:7

It's your sin and self that separates you from fellowship with your heavenly Father. It's when you choose to step out of the Light and into the shadows of the ways of the world that you walk in darkness. You have a choice, to walk in Light or darkness. You are called to be My body … to be salt and light in a sinful world. You have an unbreakable union with Me, you are eternally accepted in the Father's grace through faith. Yet, if you choose to walk in darkness, you cannot also walk in the Light.

Though you are in relationship with Me, fellowship is your drawing upon My resources and all that I am. It's a daily surrender to the Father and submission to His will, whatever that means … wherever that takes you … on the highest mountaintop or in the lowest valley.

If you claim to have faith in Me, if you say that you follow Me, your life must show evidence that you do. It's okay to admit that things are wrong, that you have problems, and that your faith is being tested. This is walking in Light. It is exposed, the darkness being brought to Light. Walking in the Light means hiding nothing, not pretending to be someone you're not. Whatever needs dealing with … bring it to the Father.

FAITH THOUGHTS

Do you struggle with trying to pretend that everything is okay when it's not? Do you try to keep in darkness what needs to be brought into God's Light? Your faith is not faith without proof. Your life should be different. You should long for God's presence and His conviction and love. Make it a point to focus on how He is changing you and cling to His grace.

MAY 24

Life in the Spirit

So I say, walk by the Spirit, and you will not gratify the desires of the flesh.
GALATIANS 5:16

When you walk with Me, you are living with Me. And you are called to walk by the Spirit, with the help of the Spirit. You are not to keep walking, living, the way you were. All of your life, every aspect of it, is to be lived according to the Spirit's power and guidance. Whatever you do, all of your plans, passions, and decisions are to be done with the Spirit. You were not meant to walk through this life alone.

Living life according to your plans and purposes is gratifying the flesh and you cannot walk in faith, believing in Me, while rejecting the Father's mercy. You need His mercy and grace. Your flesh and the Spirit will always be in opposition. It's the conflict within you, between your flesh and spirit, that keeps you from doing the things you want to do.

The Spirit keeps you from gratifying the desires of your flesh and keeps you walking in the Father's path of righteousness. There is a spiritual battle continually going on and it's important that you recognize it. Lean on the Spirit to encourage you in your fight. If you are alive by the Spirit, then you must walk with Him, step by step. Each and every day commit the entirety of your life to the Father and His purposes for you and trust in the promise of hope found in Me.

FAITH THOUGHTS

In what area of your life are you struggling between what you know you should do and what you want to do? Have you called upon the Spirit to strengthen your soul as you fight your spiritual battles? Or are you relying on your own wisdom and understanding through it all? You're not alone, the Spirit is within you ... He's with you step by step ... walk surrendered to Him.

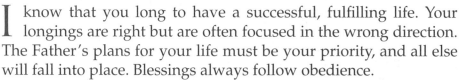

A Successful Journey

He replied, "The LORD, before whom I have walked faithfully, will send his angel with you and make your journey a success, so that you can get a wife for my son from my own clan and from my father's family."
GENESIS 24:40

I know that you long to have a successful, fulfilling life. Your longings are right but are often focused in the wrong direction. The Father's plans for your life must be your priority, and all else will fall into place. Blessings always follow obedience.

When you're faced with decisions, struggling for direction, make sure you are praying and relying on the Spirit to lead, guide, and direct you. It's in your relationships, and in a marriage that you must see more than just what they are on the surface. You are to look to the Father's guidance, seeing that there should be a desire to love and care for each other, pursuing the Father's goals throughout your lifetime.

Don't look to financial rewards and earthly pleasures, but make sure you are using your spiritual gifts in a way that can bless and serve others. When you or someone you know is ill, look past the physical illness and care for the spiritual needs as well. Rely on the Spirit to help you carefully make decisions, opening your heart to be prepared for the Father's direction to identify and complete His purposes for your life.

FAITH THOUGHTS

What do you think makes you successful? When is it that you feel success? Are you placing God's priorities for your life above your own? Don't be distracted by the temporary pleasures of the world. God's blessings are far better than anything you can dare to hope for or imagine.

MAY 26

All You Need

For though I am absent from you in body, I am present with you in spirit and delight to see how disciplined you are and how firm your faith in Christ is.
COLOSSIANS 2:5

I am all you need. I am sufficient in good times and in bad, no matter what situations you face, grace is enough. Your faith must always remain steadfast, focused on Truth, looking to Me. Regardless of your circumstances, you must continue to live in Me. If you will, hope is never lost and victory is sure.

When you're disappointed, struggling in your faith, ask the Spirit to strengthen you through the Word and overflow with thankfulness. There may not seem to be a way out or through, but I am the way when there seems to be no way. When you're facing impossible circumstances, and it seems as though you've reached the end, remember that the Father has the final say.

In Me you have everything you need ... the strength and power of the Father Himself – miracle-making power. It's the Word that will bring inner change to your heart, enabling the Spirit to accomplish the Father's will in and through you. Your fullness of life will come from a life of dedication and devotion to My cause. It's when you give your life to Me that you will live each and every day seeking to serve Me and obeying the Father's will. It's continuing to live for Me when the world calls you to live in its ways. Wherever I lead, you must follow.

FAITH THOUGHTS

Are you thanking God even when His path may lead you into pain and suffering? Regardless of where He takes you, you are safe, secure, and He will never fail you. You might not understand it all now, but one day you will, and you will not be able to behold His glory.

Surrendered

MAY 27

*Walk in obedience to all that the LORD your God
has commanded you, so that you may live and prosper
and prolong your days in the land that you will possess.*
DEUTERONOMY 5:33

Your life, in following Me, is to be one that has a heart surrendered to the Father, walking in His ways as He directs you. You are called to live with a humble heart, walking in faith, at all times and in all ways.

I came so that I could bridge the gap that your sin had made between you and the Father. Once you surrender your life to Me, your unholiness is covered and your relationship is made right with the Father. Because the Father loves you, He commands you to obey Him. He wants the very best for you. Each and every day you should begin with Him in mind, prioritizing your day around His purposes for your life. As you continually surrender your heart, you will begin to hear His voice more clearly. You will find that the time you spend in prayer, speaking to Him, comes with great reward, as you're filled with peace and hope in the most difficult circumstances.

Walking with Me will not always be easy, but it will bring about the greatest blessings in your life. Don't miss out on the joy that will come from walking in obedience to the Father, His purposes for your life will bring about miracles in your life and in those around you.

FAITH THOUGHTS

Are there ways that you are living that are contrary to what God has commanded? It's easy to view what He's asked of you as a burden instead of a blessing. Ask the Spirit to fill you with peace and show you that God is calling you into miracles in your life when you choose to obey His commands.

WORSHIP THROUGH YOUR WORRY

Why, my soul, are you downcast?
Why so disturbed within me? Put your hope in God,
for I will yet praise him, my Savior and my God.
PSALM 42:11

You have a choice: You can pray or you can panic. And you can worry or you can worship. It's your worry that keeps you from the fullness of God's goodness. In taking all of your worries to God through prayer, you can look forward to the fulfillment of His promises in your life.

When you find yourself consumed with worry, take note of what you're focusing on. It's what has your attention that will determine your direction. Where you're looking is where you'll end up. When you're facing challenges in life, faced with fear that has thrown you off course, turn to the Word of God and get back on the path of faith. When you allow your heart and mind to be fixed and focused on the things you can't control, the things you worry about take control of the direction of your life.

They end up dominating your thoughts, decisions, and actions. You've been commanded not to be anxious about anything, not to worry, and to simply pray. Look to Jesus and He'll turn your worry to worship. He wants you to bring your heart before Him, telling Him your worries, turning your anxiousness into asking, and allowing Him to transform your circumstances into a catalyst for building your faith and godly character.

You can make a shift in your focus, you can choose faith. He'll take your wasted hours of worry and replace them with purpose and peace. He'll assure you that everything is under His control and you can trust Him, even when you're not sure you can.

Enduring Love

MAY 28

*Give thanks to the LORD, for he is good;
his love endures forever.*
1 CHRONICLES 16:34

It's when you find yourself facing unthinkable circumstances, troubles at every turn that you can often find it difficult to give thanks. It's hard to see the Father's love and grace when your vision is blurred by unending burdens. And yet, amid it all, I have shown you that life can be lived in joy despite the trials and sufferings you might face. You can give thanks to the Father in the middle of it all.

If you continually look about you, you will see the Father's enduring love and grace in every aspect of your life. Expressing gratitude that will change your heart and your perspective of your problems. It's when you remember the reasons you have to be thankful that you will take your focus off of all of the things that are causing you to feel a loss of hope. It's your gratitude that will give you a heart that is more joyous and optimistic, instead of allowing the weight of your problems to cause you to be bitter and pessimistic.

Thankfulness is your faith in action. And although you may question why you're being allowed to suffer, why your prayers seem unanswered, and if you should have faith at all … I am waiting for you to come to Me. I will show you the way and help you to see that the Father is patiently working out His perfect plan while fully providing all that you need along the way. Your yesterday, today, and tomorrow is held in the loving, gracious hands of the Father. You can give thanks in this moment for the promise of the joy that lies ahead.

FAITH THOUGHTS

Find something, one thing, you are thankful for today and thank the Father for His love, grace, and faithfulness in your life. In the middle of your doubt and brokenness you can praise God for His promises.

All Day Long

*My mouth is filled with your praise,
declaring your splendor all day long.*
PSALM 71:8

There are ways that you recognize that you've been saved and other ways that you've been pulled out of troubles and been blessed without you realizing it. So, you should continually praise the Father for His wonderful goodness and grace.

There will be times when your heart or mind is battling the will of the Father. Your faith will always call you to do things that you don't want to do or aren't sure you have the ability to. If the Spirit is leading you in a direction, you can be sure it is the Father's will and you will accomplish all that He intends for you to … and then praise Him.

Let everything you do be done in His name. At times it will be difficult to set your emotions aside – fear and anxiety, feeling overwhelmed by the weight of all that you're being called to do. You know what you should do, but you struggle with it all. There is nothing for you to worry about, I am with you and I will strengthen you for the journey. The Spirit is with you to comfort you and help you through every obstacle, nothing is too difficult for My resurrection power. So trust and rest and praise the Father in every situation that you face.

FAITH THOUGHTS

It's easy to only focus on the negative emotions that flood your soul from the struggles of life. Storms can seem to never cease and neither should your praise. God always has blessings that are disguised. Don't stop thanking Him just because life is hard. It's not over, He's at work … trust in His faithfulness.

No One

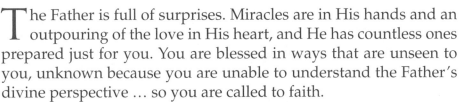

MAY 30

*How great you are, Sovereign LORD!
There is no one like you, and there is no God but you,
as we have heard with our own ears.*
2 SAMUEL 7:22

The Father is full of surprises. Miracles are in His hands and an outpouring of the love in His heart, and He has countless ones prepared just for you. You are blessed in ways that are unseen to you, unknown because you are unable to understand the Father's divine perspective ... so you are called to faith.

You can be grateful for the knowledge you've been given that has offered you salvation, you can understand the heart's desires of the Father and He has chosen and called you to share in His plans for the Kingdom. The joy that comes in following Me will leave you speechless ... the Father has great plans for your life and I am with you to lead you into them. In a world of empty promises, you might fall short of yours, but the Father is faithful. You can count on Him, it's the universe and all that is in it that is being held together by His Word.

Nothing overrides or overcomes His promises. I am your tangible witness as to what the Father is like. He is steadfast and consistent, never changing. He is ever-present, promising to never leave you nor forsake you. No one can keep the Father's promises but Him. No one can give His mercy but Him. No one can bring about justice ... only the Father can. And He does all of these things through Me. He is more than worthy to be praised.

FAITH THOUGHTS

When all else fails, God never will. He's holding the universe in the palms of His hands and He's holding you too. You may not be able to see what God is doing but if you are breathing, He has a purpose and plan for your life that will bring about joy to your life and blessings for the kingdom of God. Depend on His love, rest in His mercy, and thank Him for His grace.

MAY 31

Better than Life

*Because your love is better than life,
my lips will glorify you. I will praise you as
long as I live, and in your name I will lift up my hands.*
PSALM 63:3-4

From time to time you, will find yourself in the wilderness, where you're afraid, lonely, confused, and lacking in basic needs. Yet, it's in this moment, when all hope seems gone that you are to declare your love, praise, and thankfulness for the Father's presence in your life.

I know that it's difficult to react in praise when your natural response is to question and doubt. You wonder how the Father could allow these things to happen to you, and how He could abandon you ... know that He is not afraid of your questions. But know that in the middle of it all you must praise Him no matter what circumstances you face because He is working in your life in ways you cannot see.

You can gain a different perspective in the wilderness and the Father uses those times to draw you closer to Me. He wants you looking to Me and living as I did. He's changing you, taking you from glory to glory to completely transform you.

Your praise should always transcend your circumstances and your faith must keep going until the end ... confident that there is wonderful joy ahead because that's what the Father has promised. As long as you live, let everything you are offer up praise to the Father.

FAITH THOUGHTS

Are you continually praising God for both the good and the bad in your life? Are you thanking Him for it all, knowing that He is faithful and just and will bring about good from any evil you must endure? Thank Him right now for the thing that is causing you the most distress. Then wait for His loving arms to embrace you, as He pours out His love and grace.

All Good Things

JUNE 1

*I say to the LORD, "You are my Lord;
apart from you I have no good thing."*
PSALM 16:2

Everything good comes from the Father. Live from the place in your heart that confesses that I am Lord of your life and the foundation of your security and peace. Concede that the Father is sovereign and supplies all your needs. Realize that there is nothing given to you that is good that does not come from His hands. And His love does not change with your circumstances. It's His promises that reveal all the good things to come which provide an anchor to your faith.

If you place your trust in Me, you are assured that the Father will supply all that you need. As you trust, as the Father provides, your heart will naturally long to live a life worthy of Him. You will find yourself embracing His heart more and more, distancing yourself from the things of the world.

Even in difficulties, the Spirit will give you eyes to see the ways of the Father that are refining you and bringing you into His glory. Though there are trials, the Father is always in control and your faith will more consistently demonstrate your confidence in that truth. Let everything that you are praise the Father in every area of your life. Give thanks for the beautiful inheritance you've been given, by His power, where death brings you into My presence and where there is fullness of joy for all eternity.

FAITH THOUGHTS

You are faced with a challenge each and every day. Will you choose to praise or complain? Will you choose Jesus or the world? Will you choose sin over the eternal life you've been offered? You've been given good things and the best is yet to come. Will you choose faith and the beautiful inheritance you've been given? Choose wisely.

June 2

Awesome Wonders

*He is the one you praise; he is your God,
who performed for you those great and awesome
wonders you saw with your own eyes.*
DEUTERONOMY 10:21

Your praise welcomes the presence of the Father, placing Him first in your life because you are turning your full attention to Him. Your praise comes from an intimate relationship with the One that has given you life. As an act of your will, you make the decision to glorify the Father and it's an expression of gratitude and faith. Regardless of your circumstances, or how you feel, you must always choose to praise the Father who is worthy of it.

There is evidence of the work of the Spirit, the will of the Father, all over your life. It's your eyes of faith that will see His constant goodness and mercy towards you. You can give thanks that your needs are met, even when your desires may not be. He is always at work, always listening, and always working through the Spirit to lead you into His path that leads to overflowing blessings.

And even when you're confused or disappointed, you can be glad, you've been promised that there are wonderful things that lie ahead. Keep trusting even when it looks as though hope may be gone. I am here, the Spirit at work within you, and the Father has stored up miracles that go beyond your understanding. He's full of surprises.

 ## FAITH THOUGHTS

When you're struggling with overwhelming circumstances, are you praising God or living by your feelings that leave you weary and wondering if God even cares? Miracles happen every day and God has countless ones stored up to deliver at the perfect moments in your life. Trust in His faithfulness and make a decision to praise Him even though you can't see clearly or understand ... one day He will give your faith sight.

A Heart of Gratitude

JUNE 3

Let the message of Christ dwell among you richly as you teach and admonish one another with all wisdom through psalms, hymns, and songs from the Spirit, singing to God with gratitude in your hearts.
COLOSSIANS 3:16

I know you want to be happy. You need to feel content and at peace. You can try to achieve it on your own, but all the ways in which you try to be satisfied will only eventually leave you disappointed. The way to true contentment is in seeking Me. If you are walking with Me, you are fulfilling the Father's purposes for your life and the Spirit will fill you with a constant joy regardless of your circumstances.

When you are following Me, you will be marked by a heart of gratitude with all that you are. Worship will be your spontaneous response as you continually encounter the Father and His ways along our journey of faith together. If you focus on the Father and His will for you, you will find yourself grateful and thankfully worshiping Him for His love, mercy, grace, majesty, glory, goodness, and faithfulness.

Every aspect of your life is to be a holy experience of living gratefully under My lordship. All that you say and do is to reflect the joy of your salvation in My name. Don't allow the troubles of the world to keep you from living in the victory you are given. Rise above it all in My strength and instead of leaning on your own understanding, simply trust in the Father's promises to you and depend upon His faithfulness.

FAITH THOUGHTS

Do you have a hard time being grateful when you're in difficult circumstances that are causing you great distress? Ask the Spirit to give you peace as you look to God's promises to you to increase your faith and give you hope. Praise God even through your problems.

JUNE 4

Growing in Grace

But grow in the grace and knowledge of our Lord and Savior Jesus Christ. To him be glory both now and forever! Amen.
2 PETER 3:18

I will not leave you where I found you. You are to experience the fullness of grace, living and maturing with an ever-increasing knowledge and understanding of Me. It is the Spirit that will transform your life, becoming more and more like Me. But it requires a life that is submitted, dying to self and living for Me.

Your spiritual growth is an ongoing process, finding more and more grace to meet you in the transformation. You will need My strength to live out the purposes the Father has for your life. Without Me you can do nothing. I have promised you can do all things through Me, especially the impossible.

Long to be closer to Me, yearn for a deeper relationship, so that you can experience the immeasurable riches of My grace. If you are continually seeking Me, you will never be satisfied in remaining where you are. It's the Spirit that will drive you to greater things, to greater faith, taking you from glory to glory. When the world is crashing down on you, lift up your spirit in worship and praise. Declare Truth in your life and delight yourself in the relationship you have with Me. There is no greater joy than the joy you will experience in Me.

 ## FAITH THOUGHTS

Is your daily goal to grow to be more like Jesus? It's easy to get sidetracked with goals for your life here on earth and unintentionally ignore the eternal. Ask the Spirit to make your heart's desire to grow in the grace of Jesus. Ask that you would be given the joy of experiencing His constant presence in your life.

Help and Hope

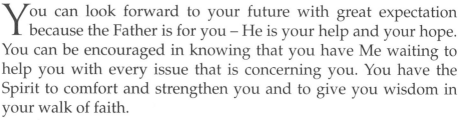

*The Lord is my strength and my shield;
my heart trusts in him, and he helps me.
My heart leaps for joy, and with my song I praise him.*
PSALM 28:7

You can look forward to your future with great expectation because the Father is for you – He is your help and your hope. You can be encouraged in knowing that you have Me waiting to help you with every issue that is concerning you. You have the Spirit to comfort and strengthen you and to give you wisdom in your walk of faith.

Life's circumstances can overwhelm you unexpectedly, leaving you weak and weary, driving you into despair, and sometimes you will need to wait on the Father to work out His plans for good. It's while you wait that the Father will be your strength, encouraging you through the hope of His promises and giving you rest so that you can continue to trust.

The Father knows all that concerns you. He knows your every need. There is nothing for you to worry about, there is no fear that cannot be overcome with your faith. It's in those difficult times where your spiritual maturity is revealed. You need to always remember that I will sustain you and carry your burdens. You should confidently anticipate that I will help you and hold you up when you're too weak to carry on. Regardless of what you're going through, stay in a place of praise and worship. Your problems may be great, but the Father is greater.

FAITH THOUGHTS

There will be a multitude of moments in life when you need help. And not just basic help, help that is dependent upon a miracle from God. Don't forget where your hope lies when you're struggling with worry and doubt. You must continually make the choice to walk by faith and not by sight.

Praise Be

*Praise be to the name of God for ever and ever;
wisdom and power are his.*
DANIEL 2:20

In your most desperate moments, you must do two things: trust the Father and praise Him for His goodness and grace. As you walk with Me, your ears will be more open to the Father's voice and your heart will be more easily led by the Holy Spirit. When you don't know what to do, pray.

Be constantly seeking the Father, long to hear from Him and be used by Him, and give Him all the glory. You can find strength, as we walk together, knowing that we are walking in the will of the Father who has all wisdom and power and sovereign authority over all creation.

When your pressures and problems never seem to cease, you should acknowledge that there is nothing you can do in your own strength, but in My strength you can do all things. The Father knows each and every day you live and all that your life will entail. His plans and purposes are for good and His blessings will come if you are continually willing to submit to Him and trust Him in all things.

When you are feeling weak and weary, come to Me and allow Me to carry your burdens as you lift your heart to the Father in prayer. If you call to Him, He will answer … He is worthy of all the praise and worship. His love for you endures forever.

FAITH THOUGHTS

In the middle of your problems, it can be difficult to feel like praising God. After all, if He was good and loving, why would you have problems at all? You can't always understand God's ways, but you can trust them. All too often, He must use difficult circumstances to bring the impurities of our soul to the surface. Be determined to surrender to His process and realize that all He does is out of His great love.

Unsearchable Greatness

JUNE 7

*Great is the LORD and most worthy of praise;
his greatness no one can fathom.*
PSALM 145:3

Daily pray that the Father brings you to your knees in humble adoration and deep appreciation of His majesty and power, which is beyond your ability to comprehend. It is only through His love, mercy, and grace that you can approach His throne and be in right relationship with Him, opening heaven's blessings in your life. His greatness deserves all the praise and glory.

Often, when you don't know what to do, you should simply worship and praise the Father for all He's done and all He's yet to do. Throughout your life you will have dark valleys of discouragement, fogs of frustration, and clouds of confusion, as well as mountaintops with miracles. Yet, in the midst of it all, through all the joys and sorrows, you should fix your eyes upon the greatness and glory of the Father. He hears and He helps, and your life is all about bringing Him glory. Every step of faith in your life should be seeking to know Him and make Him known.

 ## Faith Thoughts

In moments of worry, make the decision to worship. Make it a priority each and every day to acknowledge the greatness of God. He gives you life and breath, He pours out His grace upon you and has given you the joy of looking forward to eternity with Him. He is worthy of your praise.

June 8

In Awe

Therefore, since we are receiving a kingdom that cannot be shaken, let us be thankful, and so worship God acceptably with reverence and awe, for our "God is a consuming fire."
HEBREWS 12:28-29

The things of this life will pass away and be forgotten. Those things you worry about, those desires and troubles of the world will one day be gone. You have received a Kingdom that cannot be shaken or removed and you can worship the Father for His great love, mercy, and grace. You can look forward to eternity. This is not the end, it is only the beginning. And while you look forward to eternity, it is right here and now that you can experience the abundant, intimate life with Me.

Your perspective, each and every day, should not focus on the worries of the world, but remain focused on the Kingdom that will remain forever. All that you are should be thankful for all He has done, asking the Spirit to use your life to bring glory to the Father in all you say and do. Make it your one desire to be used by the Father, to fulfill His plans and purposes. Your faith is only strengthened through your trials, your doubt does not deter the Spirit from transforming your heart. The Father is always at work, always bringing all things together for good. You can remain unshaken because your faith is in the unshakable.

FAITH THOUGHTS

What is it that is causing your spirit to feel shaken? Life is hard and faith isn't easy. When you're trusting in the unseen, what you see seems far more believable. But God's love for you doesn't change. He knows your struggles and yet, He is promising you that you can be unshaken because His love, mercy, and grace is unshakeable.

Proper Perspective

JUNE 9

All the nations you have made will come and worship before you, Lord; they will bring glory to your name. For you are great and do marvelous deeds; you alone are God.
PSALM 86:9-10

I know that it is difficult in hard times to believe that the Father is listening to your prayers ... troubles can bring about doubt. Don't believe the lie that your struggles are big and the Father is small. All things are small to Him and nothing is a surprise or too difficult for Him. Whoever you are and whatever you've done ... wherever you are ... the Father's grace saves.

Your spiritual growth will challenge your faith. And it's in your most dire situations when you must continue to look to Me and turn to the Father. You must continually pray, asking the Spirit to remind you of the Father's character – He is always gracious, good, forgiving, and abundant in loving kindness. You need Me, every hour of every day. It is the Spirit who will comfort you in times of distress and keep you focused on the Father's faithfulness.

Keep your heart focused upon Mine and the love that carried Me to the Cross. Ask the Spirit to reveal the Word to you in new ways and help you apply it to every part of your life. Ask to be given the wisdom to see opportunities to serve Me by serving others. Ask that your entire life would be used to bring glory to the Father.

FAITH THOUGHTS

It's easy to get focused on the things that only matter in this world and not keep an eternal perspective. You must make it a priority to seek God each and every day and place all of your burdens at His feet. It's His promises to you that are going to give you the strength to live for Him. Don't miss out on the blessings stored up for you when you surrender your life to the God of miracles.

CONTENTMENT THROUGH THE CHAOS

I know what it is to be in need, and I know what it is to have plenty. I have learned the secret of being content in any and every situation.
PHILIPPIANS 4:12

Contentment is not having all you want, it's wanting what you have. The reality of life is that this is not your home. You were created for heaven, but until Christ makes everything right, you are here to stand fast and firm in your faith. You're to have hope in your salvation. Regardless of your circumstances, you're always to express the joy that you have in the Lord, remembering all that God has done in your life and recalling the blessings you've been given. You are called to a life of hope and contentment because God gives you all you need.

The world you live in is always driving you to compare yourself to others, to always feel as though what you have is not enough. It's in those moments, on those days of losing faith and hope, that you need to fall into the grace of God and simply rest. Your joy does not come from anything on this earth. Your joy is in Christ alone. And you need to keep remembering that. Only a relationship with Him will bring true satisfaction to your soul. Refuse to let setbacks in your life steal your joy, don't allow any of your troubles to destroy your relationship with Jesus. Ask Him to calm the storm within you as you face the ones around you.

Ask the Spirit to control your emotions, keeping you from soaring too high during times of abundance and preventing them from sinking to depths during times of need. God knows what you need and everything He does and allows in your life is for your good. So, whatever your circumstances, pray for strength to endure, thanking Him for the grace that He continually pours out on you. And while you're waiting for things to change, trust Him and seek to honor Him in whatever circumstances you're in.

Perfect in Weakness

JUNE 10

But he said to me, "My grace is sufficient for you, for my power is made perfect in weakness." Therefore I will boast all the more gladly about my weaknesses, so that Christ's power may rest on me. That is why, for Christ's sake, I delight in weaknesses, in insults, in hardships, in persecutions, in difficulties. For when I am weak, then I am strong.
2 CORINTHIANS 12:9-10

By grace alone you are saved. When you are facing your weaknesses, know this: the Father is for you. Though you were a sinner, through Me you are forgiven and adopted by the Father. If you belong to the Father and He is for you, who or what can be against you?

You don't need to run or hide from your weaknesses. You can embrace them because it is My power that rests on you. It's your weakness that opens the door to My power that calms the storms, raises the dead, and calls you to walk upon the water. Don't be surprised that your greatest challenges in life, your darkest moments, can be used to open your eyes to your weakness and reveal the Father's unending grace, power, and provision in your life.

It is humility that will open the door to your heart and draw you closer to the Father. I meet you where you are, with open arms, to heal your hurt and transform you into My image. You don't have to be perfect because I live in you and I am perfect in every way. Stop struggling and striving, simply surrender and let the Spirit do His work in you.

FAITH THOUGHTS

What do you feel is your greatest weakness at this moment? Do you believe that God is doing something in and through you while you struggle? Ask the Spirit to help give you peace so that you can be content regardless of your circumstances. There is no reason for you to doubt in the faithfulness of God.

JUNE 11

Great Gain

*But godliness with contentment is great gain.
For we brought nothing into the world,
and we can take nothing out of it.*
1 TIMOTHY 6:6-7

If you do not transform your mind, you'll be conformed to this world. Your emptiness is something only I can satisfy. When you are thirsty, I am Living Water. If you're trying to find satisfaction by any other means than through Me, you will only remain empty.

Your contentment will only come in trusting in the Father's sufficiency, so that you are unaffected by the circumstances around you. You must completely trust in the Father's sovereignty and His faithfulness to care for you in every way throughout your life, in order to rest in the peace that you are given.

You must trust in His love and that He is working all things together for good. And don't store up your treasures here on earth. They are temporary. Store up treasures in heaven where nothing can be taken or destroyed. It is in the way you live your life for Me, accomplishing the Father's purposes, that will bring you the joy and contentment you long for. Focus on eternity and you'll find great gain.

 ### FAITH THOUGHTS

Do you sometimes feel empty? Is it possible you're looking to anything and everything to fill you when only God truly can? If you're going to live a life for Him, it's your constant surrender that will make the difference. It's in emptying yourself that He can fill you. Look to Him, seek His peace for your soul, and trust in His plans for your life. They are far better than the ones you have.

Watch Out

JUNE 12

Then he said to them, "Watch out! Be on your guard against all kinds of greed; life does not consist in an abundance of possessions."
LUKE 12:15

The ways of the world, the earthly desires that can so easily entice you, will never bring true joy and happiness to your life, only emptiness. I am more interested in your earthly character and your direction into eternity than your fleshly success and possessions. Whatever you achieve, whatever you're blessed with in this life is to be used in ways to further the Kingdom, not selfish pleasure. Your purposes go beyond yourself.

Your contentment will not come from the things you have, but by your attitude, devotion, and the surrender of your heart to Me. Do not give in to the senseless and harmful desires that will plunge you in to ruin and destruction. If you are trusting in possessions and money for your security, joy, happiness, and contentment, you are in danger and you need to watch out.

Your focus and concern should be your eternal destination and the priority of your spiritual growth that will prepare you to live with Me forever. Your life is to be lived by faith in Me, recognizing that all that you've been blessed with has been given to you by the Father to be used for His glory. If you are walking with Me, you will have a proper understanding of being "rich" … you will find yourself rich in grace, love, forgiveness, peace, and countless blessings you never anticipated.

FAITH THOUGHTS

It's easy to get caught up in what the world sees as success and be driven in that direction to be seen as worthy in the eyes of others. But your worth comes from God's view of your life and whether or not you are fulfilling His purposes for your life. Those treasures, stored up in heaven, will bring about more joy than you can imagine in this life and the next.

June 13

The Heart's Desires

Trust in the LORD and do good; dwell in the land and enjoy safe pasture. Take delight in the LORD, and he will give you the desires of your heart.
PSALM 37:3-4

There is not a moment that you are not called to trust the Word, to believe what it says and to have faith in the Father in all things and in all ways. If you will acknowledge all that He is through all the troubles of life, you'll find Him sovereignly and lovingly guiding and directing your life in ways that will bring about countless blessings.

You are called to trust the Father in this world and the next, to trust Him for the little things as well as those that are bigger. And you must trust, even when you don't understand. It's when you follow Me that you find yourself continually looking to the Father, being called to do good, to love mercy, and to forgive as you follow His paths for your life. As we walk together, and you submit to the Spirit's work within you, living by the Word, you'll see that no matter what happens, your life is in the Father's hands. Knowing that I am with you always, trusting in His faithfulness, and relying on My strength and power will enable you to live out His purposes for your life. Ultimately, He will give you the desires of your heart.

FAITH THOUGHTS

Instead of striving for the things you want and long for, surrender your life into the hands of the Father. Be willing to go where He leads you, knowing that Jesus is with you always. In your submission to the Spirit and His work in and through you, you will continually be given the desires of your heart.

Enjoying the Gifts

JUNE 14

That each of them may eat and drink, and find satisfaction in all their toil – this is the gift of God.
ECCLESIASTES 3:13

It is the Father who has given you the ability to enjoy life and to rejoice. It's His perspective and hope that will give you the ability to have joy regardless of your circumstances. By following Me, in living for Me, you have the ability to produce divine good, to bring about miracles, and experience the Father's blessings here on earth.

The key to joy is your humility. You must learn to be content, accepting the Father's plans and trusting in His promise to care for you in all ways. You were meant to live a life that works for the Father and also rests in Him. In the middle of your struggles, give thanks for all you're called to do.

You may not know what lies ahead, but the Father does and you can find joy in the ordinary things in life. Even in the mundane there are miracles. In every little thing you experience throughout your day, you can look for the Father. Don't always try and figure out the reason everything happens, you can't always understand the Father's ways.

So, when life is good, give glory to the Father, and when there are troubles, praise Him for His protection and provision through them. Each moment of your life, good and bad, is a gift.

FAITH THOUGHTS

Is it difficult sometimes to see your challenging days as a gift? It's easy to live according to your feelings instead of the Word. When times are good, rejoice in the Lord, and when they're not, make sure you rejoice then, too, because God is at work, whether you can see it or not ... He has promised to work all things together for good. Thank Him for the many gifts He's given and is yet to give.

JUNE 15

Rejoicing Anyway

Though the fig tree does not bud and there are no grapes on the vines ... yet I will rejoice in the LORD, I will be joyful in God my Savior.
HABAKKUK 3:17-18

Though you might not always feel My presence, especially when storms are raging in your life, I know that you are clinging to faith even as you doubt. You must always look to the truth when you're being overwhelmed by lies. The Father is faithful. In everything you go through, search for Him.

Throughout My life I was constantly directing you to a relationship with the Father, in My living, praying, dying. Though My death on the Cross seemed contrary to the Father's best, He proved otherwise. When everything in your life is going contrary to what you feel is the Father's best for you, you too, must rely on the Spirit for strength to keep walking in faith. You are to worship instead of worry. It's a choice to have faith, not a feeling.

The Enemy wants to steal your joy, and in the midst of intense trials, he will always lie to you regarding the Father's ways. You must declare that the Father is sovereign over every situation and look upward instead of inward. The Father's perfect plans and purposes far exceed your current circumstances. Don't be tempted to believe anything other than that all things are in the Father's loving, faithful hands.

FAITH THOUGHTS

What situation are you facing that is causing you to worry instead of worship? What is it that you're not sure God can handle? There is nothing that comes as a surprise to Him, and although you're concerned that He's somehow overlooked your pain and suffering, He's assured you through His promises that He has not. When you are afraid and uncertainties overwhelm you, praise Him anyway.

Strength in Joy

JUNE 16

Nehemiah said, "Go and enjoy choice food and sweet drinks, and send some to those who have nothing prepared. This day is holy to our Lord. Do not grieve, for the joy of the L<small>ORD</small> is your strength."
NEHEMIAH 8:10

There will be times of sorrow and suffering, but the Father has promised that joy is coming. It is the renewing of your mind, through the Word, that will align your heart with the Father's, enabling you to see life from a more eternal perspective that will give you greater peace.

Throughout life, when you experience discouragement and disappointment, you face doubts in your faith. Do not be surprised by them. Bring them to Me. Do not allow yourself to get so exhausted from carrying your burdens that you no longer seek Me. Seek Me first. Hope is never lost. I am with you, the Spirit within you and the Father is still on His throne.

Your joy cannot be dependent upon your ever-changing circumstances. Your joy must be found in your relationship with Me, bridging your way to the Father, so that you can experience true peace in your soul. And all joy will come from being grounded in the Father's promises to you … seek them always and listen carefully for His voice whispering your name.

FAITH THOUGHTS

Is your joy tied up in whether or not life's circumstances are meeting your expectations? Your faith must be grounded in a foundation of God's promises rather than your feelings. Make it a priority to meditate on God's Word every day so that you can be filled with the peace and joy that surpasses all understanding.

June 17

Empty

"Blessed are those who hunger and thirst for righteousness, for they will be filled."
MATTHEW 5:6

I know your soul is hungry and your heart is thirsty. You have a longing for something. You are restless. And nearly everywhere you turn, things in others' lives look better than in your own. Whatever you strive for to fill you, will ultimately leave you empty. When the Spirit is beckoning you to Himself, don't turn away. Don't take the shortcuts on your path of faith. The Father has designed a specific journey, just for you, in order to perfect your unique character.

The Father has put eternity in your heart and you have an inconsolable longing that cannot be satisfied in this life. You are looking for life to be perfect here on earth, for the next chapter in your life to fill you with the joy you know that the Father wants you to have ... except, that will only come when I return.

Until then, I walk with you, I show you the way, and the Spirit works within you to develop your godly character and prepare you to live with the Father forever. There are blessings in your emptiness. I have said that you are blessed, I have given you a blessing. I have declared that if you hunger and thirst for righteousness, you are blessed because you will be filled. It's from your brokenness, grieving, and quietness in thirsting for righteousness that you will be overflowing in mercy, pure in heart, and a peacemaker.

FAITH THOUGHTS

Are you constantly feeling as though your life is missing something? Or maybe you're just empty in one area of your life? Ask the Spirit to speak to your heart and help you to get a glimpse of what God is doing ... how He is using that emptiness to someday fill you to the full. Be determined to rest in your faith and have confident expectation in God's blessings for your life.

A Spring of Water

JUNE 18

Jesus answered, "Everyone who drinks this water will be thirsty again, but whoever drinks the water I give them will never thirst. Indeed, the water I give them will become in them a spring of water welling up to eternal life." The woman said to him, "Sir, give me this water so that I won't get thirsty and have to keep coming here to draw water."
JOHN 4:13-15

What you ultimately long for is eternal life, eternal satisfaction and My peace and contentment. I know you also long to be loved, esteemed, honored, and valued, and I give those things to you too. You must open your heart to receive all that I have to offer. Don't look for shortcuts and miss your destination. Only I can satisfy your thirsty soul. Only I can fill the emptiness and aching of your heart. My special gift, My blessing, is that what I offer is lasting.

It is the Holy Spirit that I have given to you that makes a difference in your life. He helps you to understand the Father by giving you spiritual understanding. He leads you to Me and transforms you into My image. He lives in you and empowers you to live your life for Me. He takes you from where the Father found you, lost and empty, and fills you with His love, mercy, and grace.

You don't need to be weary from "drawing water" from places that will never satisfy you. You need the Living Water I offer – come and drink.

FAITH THOUGHTS

Don't try to fill your life with things that can be taken or destroyed. Ask God to reveal His purpose for your life. Ask Him to give you opportunities to draw your strength from Him and live your life for Jesus. He has promised to fill your emptiness with the fullness of His love … but you must open your heart to what He's offering.

Chasing the Wind

*"Better to have one handful with quietness than
two handfuls with hard work and chasing the wind."*
ECCLESIASTES 4:6 (NLT)

You need peace in your heart and in your life. It's your joy and contentment that reflects an attitude of faith which overcomes the temptation and sin in your life. The longing for things that will never fill you, the worry that consumes you, the quick escapes that only leave you struggling more, this all makes you restless until you rest in Me.

There will be times in your journey when you will journey through darkness, but you will have joy through it all because My Light is within you to guide your way. All the days that you are given on earth are to be rejoiced in. Make it a priority to grasp every opportunity to see My Light, and remember how My Light has led you through seasons of trial and pain.

If you're struggling, recall My past mercy and see it as a gift from the Father. If you're walking through times of joy, embrace it and savor it. Don't keep chasing after what you already have. I've given you peace that surpasses all understanding, and you can use it to stay focused on hope. Don't allow the circumstances of life to blow you off course. You are to fight the good fight of faith, standing firm, grounded in the promises of the Father and His faithfulness. Don't be tossed by the wind in doubt. Don't chase the wind. Through the storms, keep your eyes on Me.

FAITH THOUGHTS

Are you able to see the Light of God's love and mercy in your life today? Are you accepting and giving thanks for God's grace? Keep focused on His Light because the darkness of storms will come and you will need to stay focused on the memories of how He's rescued you in the past. You need to continually remember the hope you have in Him and that He is faithful and will never let you go.

You Do Not Ask

You do not have because you do not ask God.
JAMES 4:2

The purpose of prayer is so that you might get a hold of God, not the answer. Sometimes, your motives are wrong. Ask the Spirit to help you. Often, all the things you want are not truly what you need. You need My mind, My attitude, My selfless humility. These are the things that will bring you the contentment and satisfaction you're longing for.

This journey of faith is about aligning your will with the Father's. It's the key to living a victorious life of contentment in this world. If you will follow Me, living out the Father's purposes for your life, you are laying up treasures for yourself in heaven.

If your heart reflects the Father's, you will bring about great blessings for yourself and those around you. Ask that the Spirit will keep your eyes focused on Me and keep you following in My ways through faith. Know that the Father will supply all your needs, even before you ask. He has a plan for your future that is filled with goodness and hope.

When you're struggling through your doubt, questioning if you can really count on the Father's faithfulness, I will be with you to assure you that with faith all things are possible. You need only to believe … and ask.

FAITH THOUGHTS

Are you trying to make things happen on your own instead of asking God to do it for you? Are you letting go of what you should and doing what God has asked you to? Ask the Spirit to realign your will with God's and give you the strength to live out your faith by fully relying on Him for all of your needs.

JUNE 21

Peace and Joy

For the kingdom of God is not a matter of eating and drinking, but of righteousness, peace and joy in the Holy Spirit.

ROMANS 14:17

Goodness, peace, and joy do not happen accidently. They are the work of My presence within you through the Holy Spirit. Always remember that the Holy Spirit is the source of all that is good in your life. And He is the basis of the peace and joy that keeps you walking in faith. You've been given a gift.

You enjoy blessings each day, and you must always remember that life in the Kingdom is not about what you have. It's about living your life according to the will of the Father and fulfilling His purposes for your life. Continually have a heart that is thankful for the Spirit who is transforming you more and more into My image.

Be thankful that you have been given the peace that surpasses all understanding so that you can know My deep and abiding joy. The Spirit is always working within you, even through your doubt, to produce righteousness, peace, and joy. He is always at work advancing the kingdom of heaven. Be blessed because you've been chosen to be a part of it.

FAITH THOUGHTS

Try to remain in God's peace even when the circumstances of your life are not peaceful. Don't try to do it in your own strength. Call upon the Spirit to give you the power to do it. Keep focused on the joy of being called and chosen by God to fulfill His purposes and then look around you for the ways in which He's calling you to do so.

Comforted

JUNE 22

*When anxiety was great within me,
your consolation brought me joy.*
PSALM 94:19

In the midst of your worries, the Spirit will comfort you. I am your hope, you can find strength and peace in the victory that has been given to you. When worry fills your heart and fear overwhelms your soul, you must make a decision to not allow the worry and fear to settle in … faith cannot coincide with them and you cannot fully trust and allow the Father to do all that He longs to do in your life. Worry adds nothing to your life. Just seek Me and you will find Me as your help and your hope. I am all you need.

You will begin to overcome your worries when you put your trust and hope completely in Me. When you rest in My peace no matter how fierce the storm is raging, you will experience greater miracles than the ones you've prayed for.

The miracles that are done in and through you to perfect your faith, are without number. But, you must daily surrender your will to the Father's. You must let go of your expectations and rely on God's plans that will bring about greater joy than you can imagine. When you're afraid, when your circumstances paralyze you, run to Me. I will comfort you, fill you with joy and give you hope to be full of cheer instead of fear. I am your hope.

FAITH THOUGHTS

God is continually offering you hope in the most hopeless of situations. He wants you to trust Him in spite of your circumstances. You can't wait until all is "well" for all to be well with your soul. It's your choice to live in the security and joy the Lord gives to you. What if you made the decision to be joyful right now? How will that change things? Give it a try … trust God.

WAITING ON GOD

*I wait for the Lord, my whole being waits,
and in his word I put my hope.*
PSALM 130:5

God's will includes His timing. He has amazing plans and purposes for your life, but He only reveals it all one step at a time. It's when you follow His plans that He is glorified and you'll find true fulfillment ... that's worth having faith for and waiting for.

If you're not looking to God for guidance and direction, you may end up lost at sea. But you have a Light to lead you back when you're confused and dissatisfied because you've missed where God was leading you. The wisest things you can do each day is start by connecting with God and calling upon Him in prayer. Communicating with Him continually keeps you in an intimate relationship, so that you can live in His divine wisdom and power. And when you doubt, when God seems to be taking too long, know that His delays can be what prepares you for His plans. And while you're waiting, you need to be living in faith, actively living out His purposes for you, using your spiritual gifts. So, waiting is purposeful.

Sometimes you're not ready for the answer God has for you. Sometimes your heart needs to be prepared for what He wants to give. And while you wait in faith, you can count on the promise God has made to you that you will not be disappointed when you trust in Him. Remember when you feel you can't go on, when you're weak and weary, and you're not sure that God is doing anything, that He works in mysterious ways, using the waiting time to draw you nearer, trusting in His guidance and testing your faith.

But know that as He tests your faith He is also strengthening it. He's preparing your heart. So respond to His love and grace by waiting patiently, quietly, trustingly, expectantly, courageously and steadfastly.

Waiting Patiently

Be still before the LORD and wait patiently for him;
do not fret when people succeed in their ways,
when they carry out their wicked schemes.
PSALM 37:7

When you are feeling desperate, cry out to the Father in prayer. Tell Him honestly how you feel, opening your whole heart, so that you might fully receive My peace. As you wait on the Father to answer you, He is doing something. It's His timing that teaches you to trust Him more and more.

Know that I am with you, to give you peace and strength as you wait patiently for the Father to intervene in the ways He has planned in your life. I will help you to rest confidently in His goodness and trust fully in His faithfulness. And I know that waiting is hard. But as you endure, you can have hope in Me that you will receive compassion and mercy, even in the most strenuous of circumstances. Know that the Father is working out the answers even though you may not know all the details. Your life can change instantly, as God moves suddenly.

Oftentimes, how you wait may determine how long you wait. Live your life each day following Me and living out the Father's purposes for you, waiting actively and expectantly. It's when you are focused upon your problems, instead of My power, that doubt clouds your vision of the Father's sovereignty. Keep your eyes on Me, let your faith feed your hope for what you do not see and wait for it with patience.

FAITH THOUGHTS

Ask the Spirit to give you peace as you wait on God. Be determined to remain faithful in your waiting and refuse to give up. When you struggle, remember that Jesus is with you and you aren't waiting alone. Realize that your waiting is increasing your faith and has purposes that go beyond your understanding.

June 24

Pouring Out Grace

Yet the LORD longs to be gracious to you; therefore he will rise up to show you compassion. For the LORD is a God of justice. Blessed are all who wait for him!
ISAIAH 30:18

Whatever you're going through in life at this moment, I want to encourage you that the Father longs to be gracious to you and desires to bring about His glory by showing you mercy. Know that when you must wait, the Father always has a loving purpose and reason behind it. You won't always understand, but you don't need to.

There is a built-in blessing if you wait patiently, trusting in the Father's promises. He has promised you that He will make things right, that He hears you and that His mercy will turn your life around … everything that is wrong will be made right. It's in My presence and love that you will find happiness and freedom from your worries, stress, and fears. The Father will rescue you. You don't need to worry.

Whatever you need, the Father knows. Look to Him, wait for Him, and walk with Me in faith as you wait for His miracles in your life. When you are troubled, filled with doubt, confused, needing guidance and direction, it is the Spirit that will work within you to assure you that your waiting is not in vain. He will lead you to specific promises that will give you peace as you wait and will comfort you through your struggles. Help is on the way.

FAITH THOUGHTS

What specific area or situation in your life could use God's mercy and grace right now? Look to God and come to Him in prayer, praising Him for His promise to show you mercy. Trust in His faithfulness and expect His grace, then be ready for how He will show His glory, when you thought He wouldn't show up.

Watching in Hope

JUNE 25

*But as for me, I watch in hope for the LORD,
I wait for God my Savior; my God will hear me.*
MICAH 7:7

Whatever your trials and tribulations, I will bring you through. I am with you always. I am still present and I have promised to lead you out of all the darkness you're facing, bringing you into My Light. Not only will the Father hear you as you pray, but He will also save you in every way you need to be.

Look to Me for strength while you wait upon the Father. Wait for His help confidently and expectantly, knowing that at the perfect time He will deliver you from your pain and suffering. When you're tempted to give up, get up. Look for My Light. Whatever your situation, try to see Me in it. Try to see the Spirit at work. It may not be obvious, and I might not be where you expect Me to be or not working in your life in the ways you think, but if you open your eyes in faith, I'm there … in the middle of it all.

Know that as you wait for the Father's intervention in your life, the Spirit will be working within you, revealing areas of your life that need to be brought in line with the Father's will for you. Take this waiting time as a gift, to surrender more of yourself to Me and to be emptied so that you can be filled. While you wait, watch … look to Me for hope.

FAITH THOUGHTS

Are you tempted to give up in a situation you're struggling with? Does it seem like you've prayed, like you've tried everything you know, and nothing is getting better? Right now, in that situation, God is at work. When you're about to give up, look up. Don't forget that God is still on His throne and He is faithful to His promises.

Just Wait

I will wait for the LORD, who is hiding his face from the descendants of Jacob. I will put my trust in him.
ISAIAH 8:17

You've been given the privilege of waiting on the Father. With your waiting comes great responsibility to enter into His presence and praise Him, confident that He hears you, setting an example of faith as you wait in peaceful expectation.

You must believe through faith alone that the Father can and will help you. Instead of giving into despondency or despair, pray that I will bring Light into your darkness. Whatever you're going through, you'll get through it. It's waiting that engages your faith. If you're disappointed, stay expectant of what the Father will do through His love, mercy, and grace. Keep praising Him. The proof of your faith is not the miracle, it's not the change, it's your patience. It's waiting and waiting well.

You may not believe that you're going to experience a miracle, it may seem impossible … but that's what makes it a miracle … it's impossible. Except with the Father. With Him all things are possible. Know that it's your desperation that is setting you up for a revelation. The Father is going to reveal Himself in ways that He couldn't otherwise. He always uses every situation you face to give you a greater vision and understanding of who He is. If you're struggling, suffering, and in need of a miracle … just wait.

FAITH THOUGHTS

Have you asked God for a miracle in your situation? Have you already decided how He'll answer you? You need to let go of your expectations of how God needs to answer you, and simply let Him be God. Don't cut His blessings short by underestimating what He can and will do. His miracles come wrapped in His love.

Stand Firm

June 27

> *Be patient, then, brothers and sisters, until the Lord's coming. See how the farmer waits for the land to yield its valuable crop, patiently waiting for the autumn and spring rains. You too, be patient and stand firm, because the Lord's coming is near.*
> JAMES 5:7-8

You are the vineyard in the Father's field. I have made you fertile ground, prepared, planted in the Word, and I will help you to grow by My Spirit. The Father provides everything you need from day to day. And yet, He waits for you to cooperate with Him so that you will bear fruit. You will continually need to rely on Me, staying connected to Me. You will need My strength as your faith grows. Be patient and stand firm.

Faith is going to require you to believe without seeing. You may not always see or understand what the Father is doing in your life, but you must trust in His plans and rely on His faithfulness to carry you. Every obstacle you face is an opportunity for the Father to bless you. But don't expect Him to answer right away when it may not be in His timing. And don't judge His answers to your prayers. He knows what He's doing. His plans included My crucifixion, but they also included My resurrection. When you don't know what to do, when you're confused, just wait and pray.

Faith Thoughts

Don't be tempted to move ahead of God. You might not see anything happening, but beneath the surface, your faith is growing. You're seeking Him more, digging through your doubt, and the Spirit is searching your heart. It's all about the journey, not the destination. And Jesus is with you each step of the way.

June 28

Looking Up

> *... so our eyes look to the LORD our God,*
> *till he shows us his mercy.*
> PSALM 123:2

No matter what you face in life, I am with you and you can depend on and trust the Father. The Spirit is your strong helper, enabling you to endure every trial you face. Know that no matter the temptations you face, the Spirit in you is stronger and He will give you the power to overcome. You are to be strong in Me and stand in My might.

Whether you realize it, admit it, or not, you are totally dependent on the Father. No matter what you face or what you accomplish, it is all done under His sovereignty. All you have and all that you are is by the grace of God. There is no room for pride. The Father designed His plan for your life of redemption, where you will only be able to look to Him and point to Him and He gets all the glory. Your understanding of His Word and the knowledge you're given only comes from the Spirit.

Everything is through His grace and by His grace. It's your great responsibility to use the gifts He has given you and live out His purposes for your life in My strength. You are a new person, in Me, created to do good works. I will not leave you or forsake you, and the Father's mercies never cease ... look to Him always, His faithfulness endures forever.

FAITH THOUGHTS

What is it that you're facing that is causing you to look frantically about you? Are you panicked or are you praying? Are you worrying or are you worshiping? Take a moment to examine your heart and then ask the Spirit to keep your faith steadfast as you continue to trust God for all your needs.

Being Ready

"You also must be ready, because the Son of Man will come at an hour when you do not expect him."
LUKE 12:40

One day, I will return. Unexpectedly. In the blink of an eye. Be watching. Be ready. Continually ask the Spirit to search your heart and reveal sin, to bring the dark things into the Light. It is vital to our faith that you accept the truth of My Second Coming and be in a constant state of readiness. And you will need to be following Me, doing My work, fulfilling the Father's purposes for you ... disciplined and diligent.

I want you to live a life that is lived on purpose, being led by the Spirit and walking in love. Whatever you do, in work, play, and in worship, do it with an eager expectation of My imminent return. Everything should be done in preparation for My return.

You've been entrusted with time, money, and spiritual gifts. And whatever portion you've been given will be enough to accomplish all that the Father wants you to. When I return, you will have to give an account of how you used what you were given. If you are expecting Me, the King of kings, what should your life look like? You will need to immediately open the door to Me when I come and knock on your door. What will I find? You will truly be blessed if I return and I find you ready.

FAITH THOUGHTS

Look at how you live each day? Are you filling each moment with the purposes of eternity in mind? Your mission may be where you work, or in raising your children at home. Whatever you do, it should be done to bring glory to God.

JUNE 30

Blessed Hope

While we wait for the blessed hope – the appearing of the glory of our great God and Savior, Jesus Christ.
TITUS 2:13

At the appointed time, I will return. It is your faith in Me that should motivate you to godliness and promote you towards joyful anticipation of My arrival. Watch and wait, being inspired to do all that the Father has called you to do until My return. Expect and prepare for your blessed hope. Hope that is not heaven itself, but Me, face-to-face.

It is My Spirit within you that gives you hope and motivates you to live a godly life, eager to live in a way that reflects My character. Let grace teach you to live in My peace and walk in My ways. Your life of faith is not an idle one, but one that is full of opportunities to bless others, to see the Father's glory while you're on earth. And when I return, glory will be revealed, the trials of your life will be over and you'll see that your present sufferings were not worth comparing to what will be revealed to you.

You don't have a faith that is uncertain, but one that has the assurance of the faithfulness of the Father. And I am your hope. Nothing can take that hope from you. So, be looking, living each day in continual anticipation and expectancy. Let hope have its place by transforming the reality of your life, allowing the Father to be glorified through you.

FAITH THOUGHTS

Has your hope in the return of Jesus made a difference in your life? If He is coming at any time, it should affect the choices you make every day. What if right now, you lived as though glory is already revealed and that your trials don't even compare to it. What if you allowed your faith and hope to make the difference in your life right now? What if?

Good and Glory

*In the morning, LORD, you hear my voice; in the morning
I lay my requests before you and wait expectantly.*
PSALM 5:3

JULY 1

Each and every day, be looking for the Father's goodness in your life. Wake up with anticipation of how the Spirit will work in and through you to accomplish the Father's purposes for your life in order to further His kingdom.

Know that the Father hears you, in your cries for help and in your praise and worship. With each breath you take, follow Me, laying down your life before the Father and relying on the Spirit to lead and guide you. Every detail of your life, throughout your entire day, should be lived in anticipation of hearing the Father's voice and looking to those ways in which He can use the gifts and talents you've been given. And His plans will often change your own.

Be ready to follow closely, to draw nearer, and to have a heart that is humble and ready at all times. Continually lift your voice to the Father in prayer, lay your requests before Him. Commit your problems and the difficulties you anticipate to Him and then submit your decision to Him. As you rely on Him for all that you need, confidently expect the answers and direction you need to bring about your good and His glory … you'll find that the end of your day will be more blessed than the beginning.

FAITH THOUGHTS

What do you do first thing in the morning upon waking? Do you faithfully run to God before beginning each day? If you will seek Him immediately, before starting your day, you'll be more aware of His presence with you throughout your day. You'll be more strengthened to walk in faith, without fear, through your challenges, knowing that He is with you.

JULY 2

Await by Faith

For through the Spirit we eagerly await by faith the righteousness for which we hope.
GALATIANS 5:5

Without the Holy Spirit, walking through your transformation to be like Me, full of righteousness and grace, would be impossible. But with the Spirit you can eagerly hope and expect amazing miracles to happen in and through your life as you are transformed. I change everything about how you live. And it's not just faith, but saving faith, faith in your salvation that changes everything.

The faith that you have in Me to save you from your sins will be seen in your life. It's an observable faith. A life-changing faith. You've been set free of your sins, free to live for the Kingdom, placing your hope in Me and not yourself.

Let your faith be seen by your love for the Father and for others. Pray that your heart would yearn for more of Me, and that you would draw nearer to the Father. There is no greater joy and fulfillment you can experience than to walk with Me and live out the Father's purposes for your life. And you've been given the gift of the Spirit to lead, guide, and direct you as you walk, wait, and hope in faith.

 ## FAITH THOUGHTS

Are you relying on the Spirit to help you through each day, through each situation you face, until Jesus returns? Are you continually struggling to try to control what you cannot? Remember that you are to live by faith. Faith in the power of the Spirit that Jesus died to give to you. You don't have to walk through life alone, you have the power of God within you and Jesus by your side.

Waiting in Hope

JULY 3

*We wait in hope for the LORD;
he is our help and our shield.*
PSALM 33:20

The Father's love is always faithful and never falters, no matter what your circumstances or feelings. Your waiting does not rest on an outcome, but on the secure foundation of hope that I've given you. The Father is above all and sees all, He is always in control and there is never a reason to lose hope or to feel hopeless. I am your source of hope and encouragement. You can rejoice always. You can wait in hope.

Although the waiting can be hard, you have a reason to wait, a reason to keep watch, as you look to the Father's steadfast love. No matter what you're facing, His eyes are always on you and you are safe in His arms. Although you may continually face struggles, each day brings new hope and new grace. And as you face the impossible, you will learn to trust in the One, more and more, who makes all things possible.

It's often when you have no human means of escape and you cry out to the Father as your only hope, that He delivers you. Expect the unexpected and expect it wrapped in the Father's love and grace.

FAITH THOUGHTS

Are you looking to God for your help? He is with you to guide you and care for you in every way. Jesus is walking with you to assure you of the path you're to take and the Holy Spirit is always within you to comfort you and give you hope. Come boldly, continually to the throne of grace … you'll find all the help and hope you need.

JULY 4

In Quietness

*I say to myself, "The L*ORD *is my portion; therefore I will wait for him." The L*ORD *is good to those whose hope is in him, to the one who seeks him; it is good to wait quietly for the salvation of the L*ORD.
LAMENTATIONS 3:24-26

In the midst of everything bad, I am your hope. You don't have a hope based on wishful thinking, imagining that your odds will change, looking to random factors to somehow fall into place … because they won't … that kind of hope only leads to crushing disappointment and loss. And you're not looking forward in a hope that believes against all evidence that things are going to change and get better, you are hoping in Me … the hope of glory.

There's no reason to panic, frantically searching for solutions to your circumstances and worrying that nothing is going to work out. It will all work out in the end … the Father has promised it will. It's along the way, in this journey of faith, that you will be given glimpses of His glory, that you will be able to experience His miracles while on earth.

And as you wait upon His miracles, as you wait upon Him in hope, do it quietly, patiently, showing the proof of your faith. There is nothing to fear and there is no reason to feel as though all is lost. The Father has promised to be good to you, to give you your heart's desires … just hope in Me, seek Him, and rest in His Truth.

FAITH THOUGHTS

Whatever you're going through, there is hope. It's not over until God says it is and He has promised that if you'll hope in Him, there are good things ahead. Those things may not happen right away, it may not look like God is going to show up … but He will … just wait.

But Now

JULY 5

> "But now, LORD, what do I look for? My hope is in you."
> PSALM 39:7

There is no backup plan for faith. There's no other "way." I am the only Way. So, don't look anxiously about you ... you must be fully committed. Your hope must be in Me alone. I am the only hope that is stable, sure, and steadfast. It may be difficult to have hope when everything around you is uncertain or falling apart. But when you are looking at Me for your hope, it cannot be shaken. The Father has proven Himself trustworthy.

You can do nothing without Me. You need the Spirit to help you in your faith. And you must rely on the Father for your every need. You must keep your mind focused on the Word. You must filter everything in your life through it. So, in the middle of it ... in the middle of your messes in life, the lies of the Enemy are going to flood your soul like a tsunami. Be ready.

Let the promises of the Father be the anchor to your soul and your faith. Let nothing move you. And when doubt makes you question your faith, trying to drive you in another direction, look to Me, keep your eyes on Me. So, even now, when you're not sure where your life is headed, when you're uncertain as to whether you can have peace in the storm, you can choose to look to Me. Continually put your hope in Me, even when you can't see.

FAITH THOUGHTS

Are you losing hope in your situation? Are you struggling with what to do and which direction to take? Rely on the Spirit. You are not alone. God has a path and a plan for your life. He has blessings stored up for you, but it's in following Jesus that you will experience them. Hope is found in Him alone.

SECTION 3

In the Boat

When Jesus woke up, he rebuked the wind and said to the waves, "Silence! Be still!" Suddenly the wind stopped, and there was a great calm. Then he asked them, "Why are you afraid? Do you still have no faith?"

Mark 4:39-40 (NLT)

When an unexpected storm comes into your life, doubt can get the best of you. You expect, through faith, that God will show up in your timing and in your way, but He doesn't, and that causes you to question His love and whether or not He has your best interest at heart.

It's the storms of life that cause you to question God and beckon Him to answer. If you're seeking God continually, being present with Him constantly, He *will* speak. It can be a real struggle to believe consistently that God's promises are true. Difficulties in life can cause you to doubt whether or not those promises are really for you. You know you don't deserve a miracle, but you forget you're living under God's grace. Within moments, you can find your faith mixed with doubt, unsure of what you really believe and why your feelings get the best of your faith. But it's your doubts that are the reminder that you need God more. You need to know Him in greater ways. And He knows that. He allowed the storm. He allowed it with a purpose. He knows you need to witness a miracle. He knows nothing short of that will do. But He may make you wait. He may test your faith, looking to see if you just continue to frantically bail water or run to Him for help immediately. He's going to challenge you through the storm, asking you to dive deeper into your faith. And the more you come to Him, the more you'll learn to trust Him. So, it's okay to doubt. Doubt has its purpose. It's when you're about to give up, when you're sure God isn't going to show up … that He does. He always shows up … in breathtaking ways. In ways you'll never forget and never fully understand. So don't be afraid. When you're sure you have no faith left, look to Jesus and simply believe. *Be still.*

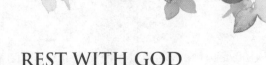

REST WITH GOD

Truly my soul finds rest in God.
PSALM 62:1

There will come a point in your life when you realize that you're not in control. The storms in your life will be more than you can handle … more than you can bear. You will only have the strength to fall on the grace of God and receive His help.

It's then that you can look to Jesus in the back of the boat. It may not seem like He cares, but nothing could be further from the truth. He's simply setting the example for you, to cease from your own striving and turn your worries over to God. He's showing you how to have confidence in allowing God to do what only He can do. And He's teaching you to rest and pray as you enter into His peace.

He's bringing your faith to a place of committing yourself to believing in His promises. As the wind and the waves become more fierce, and you become more fearful, it's seeing Jesus at rest that should show you that there is nothing to worry about … God is in control.

The storms of your life are not meant to destroy you. God won't allow that. But He will use them. He will use those difficult, unthinkable circumstances to build your faith.

Resting

JULY 6

By the seventh day God had finished the work he had been doing; so on the seventh day he rested from all his work. Then God blessed the seventh day and made it holy, because on it he rested from all the work of creating that he had done.
GENESIS 2:2-3

There is a time to cease "doing" and just rest. You need to worship and refresh your soul. It's a different kind of rest, not the rest from being weary and tired and needing to restore your strength, but a rest that restores your soul by focusing on the Father.

You will be blessed by blessing the Father, by worshiping and praising Him, and recognizing that He is more important than anything in your life. Rely on the Spirit to direct your every path and give you the strength to fully live out your faith. If you leave Me out of your life, trying to do it all on your own, you'll end up worn out and frustrated. But if you will lean on Me, you can allow Me to carry your burdens and you can enter into the Father's rest and enjoy your life, no matter what your circumstances might be.

Your life is to be a relationship with Me, living as a servant, doing what the Father has called you to do by His grace, doing what you can do and leaving the rest to Him. Living by faith should not be a struggle, it is resting. It's already believing what you do not see and being at rest in that faith.

FAITH THOUGHTS

Are you resting or always rushing? Focus on an active rest – living the life you're called to but trusting in the Father's care. You're not supposed to face your trials and tribulations on your own, you're meant to walk with Jesus and rely on the Father to protect you while the Spirit guides you. You don't have to live in fear and uncertainty, you can rest, knowing that God has everything under control.

Flying Away

*I said, "Oh, that I had the wings of a dove!
I would fly away and be at rest."*
PSALM 55:6

In your life you will have troubles, you'll face opposition and you'll have adversaries. You will struggle with your thoughts and you'll want to fly away, get away, get out. In the pressures of these moments, it seems like the perfect solution to just escape it all. But all that is allowed by the Father is with purpose. You may be right where you are, in the middle of trials and tribulations, in order to develop your godly character. He knows what He is doing.

I know you get tired. I know that you long to never have to deal with problems, to be free of the pain and suffering. But the answer is not to escape it all, but to embrace the grace given to you, allowing the thorn in your flesh to have its way, to do its work. Run to the Father, seek His guidance and then trust in the Spirit to provide you with answers that will lead you into His perfect will.

There may be issues that you don't want to face, but I'll face them with you. You can have peace in Me by obeying the Father and walking in His will, even when it includes overwhelming obstacles. You can move the mountains by faith. Escaping it all doesn't solve anything and won't bring you lasting peace. You have a call on your life, a path to take, and He promises to provide everything you need as you stay obedient and faithful. The Father's love, mercy, and faithfulness never ends.

Faith Thoughts

What is it that you'd like to escape? What problems are there in your life that you wish would go away? Look at them through the eyes of faith … God is doing something in the middle of it all. Accept your troubles as something more than what they appear on the surface. Look at them as tools in the hands of God, working to transform your heart to reflect His.

A Quiet Place

JULY 8

"Come with me by yourselves to a quiet place and get some rest."
MARK 6:31

I have told you that in this world you will have troubles … your journey of faith will not be easy, and I have not hidden that fact from you. Don't give in to discouragement. And when you find yourself exhausted physically, emotionally and spiritually, come to Me for rest. Come with Me to a quiet place and get some rest.

I'm not asking you; I'm commanding you … come with Me. You need to rest, even for a moment, even for a little while. I welcome you to a place where grace flows, where your Spirit can be refreshed and renewed. Listen to My voice in times of unrest, when your soul is desperate for peace … I am with you.

The world calls you to constant motion for things of pleasure in the world and very little time to focus on the things of eternity. You must make a constant effort to take time to rest and seek Me, to be in My presence and listen to the Father's voice.

FAITH THOUGHTS

Do you rest? Do you spend time alone with God and just sit quietly in His presence? Try to make it a priority to refresh your soul by spending time with Jesus. Fill yourself with the promises of God so that you can walk in confident hope and in the peace you are meant to have in life.

July 9

Living in Rest

In vain you rise early and stay up late, toiling for food to eat – for he grants sleep to those he loves.
PSALM 127:2

When you are living for the Father, nothing you do and accomplish is in vain. You are to find blessing and fulfillment in your purposes for your life, but that will not happen apart from Me. Without Me, your efforts will be empty, frustrating, useless, and in vain.

The Father and eternity should always be at the center of all you say and do. Only then will you have the Father's provision and blessing in your daily life. Never leave Me out of your daily life. Ask for My help. Let the Spirit do His work in and through you. Don't give up when you're weak and weary. Keep going, keep believing in My strength.

Trying to work harder is not always the answer, it is about trusting the Father more. Trust Him to meet your needs. And then learn to rest in Him. Rest in the Father's blessings for your life. Reflect on His past provision in your life and trust Him for your future. There is no reason to worry and fear. If you're trusting in the promises made to you, you don't need to overwork yourself or worry. The Father has everything under control and everything is held in His hands. Trust and pray.

FAITH THOUGHTS

Realize that working harder and doing more is not the goal. The goal is learning to walk in faith, trusting in God to lead, guide, and direct you and provide you with all that you need to accomplish His purposes. You don't need to stay up worrying, He's up all night … He'll take care of it all. You need to rest in Him.

Peaceful Living

JULY 10

*The LORD replied, "My Presence will
go with you, and I will give you rest."*
EXODUS 33:14

Your rest is in the presence of the Father. When you surrender into His power, your weakness will be made into strength. And it's My strength that will flood your soul with hope, peace, and joy. It's this strength that will enable you to face the most difficult situations. You need My presence and power in your life.

I want to be with you, to actively participate in your day-to-day struggles. I am the answer to every one of those struggles. But you must actively keep yourself in My presence. Say yes to the Father and obey all that He requests of you. You must daily surrender. If you are walking in the Father's will, you will not be worried, fearful, or anxious because you're trusting Him to care for you in every way and to bless you in all the ways you need to be.

It's your trust in Him that becomes a restful place for your soul, it is peaceful living. It is My presence that will also bring you peace at all times and in every way. It is because of My sacrifice and you being made right with the Father that you can approach His throne and dwell in His presence of mercy and grace.

You need to invite Me into your everyday moments, talking to Me and bringing all your troubles to the Father in prayer. I want you to live in My presence and in My peace.

FAITH THOUGHTS

It is going to take a conscious effort to continually invite Jesus into your everyday moments. You are supposed to live in the peace Jesus died to give you. Are you living in that peace? Or are you in a constant state of panic? Make the choice to pray about everything and to rest in God's faithfulness.

July 11

Calm and Quiet

But I have calmed and quieted myself.
PSALM 131:2

The Father has your life in His hands. When you rest, when you sleep, you should be reminded that you are not God and He has everything under control. You should walk in My peace. You should rest and sleep, knowing that the Father will protect you, watch over you, and help you through your problems. You can rest because you are never alone, the Father is watching over you and I am always with you.

I know that it's when troubles come, that you have a difficult time maintaining your peace and spiritual balance. An unshakable peace is available to you if you turn your eyes and heart to Me. I know that you wonder why the Father allows the trials and tribulations in your life, and I know that you doubt through your faith. And while it's easy to react to your pain and suffering with questions and uncertainty, you can choose to respond with faith.

You can trust in the Father's faithfulness. You can rely on His love, mercy, and grace. The answers to your worries and fears, your anxiety and your depression is found by resting in the peace of My presence. Don't be anxious, just give thanks to the Father and rest in Him. He provides you with an everlasting security. Trust in the quietness and rest in His peace. I'll be with you.

FAITH THOUGHTS

You can rest. You can sleep, realizing that God has everything under control at all times. It's easy to react to troubles with worry, anger, or despair, but you can choose to respond with faith. You can look to Jesus and find peace in His presence no matter what you're going through.

Rest for the Soul

"Stand at the crossroads and look; ask for the ancient paths, ask where the good way is, and walk in it, and you will find rest for your souls. But you said, 'We will not walk in it.'"
JEREMIAH 6:16

If you are looking for help, seeking the Father's guidance, you need to believe that He is willing and able to communicate with you. He might speak through His Word, prayer, or in other ways. A part of your spiritual growth is learning to recognize and listen to the Father's voice. Learn to listen. Rely on the Spirit to help you. When you find yourself at a crossroads, at a place of decision, a moment when your entire future depends on the choice you make, you need to stop and reflect, not rushing forward, but calling out to the Father in prayer for help.

If you want to know His will, believe that when you call out to Him, He is going to answer. Life moves quickly, but you must learn to follow Me and rest, leaning on the Spirit to comfort you and speak to your heart regarding the direction the Father wants you to go in. In your journey of faith, you must stop, stand still, and catch your breath. Slow down.

When you ask for the Father's direction, you are humbling yourself and recognizing that there is wisdom beyond your own that is more beneficial. In resting faith, you are actively living out your convictions that the Father is in control and that there is no reason to worry. I came to save the lost. I came to help you find and stay on the Father's righteous path that leads to joy and a life that is abundant.

FAITH THOUGHTS

When you are faced with difficult situations or decisions, are you taking a moment to stop and breathe and pray for God's will and direction? Don't miss out on divine direction.

When You're Weary

"Come to me, all you who are weary and burdened, and I will give you rest."
MATTHEW 11:28

There will be times that your heart feels so heavy that you can't imagine taking one more step of faith. Realize that I am with you to lead you, but also to carry you. Learn to be with Me and lean not on your own understanding, allowing Me to refresh your soul as I carry your burdens.

When you try to do everything in your own strength, it won't turn out well. When you are heavy-laden, your spirit, mind, and emotions won't be able to function well because you're trying to lift the weight yourself. You'll find yourself feeling depressed, anxious and helpless. I am with you to give you rest for your soul. You grow tired and weary trying to do it all, have it all, and be it all to please everyone. I came to teach you something different.

When you walk in My ways, you will abide in Me and also rest in Me. It's when you are overloaded, overstressed, and burdened, that you must come to Me and ask for My help. It's time for you to give up control, to allow the Father to handle your troubles. It's your weakness that qualifies you for My rest. It's in realizing that you cannot handle what you're struggling with that will enable you to accept that you're not in control. Then you must rely on My strength and power.

FAITH THOUGHTS

Are you tired of carrying all the burdens that are weighing you down? Turn to Jesus and ask Him to do what you can't. When you're feeling anxious, depressed, and helpless, it should be the first indication that you need God's help. Remember to pray about everything at all times. Don't wait.

Return to Rest

JULY 14

*Return to your rest, my soul,
for the LORD has been good to you.*
PSALM 116:7

You need to constantly remember how the Father has been good to you. And you need to realize that you are best able to face the challenges before you if you surrender your life into His hands. You can rest because the Father has promised you good and He has promised that He hears your prayers and answers them. He answers you always with My peace.

In your resting, your faith will fill your heart with love for a Father that has complete loving control over your life, showing mercy, compassion, and grace in every detail. When you don't know what to do, the answer is to pray. He has delivered you in the past and He will continue to deliver you over and over again. I want to give you peace, true peace, so that your soul can truly rest and you can enjoy life like you're supposed to.

You've been given a new life. A life in Me that gives you access to the Father's throne, calling upon His power and wisdom to help you through each day. You don't have to live in fear and despair anymore. You are a different person, walking in faith and assured of the glory to come. It's time to rest in the hope that I've given you and to follow Me into eternity.

FAITH THOUGHTS

Sometimes, when things aren't going well, it's easy to forget all the ways in which God has been good to you. It's easy to overlook the little things because the big things seem so overwhelming. But are you immediately calling out to God in your distress? Are you trusting Him to take care of you and every detail of your life? Are you resting in His faithfulness?

JULY 15

Refreshed and Satisfied

"I will refresh the weary and satisfy the faint."
JEREMIAH 31:25

The only One who can satisfy your soul is the One who created it. It's when your heart and mind are over-burdened, weary and worn from everyday life, that you can easily find yourself exhausted from all the stress. And your spiritual fatigue is just as damaging as the physical.

When your soul is weary, you'll find all of yourself weary. It's often when you've reached complete exhaustion that you lose your hope, your joy and your sense of purpose. Being spiritually broken can lead to guilt, grief, and disturbing discouragement.

The Father sent Me so that I can refresh your soul. I can calm your restless heart. I can fill the spiritually broken and empty places. The Father has promised to refresh you and satisfy you. Come to Me for the rest and refreshing. Spend time with Me and in the Word. And then surrender all of your life, the good and the bad, and those impossible situations that only I can handle. If you are tired, you are one prayer away from rest and refreshment. You are not alone and you don't have to suffer anymore. I am waiting to lift your burdens and to fill you with My peace that will restore your soul.

FAITH THOUGHTS

Do you turn to Jesus immediately when you're tired and weary? Do you look to Him for your strength or do you just give in to the overwhelming despair? Jesus came so that you could have peace and call upon His power in your life. If you're exhausted physically and spiritually, you need God's Spirit to fill you with His power and give you rest. Don't wait one more minute to pray for His help.

A Standing Promise

*Therefore, since the promise of entering his rest
still stands, let us be careful that none
of you be found to have fallen short of it.*
HEBREWS 4:1

As long as you trust in the promises of the Father, you can face anything in life without fear. And you don't have to live life in a constant state of stress and exhaustion, you've been promised that you can enter into the rest of the Father at any time. It is your choice to accept that promise. It is the door of faith that opens the opportunity for you to trust and rest in Me.

You are sealed for future glory, but I also want to save you today. Your joy can come in this moment, resting in being saved, sealed, and cared for … you lack nothing. You always have the opportunity to enter into My rest, but it's your unbelief that will keep you from experiencing it.

It requires trusting in the promises of the Father, and it's often your unbelief that keeps you from moving forward in His purposes for your life. My rest is actually faith in action. It's because of My sacrifice that you can now bring your shame, embarrassment, and need for mercy to the Father. And in exchange, you receive encouragement, direction, and help. You have full access to the love of the Father through grace. You must continually make the decision to enter into the rest you've been given, surrendering your heart and yielding to the Father's will for you.

Faith Thoughts

Are you daily making it a point to enter into God's rest? It's through your faith in Him that you can be certain that hope is never lost and you have access to the presence and power of Jesus. Whatever you face in life, you can face with joy because you know that if all things are in God's control, they are full of His goodness and grace.

JULY 17

The Offering

He makes me lie down in green pastures, he leads me beside quiet waters, he refreshes my soul. He guides me along the right paths for his name's sake.
PSALM 23:2-3

As I lead you into green pastures, you will find a place where you can rest under the watchful eye of the Father. I do not force you to lie down and rest, it is an offer to enter into My rest and peace every single day.

Know that I am leading you along right paths. You will always have everything you need. Your focus tends to be on staying busy, achieving what the world sees as success, and you need to slow down. The Father longs for you to have peace and rest. As you follow Me, you'll find that we will slow down, be quiet and still with the Father, and experience His deep love.

We will immerse ourselves in His grace. And you will find Living Water as you fellowship with Me, so that you will never thirst again. I lead you through green pastures and along still waters for your sake, it's all for the Father's glory. As the Father supplies your daily needs, it is in His offering of peace and rest that He desires to restore your soul … to revive you.

FAITH THOUGHTS

God wants you to be revived through His peace and rest. He daily offers you a place in His arms where He can comfort and assure you of His care. Don't allow the stressors of life to distract you from His mercy that can allow you to rest through even the most difficult circumstances.

Living Out of Rest

JULY 18

For anyone who enters God's rest also rests from their works, just as God did from his.
HEBREWS 4:10

Do not stop short of entering into the Father's rest. You must strengthen your faith and care for your soul by daily building your faith … walking with Me and trusting in the Father. If your soul is weary and worn from the troubles of the world, come with Me and rise above it all … come rest with Me.

You've been given spiritual blessings to help you through your journey of faith. Make sure you access them by fellowshipping with Me and relying on the Spirit to lead and guide you into the Father's perfect will for your life.

Through Me you have been given peace with the Father, free of guilt and condemnation. Your sins have been covered by My blood. Your hope, your strength, your rest comes from your constant reliance on My presence and power. You are going to pass through fires and temptations of sin … your faith will be tested. But in it all, hold fast by drawing near. Draw near to Me. Come to the Father. He loves to pour out His grace, magnifying His awesome glory.

FAITH THOUGHTS

Are you accessing all of the spiritual gifts and benefits you've been given through your faith? Are you resting because God is at work? Are you trusting that everything is under His control and letting go of your worries? Be determined to live your life out of rest – knowing that you have hope.

THE POWER OF YOUR PRAYERS

"If you believe, you will receive whatever you ask for in prayer."
MATTHEW 21:22

You should never underestimate the power of prayer. God listens to your prayers and answers them. You have access to divine, supernatural power. It's as you spend time with Jesus, in the boat, that you'll learn more and more about faith, about who you aren't and who He is. And you'll find out that God will show up just when you think He won't.

The secret is in going where He wants you to go and doing what He wants you to do … even if His plan takes you into a raging storm of life. What you must remember is that God is faithful. And He's promised that if you knock, He'll open the door. If you need Him to part the sea, He will. And through your doubt, you'll find that it's the Word that has divine power to demolish the lies. Stay in the Word and take every single one of your thoughts captive.

Know that your prayers will be a miracle in and of themselves. They will provide you timely direction, keep you from walking down wrong paths, eliminate worry and anxiety, bring about peace that transcends all understanding, and keep you from becoming discouraged, giving strength to your faith in the most unthinkable difficulties. God's answers may not always be "Yes". But if you will come purposefully and passionately, you'll come to understand that He has a perfect will that is for your best. If you'll pray for the desires of your heart and trust in His will … you'll find He'll do more than you ask for or imagine.

An Open Door

JULY 19

"Ask and it will be given to you; seek and you will find; knock and the door will be opened to you."
MATTHEW 7:7

I know that at times you are unsure what you want in life or how to accomplish all that you're supposed to. Don't try to do it on your own. You aren't meant to. Pray and ask the Father for help. And then wait and listen. All too often you pray and do not truly expect an answer. Expect what the Father has promised. He promises that He hears you and He will answer.

Too often you give up before the answer, before the miracle. Don't give up. Be persistent and keep asking. Continue seeking Me and following Me. Focus on the Father's will for you and look to the Spirit to reveal the ways in which you can bring glory to the Kingdom.

The Father will take care of all your needs. Let go of your worries and place them all in the Father's hands. You can trust Him. Look at where you were, where you've been, and all that He's done to bless you. Though you're convinced that your future is uncertain, you can look to the Father's faithfulness in the past and be assured that He never changes. He will be faithful in your life today, tomorrow, and every day thereafter. Continue to seek and live in that grace.

FAITH THOUGHTS

When you're in need, do you immediately ask God for it? And if you do, are you truly expecting an answer? You've been assured that He hears you and will answer you, so your faith needs to come to a place of truly believing that and then looking expectantly to Him to answer. Don't give up before the answer ... before the miracle.

July 20

Whatever You Ask

*"And I will do whatever you ask in my name,
so that the Father may be glorified in the Son.
You may ask me for anything in my name, and I will do it."*
JOHN 14:13-14

When you pray in My name, whatever it is you ask, ask that your will is in agreement with the Father's. Pray in My authority, as everything is under My feet, and all of My power will be given to you. You can do all things through Me.

If there is anything that will glorify the Father, you can be sure His answer will be "yes". And He will provide you all that you need to accomplish what He's asked you to do, what He has laid on your heart. The purpose of prayer is to bring you in touch with the Father, to communicate with Him, to bring your will into alignment with His.

When you don't know what to pray, you have the help of the Spirit. I sacrificed My life so that I could live in and through you, accomplishing more than even what I did during My time on earth. You are chosen and blessed, called to live your life for Me. Live it well, live it with eternity in mind and the Father's love in your heart. And whatever you ask, make sure it is in My name, to glorify the Father.

FAITH THOUGHTS

What does your prayer life look like? Are you placing God's purposes for your life ahead of your own desires? If you'll always keep eternity in front of you, God has promised to give you the desires of your heart. Continually pray that your life, all you say and do, will glorify God.

Keep on Praying

*And pray in the Spirit on all occasions with
all kinds of prayers and requests. With this in mind,
be alert and always keep on praying for all the Lord's people.*
EPHESIANS 6:18

You have been given every spiritual blessing through Me. You are adopted, predestined, and chosen by the Father. You are sealed with the Holy Spirit. I want you to learn to enjoy all that you've received in Me – to walk in faith, to live out your spiritual reality in Me. And yet, as you do, you must realize that you are in a war. One that is unseen and invisible. It is truer than any flesh and blood war, a legitimate struggle in the spiritual realm.

You will win every spiritual battle through prayer. Pray at all times and make sure you keep alert with all perseverance, boldly approaching the throne of grace. Every great miracle begins with prayer. Sometimes it is one person's simple prayer, sometimes it is a prayer of desperation through trials and tribulations, and sometimes it is a prayer that is a result of sin.

No matter the reason, the Father is listening to your heart. And your prayers should never cease. My life on earth was a constant conversation with the Father. He walked with Me throughout every day and you must walk with Him each and every moment of your life as well. And He is closer to you than He's ever been, His Spirit is within you, an ever-present help.

FAITH THOUGHTS

Are you facing difficult situations? Pray. Are you being tempted to do things that are outside God's will? Pray. Are you filled with sorrow from pain and suffering? Pray. Do you need help in making decisions and guidance through troubles? Pray. Don't wait. Create a habit of always praying about everything, always.

July 22

In Everything

Do not be anxious about anything, but in every situation, by prayer and petition, with thanksgiving, present your requests to God. And the peace of God, which transcends all understanding, will guard your hearts and your minds in Christ Jesus.
PHILIPPIANS 4:6-7

Your first reaction to everything, to every situation you face, should be to turn to the Father in prayer. You may not be able to change your world or your circumstances, but you can pray about them. Life will cause you to face anxieties and you may face fears and uncertainty, it is your choice how you respond to them. And you must choose to react in faith.

If you are at peace in the most difficult circumstances, it is evidence of the Spirit at work within you, giving you peace that surpasses all understanding. It is the practice of prayer that allows you to express your dependence on the Father.

I lived My life in prayer and so should you. I walk with you to teach you that you can trust the Father. He loves you, walks with you, and nothing is beyond His power. It's when you pray about everything that you will find My peace. You can rest, knowing that nothing happens without the Father's knowledge. Things may not happen the way you want them to, but the Father is always in control and His love for you never changes. Whatever it is that is weighing on your heart and mind, lift it all up in prayer.

FAITH THOUGHTS

What is it that is weighing on your heart and mind? What is it that you're worrying about that you should be praying about instead? Don't try and control what only God can and refuse to worry about things that He already has under His control. Whatever you do, don't forget to pray.

In Confidence

This is the confidence we have in approaching God:
that if we ask anything according to his will, he hears us.
1 JOHN 5:14

I want to encourage you to pray more faithfully. You've been promised that when you pray, the Father hears you and He will answer you. Prayer is not an option, it's essential. If you're not praying, you're not living by faith. If you're not praying, you're trusting in yourself, instead of the Father. It's when you draw near to the Father's throne with confidence that you will receive mercy and grace to help you.

Your confidence can never be in yourself, but only in Me, whose blood has given you the access to approach the Father's throne. Your prayers may not be answered right away. The answers may not come for years. But you can know that the Father has already answered in this moment.

Yet, you are to continue praying until your request is actually granted … until your faith is rewarded. As you wait, as you pray, you can begin thanking the Father, worshiping and praising Him no matter what His answer will be. You must persevere in prayer, even when you don't understand the Father's will or His ways. Pray at all times and do not lose heart.

FAITH THOUGHTS

Have you prayed about something in your life, asked God for something specific and you're just waiting? Stay focused on worshiping and praising Him that He's already answered your prayer, even though maybe you haven't seen His answer in your life yet. And as you wait, wait well … do not lose heart.

JULY 24

Calling in Prayer

*Then you will call on me and come and pray to me,
and I will listen to you.*
JEREMIAH 29:12

You must be diligent in your faith. It's easy to allow worldly things to consume your life and allow division between you and Me. You must be careful not to be conformed to this world, but to be transformed by the renewing of your mind so that you can do what is the good and acceptable and perfect will of the Father.

You were not created to live a distracted life. You were created to live a life full of Me and all of My power. Your focus is to always be directed toward Me, allowing Me to lead you as the Spirit works within you to follow the Father's will. It's extremely important that you stay focused on Me, the author and finisher of your faith.

It was because joy was set before Me that I endured the Cross, despising the shame, and then sat down at the right hand of the throne of the Father. Do not lose faith, you will miss the blessings stored up for you. If you keep your focus on Me, drawing nearer and allowing Me to lead you, you find your heart transforming, longing for Me more and seeking My presence continually. As you follow Me, we will talk to the Father in prayer, calling on Him for guidance, comforted by His presence, assured that He is listening.

FAITH THOUGHTS

Do you sometimes feel like no one is listening to you, especially God? He has promised that if you call to Him, He hears you and He will not only listen, but will also answer you. As you pray and then wait, listening for His voice, turn to His Word and be filled with His promises, so that you will have hope to hold on to.

The Divine Exchange

*Look to the L*ORD *and his strength; seek his face always.*
1 CHRONICLES 16:11

Seeking the Father is all about your heart … your personal spiritual growth process. It's the more you grow in Him that you find that you can go to Him for your every need. Look to Me for guidance in how to fellowship with the Father, praying at all times, and seeking His direction and will. And when you're uncertain and growing weary in your faith, find your strength in Me.

Seeking the Father is yearning to know Him, His ways, and His thoughts. His thoughts may be above yours, but with the help of the Spirit, you can know them. And I am the One that gives you the fullness of the Father Himself. It's in knowing Him, knowing His will, and relying on His wisdom that gifts are given to you as His child. And as you pray and wait upon the Father, there is a divine exchange. You are renewed, refreshed and strengthened through the Spirit. It's the Spirit that fills you with the knowledge of the Father's will and gives you spiritual understanding. Grace continually abounds, and the Father's mercy is never restrained.

His favor flows like a river and His Light banishes darkness. It's the joy in hope you have in Me that guards your heart and mind, as you trust in the Father to work out His plans for your life.

FAITH THOUGHTS

Each and every day you should seek God. Seek Him for all that He is and yearn to just know Him. Ask that the Spirit would reveal more of Him to you and give you understanding as you trust in God's plans for your life. When you're weak and weary in your faith, look to Jesus as your strength.

Watch and Pray

"Watch and pray so that you will not fall into temptation. The spirit is willing, but the flesh is weak."
MATTHEW 26:41

The Enemy will try to pull you in directions that are not within the Father's will for your life. You must be alert in your faith at all times. Prayer is one of the ways in which you can communicate with the Father and the way in which He can guide and direct you through His Spirit. Without prayer, you are unable to walk in the Father's will.

The more you pray, the more you are touched by the Father. As you pray, you are able to receive the divine power needed to bring about the Father's plans for your life. There are always certain areas of your life where you are more vulnerable to temptation and susceptible to sin. So, you should always pray.

Make sure you are continually bringing your specific needs and weaknesses before the Father's throne, just as I did. And then expect to receive His help. Continually come into the Father's presence, pray continually, be moved by Him, receive His provisions, be transformed moment by moment. Rely on the Spirit to help you grow in your faith as you diligently seek the Father's will and plans for your life, following His paths and following Me.

FAITH THOUGHTS

What area of your life are you tempted to go your own way and do what you know is not a part of God's will for you? Ask the Spirit to work within you to overcome those temptations. Bring your weaknesses and your worries before God's throne and expect Him to strengthen you in your faith as you passionately follow Jesus.

Joyful in Hope

JULY 27

Be joyful in hope, patient in affliction, faithful in prayer.
ROMANS 12:12

Whatever trials come your way, you can be joyful in the fact that you will live with Me forever. Yet, in the meantime, through your faithful prayer and patience, you can continue to look to Me until that day comes. Through each day, the Spirit will transform your heart and mind, enabling you to face your troubles with faith instead of worry and fear.

It's your transformed attitude that will be mercy-motivated, reflecting My character and enabling you to face the most unthinkable of circumstances. The Father's mercies call you to joyful, prayerful perseverance through the toughest of times. And in times of trial, when you pray for relief, know that you should also pray that you would be strengthened with My power so that you can learn to endure those trials with joy and thankfulness.

Make it your first priority to pray that the Spirit would work within you, transforming your heart and taking you from glory to glory. Most often your difficulties are there to test your faith, to drive you to your knees in prayer and to call upon Me to help you persevere through them. Begin each day by focusing on the hope you have in Me, so you can live fully in the joy you've been given.

Faith Thoughts

Is your life full of joy in hope? Do you joyfully persevere through your troubles or complain endlessly through them? Are you devoted to prayer or is it a last resort? Make a conscious effort to work on your prayer life. Be devoted to seeking a more intimate relationship with God, so that you can live in the joy He has given to you.

July 28

Hearing from Heaven

Hear the supplications of your servant and of your people Israel when they pray toward this place. Hear from heaven, your dwelling place; and when you hear, forgive.
2 CHRONICLES 6:21

When life is hurried, when you're driven to panic, you forget that you are supposed to be constantly, restfully rejoicing. Your daily life brings about the stress of anticipation, preparation, and expectation, and your soul craters beneath the weight of it all. There have been times in your life when it was easy to have faith, it was easy to trust the Father, and it seemed effortless to follow Me, but now, in the middle of your troubles, your faith cannot seem to take one more step.

Pray at all times. And then listen. The Father will use His Spirit to speak to your heart, to quiet you with His. Confess your worries in prayer, tell the Father your fears, and then let Me carry your burdens. Surrender your heart and allow the Spirit to reveal any sin. Recognize that your place is upon your knees, acknowledging the Father for all that He is. Draw near to Him and always confess sins … He will restore you. It's through My blood that the Father continually forgives and you can constantly live in My peace and within His love.

 FAITH THOUGHTS

Each and every day you'll need to ask the Spirit to search your heart. There may be sins that are separating you from God that you haven't acknowledged or are hesitant to. Faith will sometimes seem easy and at other times nearly impossible, but Jesus is with you through it all. Keep your eyes on Him and walk in His peace.

The Secret Weapon

JULY 29

Pray also for me, that whenever I speak, words may be given me so that I will fearlessly make known the mystery of the gospel.
EPHESIANS 6:19

It is through prayer that you call down the power of God into your life. It is prayer that is one of the greatest weapons in spiritual battles. Don't lose the battles because you simply forgot to pray. And when you pray, speak the Father's words. It's His Word, the promises He's made, that holds His power.

As you follow Me, as you live out the Father's purposes for your life, the purpose that is always assumed is that you would speak of the gospel to whomever the Father sends your way. You will need the Spirit to give you the courage to say what you need to say and to be able to speak confidently and lovingly, pouring out grace to whomever will listen. And there will be times when you will find it difficult to share the gospel. Either out of fear for your own reputation or fear of someone else's response. Anxiety will overwhelm you and you'll be tempted to walk away.

Face the Enemy, who is trying to keep you from boldly speaking of Me, with your faith. Know that the Father will protect you and bless you for proclaiming His glory. There is no greater purpose for your life than fulfilling the Father's plans to build His kingdom. You've been chosen … pray that you will accomplish all that you're supposed to in My strength.

FAITH THOUGHTS

It's easy to overlook prayer when you're overwhelmed, but there is no other way to fight spiritual battles. Pray in Jesus' name, calling down all the power in heaven to do what you're called to do and accomplish the impossible. Stand firm in your faith by standing firm in God's Word.

July 30

Answering the Call

Answer me when I call to you, my righteous God. Give me relief from my distress; have mercy on me and hear my prayer.
PSALM 4:1

You can always rest assured that the Father hears you when you pray. And you can count on His righteousness which will answer you in the right way and at the right time, every time. And yet, He has no obligation to answer – He does so out of grace. You can have confidence in your Father and rest in Him, which is your great reward.

When you are in distress, look back on the times when your heavenly Father heard your cries and helped you. Let His faithfulness give you hope for the future. Always reflect on the ways that the Father has delivered you in the past and trust that He will do it again. Always remember to call upon grace.

The Father may seem slow to answer, and He may not answer in the way you thought He would or should, but He hears you and you can trust that He will always do what is best. Pour out your heart continually and then trust in His ways. You may have troubles that never seem to end, the Father may appear distant and heaven seem silent, but if you have trusted in Me, the Father knows your circumstances, hears your prayers and simply calls on you to trust Him.

FAITH THOUGHTS

Do you sometimes feel like God doesn't hear you? Things don't seem to be changing and often seem to be getting worse, as you cry out from the bottom of your heart. And yet, in your waiting, God asks you to rest and trust that He will answer you, in due time, when He is certain that you are ready to receive that answer.

Devoted in Prayer

You will pray to him, and he will hear you ...
JOB 22:27

The power in prayer is that the Father hears you and in spending time with Him, He transforms your heart and you become more like Him ... faithful. The Father has promised to hear you and answer you. It may not be the answer you're expecting, but it will be the answer you need the most. Trust in His plans for good for your future. He has given you Me as your hope.

Always pray that you will be led by the Spirit and not lean unto your own understanding, choosing your own path. It's submission to the Father that will give you peace. It's the Father's love at work in you to remove the barriers of pride, fear, and insecurity that keep you reconciling your life to Him through Me. His works within you are always born of love, mercy, and grace. He daily pursues you, in order to bless you, and it's His desire to give you the desires of your heart.

If you are not in the right relationship with Him, it creates conflict in your life, leaving things undone and tossed about by changing circumstances. Your following Me makes you an enemy of the world, and a friend of the Father. Your transformed heart will drive you to want more and more of the Father's grace. It's in walking with Me that you find yourself moving from living a life in this world to Kingdom living. You must become less, He must become more. It's time to allow your pride to be crucified and embrace your new life that is filled with grace and more grace.

FAITH THOUGHTS

God has given you prayer out of His love and grace. It's the way in which He can communicate with you and build His relationship with you. Never stop praying. Prayer cannot only change everything, it can change you, transforming your heart and life to bring glory to God.

STANDING FIRM IN FAITH

For we live by faith, not by sight.
2 CORINTHIANS 5:7

Living by faith will not be easy. It will be difficult at best. But you have divine, supernatural power living within you, to help you, to carry you, to help you stand firm in your faith … in the worst of circumstances.

As much as you pray, knowing that God hears you, it's a lack of trust and the fear of stepping out in faith that limits His answers. You can't back away from dependence on God. Faith requires that you are strong and courageous, with the help of the Spirit. You can't do it on your own. Don't allow your faith to be shaken. Keep your eyes on Jesus at all times. Remember, He's resting in the back of the boat. Don't get trapped by unbelief and fear. Expect a miracle.

Show your faith in good times and in bad. Stand firm in what God has promised you and don't allow your faith to waiver. Your pursuit of God, walking in faith, will require that no matter what you're facing you keep walking, keep seeking, and keep yearning.

It's right now, in the middle of a raging storm of life that you'll have to live by faith and not by sight. And the storm comes with great purpose. You're not meant to see through the destructive wind and rain. And it's right in the middle of it that God has told you to consider it all joy. Yet, He's also promised something else: "blessed is the one who perseveres under trial because, having stood the test, that person will receive the crown of life that the Lord has promised to those who love Him" (James 1:12).

You see, in the storm, when you want to give up and give in, God is doing something miraculous. He's refining your faith, bringing you to a place of anchoring yourself in the hope of Jesus, learning to trust and rest in His presence and power during every moment of your life.

Faith Comes by Hearing

AUGUST 1

Consequently, faith comes from hearing the message, and the message is heard through the word about Christ.
ROMANS 10:17

Living with faith is the foundation to living an abundant life. The Father is faithful no matter what, but it's your faith that allows you to have trust in that faithfulness, giving you the peace you desperately need in all the challenges of life.

If you will depend on the Word of the Father and what He has spoken to determine your present reality, you will find yourself living in a place of victorious faith.

The promises are what build your faith. The more you read the Word and trust in the Father's faithfulness, the more your faith will grow. No matter what circumstances you're going through, the Father has something to say about it … a promise for it. Ask that the Spirit will continually draw you near to the Father and drive you to meditate on His Word day and night. Let faith be your focus.

Don't allow the troubles of the world to distract you and keep you from holding on to the hope you've been given. It's your faith that will open your heart to Truth, keeping you from walking in darkness. And it's faith that will continually lead you into the unknown, but always brings you into the presence of the Father. It will be the promises that will lead you safely through the unexpected and give you hope when hope seems gone. Each and every day, seek Me and seek to know the Father's heart continually through His Word.

FAITH THOUGHTS

Are you strengthening your faith? Your spiritual growth requires that you learn to have faith and trust in God. That can only happen by spending more time in the Word. What was it that God spoke to you today when you read His Word and listened to His voice?

AUGUST 2

The Assurance

Now faith is confidence in what we hope for and assurance about what we do not see.
HEBREWS 11:1

I know that there will always be times when you need encouragement in your faith. The pressures of life are real and in an instant you can feel weary or discouraged. Sometimes, you just need to come to Me and take a break. Pray with Me, so that your soul will be refreshed in My hope.

It's when you experience problem after problem that your spirit grows weak and you find your faith being tested. It is through these times of testing that perseverance is developed within you and your strength will come through believing in the Word. In drawing nearer to the Father, you will find true confidence in His faithfulness as an ever-present help, a refuge and your strength.

Ask the Spirit to give you courage to continue to trust even through tough times of great need. Remember to thank the Father for His trustworthiness and focus on persevering in faith through remembering My work of reconciliation. Be confident in hope because you confidently believe in Me. Be assured that I am with you always, and the Father is looking after your life in detail at all times.

 ## FAITH THOUGHTS

Do you need to be encouraged in your faith? Look for ways that God will do that in your life. His favor is always upon you, but sometimes you may not recognize the little ways He pours out His grace. Remember that faith does not walk by sight, so when you can't see … keep trusting … God has never failed you and He never will.

Through Faith

August 3

I pray that out of his glorious riches he may strengthen you with power through his Spirit in your inner being, so that Christ may dwell in your hearts through faith. And I pray that you, being rooted and established in love …
Ephesians 3:16-17

Though you walk in My strength, you have many weaknesses because you are living in a world of sickness, opposition, sin and death. Don't be tempted to look anywhere other than Me for strength and power to overcome the troubles of the world.

You need the Spirit to strengthen your inner being. If the Father has already displayed His limitless strength and power in raising Me from the dead, then there is no reason for you not to trust that He will pour out that same power in your own life. Your sins have been covered, come to His throne, boldly, praying and expecting His blessings.

Your hope is in Me, I've made the way for you, and now you have the blessings of Me living within you through the Spirit. I dwell in you through your faith. It's in believing that you've been raised with Me, giving you security and a hope of future redemption.

Faith is trusting in the Father's Truth. And through your faith, your heart can be grounded in His deep and unshakable love. When you are weak, I am strong. Embrace your challenges knowing that I live in you and everything is under My feet.

Faith Thoughts

Are you living each day with the full awareness that Christ lives in you? The power that raised Him from the dead is alive in you. Doesn't that change everything? If it hasn't altered anything in your life, ask God why. What is it in your heart that needs to be changed? What is it in your faith that needs to adjust to the truth? Pray that He will establish your soul in His love and strengthen you with power through His Spirit.

Choosing the Way

I have chosen the way of faithfulness;
I have set my heart on your laws.
PSALM 119:30

Life is all about choices. You choose every day how you will live, what you will do. And you must choose whether or not to follow Me and serve the Father. It's up to you how much you will trust the Father and when the storms of your life are raging, whether or not you'll rest with Me.

The more dedicated and determined you are to seek Me, the more you will walk down paths of righteousness. You won't always get it right, you will stumble in your faith, but the Father is loving and forgiving and waits for you to come to Him. It's your choices in life that reflect the condition of your heart. All you do and say should point others to Me. But you can't do this alone, you can't live this life of faith in your own strength. You must follow Me and rely on the Spirit as your Helper. Each and every day you must choose who you will serve, yourself or the Father. If you want to see the evidence of the Father's goodness in your life, seek His promises and ask the Spirit for insight and understanding.

Remember all that the Father has done for you, and rest in His grace that assures you that He is faithful, regardless of your faithfulness. The Cross, the empty grave, and grace that consumes you ... this is the Way that the Father has made ... choose this Way.

FAITH THOUGHTS

Are you conscious about the choices you make in your life, the big ones and the small ones? Are you placing God first in your life, making all of your choices reflect His priorities for your life and the Kingdom? Ask the Spirit to help you to be faithful and to set your heart on God's.

The Glory

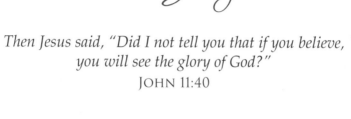

Then Jesus said, "Did I not tell you that if you believe, you will see the glory of God?"
JOHN 11:40

You should continually be taking your problems and concerns before the Father in prayer and allow Him to pour out His grace and mercy upon them. If you're lacking faith, what impossible thing is keeping you from believing? What is it that you doubt the Father can do? You need to expect things to change. Don't stay stuck in your troubles, not believing that the Father can turn things around.

Whatever is dead in your life can be brought back to life. Don't lose hope. You might be hurting right now, but the Father can make all things new. Sometimes you don't need to even know what to ask for ... you just need to know Me. When you believe in Me, you can trust Me to bring miracles into your life by walking with Me and drawing nearer to the Father and stronger in your faith. The Father has a supernatural solution to every single problem you face in life.

The joy is in having fellowship with Him and realizing that all things are under His love, mercy, and grace. There is no reason to worry, the Father has everything under control. So, you can live in the hope you've been given and look forward to going from glory to glory.

FAITH THOUGHTS

God stands right where your needs are. What miracle do you need from Him? Do you believe that He still does miracles? Believe that you will see His glory, believe that you will see your miracle, and then live each moment as if the miracle has happened. Let God's faithfulness change the way you live your life.

AUGUST 6

The Testing of Faith

*Because you know that the testing of
your faith produces perseverance.*
JAMES 1:3

Trials are going to come your way, I've promised that in this world you will have trouble ... it's a fallen world. But they are meant to transform you, mold you, and develop you through sanctification. Your struggles are used for great purposes in the hands of the Father. Things aren't what they appear on the surface.

So often, you believe that if you're walking with Me, trusting in the Father, your life should just be "easier". But, following Me is against the ways of the world and you will experience various trials. You will face trials, but you can face them in faith. Know that joy should be found in every circumstance because you should be focused on the work the Father is doing in and through them.

Everything in your life, the good and the bad, is meant to guide you towards My likeness. Do not give in to the temptation to abandon your faith, I am with you through it all. Let faith do its work. Be confidently grounded in Me, placing all of your confidence in the hope I've given you, and not depending on your own effort or resources. Faith is believing that the promises the Father has made you that you cannot see will someday be reality, because He is faithful.

Whatever you're going through will be worth it. The Father will prove Himself to you, making His promises real in your life. Don't miss the good part that comes from the hard parts.

FAITH THOUGHTS

Whatever struggles you face, Jesus is in them with you. You're not being refined in the fire on your own, Jesus is with you. There is nothing to fear. Know that if your faith is being tested, there are blessings on the other side of it. You can have confident hope because of God's faithfulness.

The End Result

Though you have not seen him, you love him; and even though you do not see him now, you believe in him and are filled with an inexpressible and glorious joy, for you are receiving the end result of your faith, the salvation of your souls.
1 Peter 1:8-9

You might think faith is hard, but you are continually believing in what you don't see. You depend on things you can't see every day like gravity and the air you breathe. Faith in Me is just as natural, just as easy. But your heart is doubtful. I know it's hard to understand the Father's grace, hard to believe He would love you the way He does. But it's true. You can live in joy because you can always come into His presence by your faith.

Though you face troubles every day, there is a joy that resides in your heart that comes from the fact that I died for you and help to lead you in your life now. You don't have to see Me, you can trust that I am with you and you can see the evidence of My work in your life.

You are loved, saved, and understood. You can walk in My peace, even through the most challenging situations of your life. You don't have to fear the end, because the end of this world will just be the beginning of eternity. You have real hope. And hope is the end result of your faith in Me.

Faith Thoughts

It's always easy to believe in the things we can see, it's believing in the unseen that requires faith that is often difficult to have in trying circumstances. Accept the love and grace that God has for you and look to His mercy when you are drowning in the weight of your troubles. He is your ready help in times of trouble.

Overcoming the World

For everyone born of God overcomes the world.
This is the victory that has overcome the world, even our faith.
1 JOHN 5:4

I have risen, not only so that you can have eternal life, but also so that you can overcome sin on the inside and the devil in the world. If you believe in Me, you've been given the victory because I have overcome the world.

I know that sometimes life can seem like a series of small victories followed by large setbacks. It can feel like you're never moving forward in faith. You allow your disappointments and frustrations to drag you down. You so easily forget that you have victory through Me. Victory over sin and death.

You can face anything because I dwell in you. It's My Spirit that works mightily in your heart to sustain your faith and trust in the Father. You can face each and every day confidently because the real victory is yours.

I have come, by My death and resurrection, and have overcome the world. I want you to live in that very real victory. You don't have to think or live as the world does. You shouldn't. You are a new creation and the Spirit is constantly transforming your heart. You should not be living in defeat, I have given you the victory.

FAITH THOUGHTS

In what ways do you feel defeated in your life? Jesus wants you to live the victorious life He died to give you, so make the choice to live differently from the rest of the world. Call upon the Spirit continually to transform your thoughts and fill you with hope for every difficulty you face.

Move Mountains

AUGUST 9

*"Truly I tell you, if you have faith as small
as a mustard seed, you can say to this mountain,
'Move from here to there,' and it will move.
Nothing will be impossible for you."*
MATTHEW 17:20

What if you lived as if nothing were impossible for you? What if you lived in the faith you profess? Just because you failed in faith yesterday doesn't mean you have to have little faith today. Today is a day for great faith. Today is a day to have the faith that will move all of your mountains.

Your faith is the channel through which the Father chooses to manifest His glory that leads others to Him. If you have little faith, then little glory is seen in and through you. Now is the time to have great faith. Do not be content with having a little faith. Ask Me to increase your faith, to help your unbelief. And as you believe, as you pray in faith, stay at the Father's throne until He blesses you with an answer.

I want you to live in the hope and joy of knowing that nothing is impossible for you. I want you to live humbly, seeking My power to work in your heart and in your life. When you face mountains in your life that appear immovable, I want you to have faith to tell it to 'move from here to there' and then watch the miracle.

FAITH THOUGHTS

In what area of your life do you need a miracle? What is it that you're certain God cannot or will not do? No matter how big your problem is, God is bigger and there is nothing that is too difficult for Him. He's inviting you to be a part of your own miracle. He's simply asking you to have faith and believe in what you hope for.

August 10

Living Water

*"Whoever believes in me, as Scripture has said,
rivers of living water will flow from within them."*
JOHN 7:38

You have a chronic restlessness, an insatiable thirst of your soul. If you will come to Me, and immerse yourself in all that I am, you will find a source of lasting and complete joy. What I give you will bring a fullness and completeness in your soul to the point that it is overflowing. When your soul is empty and thirsty, look to Me.

You have a spiritual hunger so that you might look for Me and find Me. It's a way to draw you closer to Me. Just as you are physically hungry or thirsty, and seek food and water, you are spiritually hungry and thirsty ... you need Me. And in many ways, your spiritual thirst for Me should never be quenched while you are on earth.

Each time you come to Me, you should have a desire to know Me more. The more you know Me, the more you will understand the Father's love for you and the significance of My sacrifice. The Father has a deep unfailing, unending, reckless love for you. It's a love that led Me to lay down My life for you. Once you recognize Me as Savior, the Holy Spirit dwells in you, teaching you, guiding you, correcting you, encouraging you, and drawing you closer to the Father. What greater love is there than the love the Father has for you?

Faith Thoughts

You are supposed to feel an emptiness that continually drives you to Jesus. When you are struggling with your life and its purpose, when things just don't seem to make sense, look to Jesus. He will satisfy your soul, filling you with His peace and power and an assurance that you can live in joy because of the true hope He's given you.

Saved through Faith

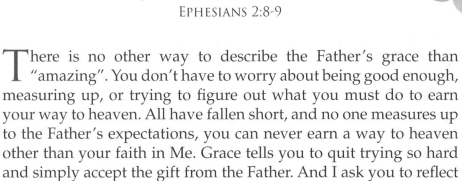

*For it is by grace you have been saved, through faith –
and this is not from yourselves, it is the gift of God –
not by works, so that no one can boast.*
EPHESIANS 2:8-9

There is no other way to describe the Father's grace than "amazing". You don't have to worry about being good enough, measuring up, or trying to figure out what you must do to earn your way to heaven. All have fallen short, and no one measures up to the Father's expectations, you can never earn a way to heaven other than your faith in Me. Grace tells you to quit trying so hard and simply accept the gift from the Father. And I ask you to reflect that grace by living a life that honors Mine and the price that I paid.

It's your present hope that creates your present faith. And your faith is not blind, it is not a leap in the dark, where you don't know what's on the other side, hoping things will somehow work out.

It's the faith that understands that although the Father is invisible, His promises are certain, He is faithful, and He has been seen in Me … God in the flesh. Your faith is the surety of the Father's promises based on His character. It's looking to Him and trusting that His grace is sufficient.

You've been granted faith by grace. And you don't have to worry about the amount of faith you think you need. It's about the object of your faith and whether you are placing your faith in Me. You are to place your life in My hands and not worry, assured that I am strong enough to save you.

FAITH THOUGHTS

You don't need to work hard at faith, you've been given it by grace. You just need to live in the faith you're given. You need to have hope because Jesus is no longer in the grave. You need to trust because God has proven Himself trustworthy. Just receive the grace God continually offers you.

August 12

Believe It

"Have faith in God," Jesus answered.
MARK 11:22

I want you to understand that you can do amazing things if you believe. My entire life on earth, all of My teachings demonstrated that I want you to place your complete confidence in the Father's character as the Redeemer and in the Father's power as the Creator. I want you to know that the Father is intricately involved in your life and in the lives of those around you. His love is an active love, always at work, always bringing about good.

The outcome of your prayers does not depend on your ability to have strong faith, the outcome depends solely on the Father. Miracles are possible, but they are not guaranteed. You are to ask for them. You are to pray to the Father for what you need and trust Him in everything. Sometimes you forget how important prayer is. You try to do things in your own strength instead of Mine. And you can be sure that as you look to Me in complete faith, I will overcome any and all obstacles in your life that keep you from fulfilling the Father's purposes for your life.

Each and every day, ask the Spirit to guide you to a promise that the Father has made to you and let it help you to live more confidently and with greater expectancy. Pray at all times and trust continually. Have faith in the One who is faithful.

Faith Thoughts

You don't need to try to have more faith, you need to live confidently in the faith that you have. God has given you a measure of faith. Enough to take you to the next step in your journey with Him. Keep believing, regardless of how things might appear. You're trusting in the unseen, the One who holds the power to do anything.

Guaranteed Blessings

As Scripture says, "Anyone who believes in him will never be put to shame."
ROMANS 10:11

There is a constant message of grace that should resound in your heart … if you put your trust in Me, in My sacrifice for your salvation, you'll never be disappointed. You must continually put your confidence in Me and what I've done. If you are placing your faith in Me, you are blessed. You don't have to worry about anything.

I am able to bless you and make all grace abound in your life simply because I love you and you've put your trust in Me. It's in trusting in Me that you can live securely in an insecure world. The empty grave has guaranteed you the blessing that the Father is on His throne, full of love and grace, loving you in every moment of your life.

It's the Spirit dwelling in you that will lead you into the Father's will for your life and He will be the one to strengthen you and comfort you along your journey of faith. When you feel that your faith is failing you, turn to the Word, look to Me, seek the Father's voice through His promises to you. Don't allow the doubt of hardships to cloud the vision of hope that you've been given. When you're tempted to give up, simply decide to keep going, and keep believing. Walk by faith.

FAITH THOUGHTS

It's because of your faith in Jesus that you have guaranteed blessings. You can live in confidence each moment of your life that your future is sealed in eternity. You can offer up thanks and praise to God for being faithful in your life. And when you grow weary in the journey, lean on the Spirit for strength and keep walking by faith.

EXPERIENCING THE GOODNESS OF GOD

*Taste and see that the L*ORD *is good;
blessed is the one who takes refuge in him.*
PSALM 34:8

God is good ... *all* the time. In the circumstances that are tearing you apart and wearing you down, He is good. There is never a moment when He is not. That truth is extraordinarily difficult when you're dealing with loss of health, relationships, or finances. When everything is falling apart, it's difficult to see that in the hands of God, everything is really falling into place.

All too often, you believe God is good, but you aren't sure He'll *always* be good. It's easy to allow fear to stop you from fully believing God's promises when you are focusing upon the wind and the waves in the circumstances around you. But don't worry, God's mercies never cease, you can have a second chance to get out of the boat and walk upon the water. You're meant to walk in the fullness of life, in God's goodness, in abundance because of what Jesus has done. When you begin to doubt and feel yourself sinking, you're going to have to renew your mind in the Word. You're going to have to refresh your memory and strengthen your heart to walk forward in faith.

You'll lose heart, unless you believe that you'll see the goodness of God. You can pray big. You need to ask God for the impossible and for life-changing miracles. And you need to trust Him when He's promised that you haven't even seen or heard all that He has prepared for you. You need to trust what He's promised. That's the bottom line. He's the One who gives every "good and perfect gift" ... He's the One you need to turn to in the storms of life. He's the One you need to run to. And then you need to trust and rest through the storm.

All the Time

With praise and thanksgiving
they sang to the LORD: "He is good."
EZRA 3:11

You can continually sing praises to the Father because He is good … all the time. If there are times where it seems almost impossible to thank the Father, ask Him for grace to learn to be thankful in spite of your difficult circumstances. I lived life on earth in constant worship and praise because the Father is good at all times and in all ways. Our praise should never stop.

It's when you praise the Father in every circumstance that you bring Him joy and please Him. He gets the glory every time you offer up praise. When you are praising Him in the most difficult of situations, you are powerfully pointing others to a place where they too can be offered salvation for their souls.

Your faith is not just for your benefit, but for all who witness it. If you're having a difficult time finding something to praise the Father for, praise Him that you have breath to live in this very moment. Start there. And then think of all the things that help you to get through your day.

Ask the Spirit to work within you and give you spiritual eyes to see what you struggle to see during difficult times … God is good, at all times and in all ways.

FAITH THOUGHTS

Do you take advantage of opportunities to praise God in all your circumstances? What is one thing you can thank Him for today? What is one small way you can praise Him in this moment? What do you need to change in your life, in order to make it a priority to praise Him more?

Level Ground

*Teach me to do your will, for you are my God;
may your good Spirit lead me on level ground.*
PSALM 143:10

Cry out to the Father in prayer and trust that the Holy Spirit will bring an answer and His power into your life. Don't give up in circumstances that seem insurmountable. Pray that the Father would bring His blessings and deliverance into your life.

All too often you pray without expectation of an answer because of your fear and doubt. It's vital that when you pray, you wait and expect the Father to answer you. It's proof of your trust in Him. When you pray, don't walk away and live the same way as before you prayed. Stay in your position of prayer and wait on the Father because sometimes His answer may come right away. Take a moment to sit silently in His presence and just praise Him.

There are so many unknowns in life and you will need the Spirit to instruct you through all the obstacles to your faith. The Spirit is with you to give you the Father's input and wisdom when you desperately need His guidance. It's the Spirit that will comfort you and lead you down the right paths. When you're confused, overwhelmed, or lost, the Spirit is waiting to help you and direct you. It is the Father's goodness and love that pours out His gentle Spirit to lead you into the Father's perfect will.

FAITH THOUGHTS

Are you praying to God with expectancy? In what area of your life do you need to pause and ask God for direction? Are you relying on the Spirit to lead you? Or are you trying to make your own way, struggling to solve your own problems? Let faith lead your heart and trust that God is good and will help you. Pray diligently for His blessings in your life and then watch and wait.

Given

AUGUST 16

*Now to each one the manifestation of
the Spirit is given for the common good.*
1 CORINTHIANS 12:7

The Father does not change like shifting shadows, He is always faithful and dependable, giving you every good and every perfect gift. They all come from His hand. He is the giver of good gifts, and never ceases, as He is the same yesterday, today, and forever. He does not give conditionally, He gives because He loves. And you are to live in Me and I through you.

Every morning you wake up is a gift from above. It's the Father looking down on you and loving you for another moment. If you'll begin to understand that all you are given comes as a gift from the Father, you will begin to look at even the very simple things in your life differently. Continually give praise for every blessing that the Father gives you, recognizing His heart and hand in your life. It is the Father's unchanging character and the faithfulness of His promises that is your grounds for having strong hope … for walking forward in faith in every area of your life. You have the assurance of His goodness.

In a world where everything is ever changing, you can find peace and comfort in knowing that not only am I with you, but the Father's love for you never changes and His blessings never cease.

FAITH THOUGHTS

Do you recognize that every good gift comes from God's hand? Pray that the Spirit would give you a new awareness and a thankful heart for all that He freely gives to you. Ask that with each breath you take you will be reminded of the gift of life you've been given and be thankful that His love is something you can rest in every day of your life.

Good and Upright

Good and upright is the LORD;
therefore he instructs sinners in his ways.
PSALM 25:8

You need divine wisdom and understanding in order to walk uprightly before the Father. You must constantly seek His Word, listening to His voice through it. You'll need to absorb Truth and rid yourself of your constant desire to go your own way. Draw near to the Father and meditate in prayer, asking that the Spirit will help you to apply the Word to every area of your life.

The Father wants you to make right decisions, bringing your life in line with His will. He's promised to give you instruction and direction. Whenever you pray, pray for a clean heart, a clean mind, a surrendered will and willing spirit. And remember to pray persistently, trusting in the promises as you remain in My peace. Although you want quick answers, the Father has told you to pray continually without giving up. And be listening.

Don't miss the Father's direction because you get impatient and move forward without His direction. It's your persistent prayer that draws you closer to the Father, putting you in a position to hear Him clearly. It's trusting in the promises that will lift you above your doubts and into a place of quiet rest. Although you may not have the answer yet, if you are waiting with hopeful expectation, you'll experience My peace which surpasses all understanding. As peace rules your heart, you'll be rid of confusion and be ready to receive the Father's clear direction without doubting.

FAITH THOUGHTS

Ask God to give you a greater desire to know His will. Ask Him to help you manage your time better so that you can use more of it to meditate on His Word. Ask that the Spirit would help you apply what you learn to every area of your life. Pray that others will see Jesus living in you in order to bring glory to God and pray for a thankful heart.

No One Is Good

"Why do you call me good?" Jesus answered. "No one is good – except God alone."
MARK 10:18

The Father has a special love that moves Him to work all things together for good. Though you are undeserving, the Father pours out His mercy and grace anyway. And He is love, I am His love poured out. It's His mercy that is an overflow of His goodness and love. He is the only One who is good.

It's by your faith that you believe in the Father's goodness, even as you walk through the most difficult of trials. If you're having difficulty seeing the Father's goodness in your current situation, know that His mercies are new every morning and He will never leave you or forsake you. These are His promises.

As you follow Me, walking obediently to the Father, you can know that behind every one of His restrictions, exhortations, or commands is His goodness. The Father is always leading you and protecting you from the consequences of sin. You've been created with free will so that you might choose to love Him, but that means that His permissive will may allow bad things to happen. Sin does not diminish the Father's goodness.

If you have faith, He will bring good out of the worst circumstances. If you're struggling through difficult situations, keep the faith, remember that the Father cares for you and is good. Although you may not understand His ways, you can fully trust them.

FAITH THOUGHTS

What situation are you facing that is making it difficult to believe that God is good? What if you just choose to believe that God is good even if it doesn't seem like it? What if you chose one of His promises to pray over and looked confidently in hope to Him to fulfill it. Whatever it is you need, trust in God's goodness and believe Him for it.

August 19

Full of Compassion

The LORD is good to all;
he has compassion on all he has made.
PSALM 145:9

You are able to share the Father's heart with others by living compassionately. It means following Me, stepping outside of yourself and loving others when they are weak. A compassionate heart will continually give grace and love to those who need it most, and not much else moves the heart of God more than compassion.

Since the Father has seen you in your imperfection and chose to love you, not casting you aside, He offered up My life as a sacrifice to save your soul. Your heart, too, should be stirred in compassion, to see the hurting and share the Father's heart. Don't allow yourself to get self-focused, caught up in your plans and your wants and needs. Live humbly and sacrificially, just as I did. The world is in desperate need of compassion. The world needs more of the Father's mercy and grace. And it's His heart's desire to use you so that you might show His mercy and grace as a reflection of His unconditional love.

He is calling you to be light in the darkness, so that others might see His compassionate heart. Continually pray to receive a fresh revelation of the Father's kindness, tenderness, and forgiveness. Open your heart so the Spirit can transform you into My likeness. And allow the Father's heart to become your own.

FAITH THOUGHTS

Are you continually asking the Spirit to work within your heart so that it reflects God's? You have purposes for your life that are for furthering the Kingdom and it's your acts of compassion that will not only make a difference in the here and now, but also in leading others to God.

Good Gifts

AUGUST 20

"If you, then, though you are evil, know how to give good gifts to your children, how much more will your Father in heaven give good gifts to those who ask him!"
MATTHEW 7:11

You have the great privilege of approaching the throne of the Father through your faith in Me. Prayer is not only essential, it's the very foundation that the Father has given you to keep you close to Him. Prayer enables you to discover who the Father is and where you are in your relationship with Him. Prayer is the door to your relationship with the Creator of the universe.

Most often, when you come to the Father in prayer, there is a deeper need. He wants what is best for you, so He will always answer in His perfect and loving way, even when that means delaying or denying a request. You must trust in His sovereignty and in His unfailing love.

Asking makes your request known, prayer brings to your attention what you recognize as the need. Prayer isn't a way of manipulating the Father to get what you want, it's how you discover what the Father wants for you. You shouldn't have a desire to change the will of the Father, but for your will to be conformed to His. So, when you approach Him, ask Him what is in your heart.

Be persistent in your prayer, understanding that the Father will answer in His perfect way and in His perfect timing.

FAITH THOUGHTS

You need to trust in God's promises to you. You need to believe that He only wants good things for you. He's not only promised to care for you in every way, but He has promised to give you the desires of your heart.

AUGUST 21

Remaining Confident

I remain confident of this: I will see the goodness of the LORD in the land of the living.
PSALM 27:13

You can walk by faith in the goodness of the Father as you trust Him with your everyday life. It is His goodness that continues to work all things together for good. The Father is caring for you in every detail of your life, there are no accidents. You live in the care of a sovereign Father.

Though you experience trial after trial, the Father has a plan, purpose, and an offering of My peace through it all. In your troubles, you can remember how the Father has delivered you before, how I have been with you all along, and then you can look forward to a future of hope. Understand that if you never had problems, you would never know that the Father could solve them.

So, when you're facing difficulties that seem insurmountable, you can be sure that the Father will use them to show you that nothing is impossible with His power. Your trials and tribulations serve purposes that go beyond your understanding and it will require your confident faith in the Father's goodness to bring about joy and hope in your heart as you trust Him completely in all things and in all ways.

FAITH THOUGHTS

Are you confident in your hope or does it rely on your feelings at the moment? Life can bring about challenges that are so overwhelming that you'll know that no one other than God can help you. You'll be certain that you need nothing short of a miracle and you'll be drawn to the throne of grace. Through it all, remain confident in God's faithfulness ... trust in every one of His promises.

Intended for Good

AUGUST 22

You intended to harm me, but God intended it for good to accomplish what is now being done, the saving of many lives.
GENESIS 50:20

Know that when you're dealing with hardships and struggles, the Father's ultimate goal is His glory and your good. It may not seem like it at the time, but He redeems all things and brings beauty from ashes. I am with you to strengthen you, to help you bear up under the weight of your troubles and endure in your faith.

The Father is sovereign in everything. And because He is in it, all of your trials, the evil against you, will not prevail. It's through your faith that you will be able to see the invisible hand of the Father working in your life, even when it appears as if nothing is happening. The Father will never violate free will, even if it includes evil being done, so everything, good or evil, has consequences on earth and in eternity.

It's because the Father is in your situation, that you can rejoice that no weapon formed against you shall prosper and every tongue that rises against you in judgment, He will condemn. Know that in the end, the Father wins. In the end, everything in your life is to be shaped by the goodness and grace of the Father. I have paid the price for victory. Nothing else is required.

FAITH THOUGHTS

Sometimes things may appear to be "bad", moving in the wrong direction, and you'll be tempted to lose faith. You'll doubt and lose hope. But hope is never lost because Jesus is no longer in the grave. So, whatever your circumstances, whatever challenges you're facing, remember that God is in it. If He's allowing it, He does so out of His love, mercy, and grace.

Love Poured Out

You are good, and what you do is good;
teach me your decrees.
PSALM 119:68

The Father is good, in and of Himself. All goodness originates and flows from Him as the Source. I am the evidence of His love, mercy, grace, and overall goodness. It is through My sacrifice that He has ultimately poured out His love.

In all that the Father does, it must be good because that is who He is. He can only do good. It's His great love that has kept you from complete destruction, that has offered you salvation, not punishment. His goodness is seen in His longsuffering. And it's His patience and goodness that leads you to repentance. His desire is that you would seek His goodness, grow in goodness, and live out His goodness as the fruit of the Spirit.

You must believe that the Father is not only good toward you, but that His goodness is the very essence of who He is. He knows what you need and is faithful to provide for you in every way. If you will trust that the Father is good and that He will take care of you, you will find contentment and peace. You will find your soul satisfied.

FAITH THOUGHTS

Are there things in your life that are causing you to struggle in your faith? Are you believing in God's love for you, but doubting that He'll completely take care of every area of your life? Look to Jesus, He'll show you that you can be at peace, you can be content, you can rest in a raging storm of life because God has everything under control.

Riches of Kindness

AUGUST 24

Or do you show contempt for the riches of his kindness, forbearance and patience, not realizing that God's kindness is intended to lead you to repentance?
ROMANS 2:4

Don't take for granted the riches of the Father's kindness, tolerance, and patience. It's those riches that lead you in repentance to stay in right relationship with Himself. In His love and kindness, He calls you to a new life, one surrendered and humbled, and one that is lived for Him.

The Father wants you to experience lasting change. A change in your heart, a change of attitude in the way you live. Don't worry so much about your outward appearance, ask the Spirit to cleanse and transform your heart. The Father will continually confront you with His amazing grace so that you might fully realize that you have been given undeserved mercy that goes beyond your ability to understand. The Father has humbled you through repentance in order that you might see that I have done everything that needs to be done.

There is no price that you need to pay. I have given you open access to the Father's throne of grace and you are His for all eternity. You need only believe, once and for all.

FAITH THOUGHTS

God's love for you is to humble you and assure you of hope. Whatever it is you're struggling with in your life, the things that are keeping you from living in perfect sync with God, you can bring it to the throne of grace. You can ask God to handle it. You can rely on the Spirit to strengthen you to once again place God where He belongs in your life ... first.

Abounding in Love

*You, Lord, are forgiving and good,
abounding in love to all who call to you.*
PSALM 86:5

There will be times when your troubles will go on and on, and you will question the Father's love. And yet, if you are following Me, you will need to have humility, and a persistent faith that does not let go.

Don't allow sin in your life to erode your faith and confidence in the Father. Don't let it keep you from hearing His voice or allow it to tear down what He is trying to do in your life. Ask the Spirit to strengthen your faith so that when you're facing troubles you do not panic, but instead, turn to the Father in confidence and praise. Ask that your words would reflect the Father's heart.

Sometimes when you don't know what you should do, you should just pray. When you're struggling with overwhelming problems that are beyond your ability to handle, you're invited to the Father's throne of grace where you can receive mercy and grace to help you in your time of need.

You cannot exhaust the love of the Father. Know that the Father is always willing to forgive, and if you don't think you deserve the Father's love, you should know that's exactly what grace is … blessings for the undeserving.

FAITH THOUGHTS

When life is hard, it's easy to forget that God is good. His love and goodness work behind the scenes, bringing all the things that are causing you to worry into His will, so that you'll be blessed from all the brokenness. You cannot exhaust God's love for you, so keep praying and keep walking in faith even when you can't see.

Greatness and Glory

AUGUST 26

*And the L*ORD *said, "I will cause all my goodness to pass in front of you, and I will proclaim my name, the L*ORD*, in your presence. I will have mercy on whom I will have mercy, and I will have compassion on whom I will have compassion."*
EXODUS 33:19

The Father's glory is in His goodness. He declares that He is mercy, grace, and steadfast love, poured out in My blood. He is full of grace and compassion. He is just, righteous and holy. Together it's His love and holiness that make Him good. And He has promised that His love will never end.

My life is the greatest display of the Father's goodness. My death on the Cross is the greatest display of the Father's love and holiness. It's your faith in Me that gives you the same glory. The glory that is goodness, love, and holiness as you live out your life with My Spirit within you.

As the Spirit dwells in you, you will become more of an accurate reflection of the Father's glory. You are a representation of Him, just as I am. You don't need to be "qualified", the Father will equip you with everything you need to accomplish His purposes and He has already given you specific spiritual gifts.

Don't be surprised when you face spiritual battles. The devil will try and stop you from living in the Father's goodness and glory. Regardless of what is thrown your way, you must stay focused on the Father's love for you. Walk with Me through whatever trial the Father has allowed with the confidence that whatever the Enemy has planned for evil will ultimately be used for good.

FAITH THOUGHTS

God loves you far beyond your ability to comprehend it. Jesus sacrificed His life so that you don't have to be condemned in your sin, but so that you can live your life free through grace and bring glory to God.

BEYOND YOUR BROKENNESS

*The LORD is close to the brokenhearted and
saves those who are crushed in spirit.*
PSALM 34:18

When you find yourself in the raging storms of life, you're often going to experience brokenness. You'll find yourself so crushed that you're not sure you have the energy to take another breath. But you will. And as Jesus gazes into your eyes, His peace will consume you and you'll find that even if it's not God's will to calm the storm in your life, He'll calm the one in you … you will find rest with Jesus.

It's when you're broken, and your heart is heavy beyond words, that God is closest. No matter what you're going through or what is yet to come, God's love, mercy, power, and grace can heal the fractured or shattered pieces of your life. Regardless of the hopelessness you're facing, you can respond with the faith that says, "Though He slay me, yet will I hope in Him" (Job 13:15).

You won't feel like trusting God. You won't feel like having hope. You'll want to sit in your brokenness for a while. But it's the Spirit dwelling in you that is going to lift you up and renew your strength. He is going to comfort you and give you peace while putting together the pieces of your heart and mending your soul. It's when your pain is the deepest and your doubt the greatest, that Jesus stands with you through it all.

Listen, He's not going anywhere. He's with you to the end. He loves you on your best day and your worst, and His power will heal you when you're broken, and He'll hold you until you're whole again. When you're hurting and suffering, that's when you need God most. Run to Him, don't walk. He's waiting with open arms.

Delivered

*The Spirit of the Sovereign Lord is on me, because
the Lord has anointed me to proclaim good news to the poor.
He has sent me to bind up the brokenhearted, to proclaim
freedom for the captives and release from darkness for the prisoners.*
ISAIAH 61:1

You need Me, and all need salvation. You need My favor. You need comfort instead of pain, joy instead of sorrow. I am the only One who can truly give you these things. Always look to Me. I am what your heart needs most. I am the fulfillment of all you need. All that the Father has promised you is found in Me.

I came for the poor, the afflicted, the brokenhearted, and the sinners. I came to set you free. You can experience great joy in the here and now because I have risen and because you've been given eternal life. My Spirit is upon you – your strength when you are weak and your guide when you are filled with confusion.

It's My Spirit who moves within you to transform you and fulfill the Father's purposes for your life. It's because of the gift of the Spirit that I can say, "I will be with you always", and it is the Spirit that works within you to shape you into the image of the Father.

Through the Spirit, your broken heart is bound up. It is through the Father's love that your soul can be comforted and completely healed. Even though circumstances may appear hopeless, where the Father is, there is always hope. Pray that the Spirit would move within you assuring you of hope where there is hopelessness.

FAITH THOUGHTS

Are there times when you simply feel that all hope is gone? Do you struggle with wanting to give up? Keep looking to Jesus and ask the Spirit for direction and guidance. When your heart is breaking, it is the Spirit who will comfort you and assure you that there is hope ... and you'll see God break through just when you think He won't.

Broken

My sacrifice, O God, is a broken spirit; a broken and contrite heart you, God, will not despise.
PSALM 51:17

You can always come to the Father because of what I've done. He doesn't see your sin. I have covered that for you. You will always make mistakes and you will always need to approach the throne of grace. So when you come, do it with a humble heart, asking for mercy and forgiveness. Don't spend your time looking inward for the answer to your problems, look to the Father and His promises for every solution.

It's when you come to Me with a humble heart that you express your need for Me and the salvation you've been given. You should desire to be dependent on the Father's mercy. If you humble yourself, you will be rid of the pride that the Father opposes, and He is able to pour out His mercy upon you. You need to be satisfied in His grace, rejoicing in your salvation.

Now is always the time to pray for a renewed spirit and clean heart. Make sure you are continually repenting as the Spirit searches your heart, revealing any wickedness within you. Always be ready to turn away from your disobedience, admitting your mistakes, and turning to the Father for forgiveness. It is always ready and waiting for you, to restore your soul and draw you closer to the Father.

FAITH THOUGHTS

Are you continually asking the Spirit to search your heart and show you if there is anything that is keeping you from being in right relationship with God? As part of your faith, you will need to continually confess sins and constantly rely on the mercy of God to draw you closer and restore your soul. Pray for your faith to be strengthened and your heart humbled always before God.

Every Tear

"'He will wipe every tear from their eyes. There will be no more death' or mourning or crying or pain, for the old order of things has passed away."
REVELATION 21:4

You are surrounded by troubles because the world is filled with chaos. And you will need comfort. Even in your biggest challenges and disappointments, you can have a hopeful expectation that one day there will be no more crying or pain. Everything will be made new. All that is broken will be redeemed.

Your faith is not wishful thinking. Your heart's desires will come to pass. While you wait for that moment, you can follow Me, allowing My Spirit to lead you in My ways ... embracing those who grieve and wiping away their tears. It's through your faith that you can offer hope to a fearful world.

You must live in faith, even amid the suffering. You can have peace because the Father is caring for you at all times, bottling your tears. He knows your tears of sorrow, the sufferings you endure. Take heart in knowing that the Father fully knows your struggles, the desperation in your prayers, and that you can trust Him to comfort you and heal your broken heart.

FAITH THOUGHTS

Do you struggle with uncertainty and hopelessness in your life? You must cling to the truth so that you can withstand the temptation to lose hope. You have a secure hope that the future with God will exceed and abundantly be more than you can ever dream or imagine. Pray that you will focus on the promises so that you will not lose hope.

AUGUST 30

Said and Done

Heal me, Lord, and I will be healed; save me and I will be saved, for you are the one I praise.
JEREMIAH 17:14

The reason I came into the world was to bring healing. You can praise the Father for His goodness, for bringing healing to your soul, for salvation. It is only through Him that all things are possible, and He is worthy to be praised. If He has said it, it is done.

I know that you often feel a void within yourself, the world can lead you to feel that way. You try so many things to fill it, but it is never what you need. Your temporary pleasures last only for a moment, the only thing that will fill your emptiness permanently is Me. I know how to heal, fill, and save you. And My way is the way everlasting. Your attempts to heal your spiritual emptiness are all pointless.

True healing, spiritual, physical, mental, and emotional must come from Me and it's essential. You must humble your heart and come to Me for help. I have given you the Spirit to transform you, to comfort you in your afflictions and strengthen you in your struggles. So, take a moment to rest, to look to Me, to stop trying to heal yourself and solve your own problems without the help of the Father. Turn to Him and be saved.

FAITH THOUGHTS

In what way do you need healing? Whatever it is that you're missing in your soul can be healed and filled by God. Don't try to fix things on your own, you don't have the full picture. Only God knows your life from beginning to end and can guide and direct you properly into His great blessings for you.

Help in Weakness

In the same way, the Spirit helps us in our weakness.
ROMANS 8:26

You were never created to be self-sufficient, to have no need of a relationship with the Father. It's your weakness that can be a tremendous source of strength when you allow the Father to meet you powerfully through your humility. Ask the Spirit to work within you to give you peace and a humble heart as you come to the Father in prayer.

The Father values an acknowledgment of weakness and humility. I came for the needy and the lost. I spent valuable, limited time with prostitutes, tax collectors, lepers, and sinners. Though you can never be perfect, you can have renewed hope in Me. It's your weakness that beckons you to the throne of grace where you will find the help that you need. Instead of your perfection, the Father is simply asking for an honest and humble heart.

You must always be in a place of declaring your need for the Father's grace. It's then that you will receive His power. Trust in the almighty, all-loving, and ever-present Father. You don't need to try and attain perfection in this life. You don't need to try to find value and identity in what you do. Look to Me as your strength. Allow My love, power, and help to be the foundation of who you are. Live in the Light of My truth and I am with you always. Live with the peace and hope of the Father's limitless grace and power.

FAITH THOUGHTS

When you feel weak, there is no reason to worry, just turn to God. In your weakness, God's power will be your strength, and there is no greater power. So you can be thankful even when you're confused and don't have things figured out. You can live in peace and hope knowing that the God of miracles is with you and for you, a ready help in times of trouble.

SEPTEMBER 1

Joy and Gladness

*Let me hear joy and gladness;
let the bones you have crushed rejoice.*
PSALM 51:8

In your trials and tribulations, often there is nothing you can do, and nothing you should do, other than pray. Pray for a miracle. Pray for a sign of hope in your situation. And sometimes, your hope might be turned in a different direction. Sometimes what you're hoping for is not what is the Father's best, and the Spirit will move you in another direction. You can be assured that the direction the Spirit leads you will always be to a place of deliverance and rejoicing.

I know your brokenness firsthand. I was pierced for your transgressions, crushed for your iniquities, the punishment that brought you peace was on Me and by My wounds you are healed. My submission to becoming broken has led to the healing of your wounds. But brokenness is not the end. It wasn't the end of My story and it's not the end of yours.

It's through Me that you can experience physical, emotional, and spiritual healing. And one day you will be fully healed from your brokenness and pain and every tear will be wiped away, remembered no more. You don't have to be ashamed of your brokenness, it is the avenue by which you are healed. And it's your brokenness and healing that can encourage and comfort others while leading them to My loving arms.

FAITH THOUGHTS

You will experience pain in this life, but you have a Healer. God uses your sufferings to strengthen your faith and be a witness to others. Nothing is wasted in the hands of God. So, when you're sure that you've reached the end, when you're feeling broken and without hope, come to God in prayer and rejoice now for the joy and gladness that lies ahead through His faithfulness.

A Broken Spirit

My spirit is broken ...
JOB 17:1

It's the failures and defeats, disappointments and rejection, unforeseen events and reactions, and mistakes that we and others make that can lead to brokenness. And it's when your spirit is broken that your emotions can flood your soul into despair, depression, and hopelessness.

Regardless of who you are, everyone can have a broken spirit. And it's in that brokenness that you find the deepest need for the Father. Your broken spirit will remind you of why you need an intimate relationship with Him. You'll find that you need to live in constant prayer, bringing your problems and concerns to Him, seeking His help and depending on His faithfulness. It is through the Spirit that you can have joy and peace, even in your brokenness. As you pray, fill your mind with the Word, let those thoughts of complete defeat be transformed into victory through the promises the Father has made to you.

No matter what happens in your life, it's always time to turn to the Father. It's always time to focus on His will. Let the Spirit direct your mind and ask that the Father would heal your broken spirit, so that you might have renewed faith, ready for anything, living in the joy and hope I died to give you.

FAITH THOUGHTS

Are there times when you just feel broken? Are there moments when you're not sure that you have any faith left at all? God knows. He knows your heart and He's given you His Spirit to lift you up when you can't find the strength to do it yourself. Life is full of disappointments, but through God's promises, you can live with hopeful expectations even when life is difficult.

Restored

And the God of all grace, who called you to his eternal glory in Christ, after you have suffered a little while, will himself restore you and make you strong, firm and steadfast.
1 PETER 5:10

In everything, you must keep an eternal perspective. All of your troubles are only momentary when compared to the glory that you will experience in eternity. All that happens to you in this life, the good and the bad, the joys and the sufferings, are only for a little while. I want you to be encouraged that your suffering will not last. And the Father will restore, confirm, strengthen and settle you. It is the Spirit that will empower you to stand firm in your faith in the midst of all things.

It's because of the Father's promises that you can be strengthened in the midst of troubles. Know that your sufferings are used in the hand of the Father to purify you. Your suffering is not wasted. He uses everything to transform your heart into the likeness of His. You can stand faithfully in dark and difficult times with absolute confidence and joy because of what I've done. And at the end of the day, you may not understand, you may be consumed with confusion, but the Father is faithful and you must simply trust in who He is and what He has promised.

Remember that your sufferings will remind you that you are not in control, the Father is, and it's in prayer that the Spirit will remind you of the Father's grace. He is holy and you need His mercy.

FAITH THOUGHTS

If you continually focus on eternity, all of your troubles will have a new perspective. It's when you truly trust God that you can enjoy His glory and be more enabled to endure and persevere through your difficulties. Make sure you're taking time in your day to meditate on the glory of God that you will get to enjoy for all eternity when you see Him face to face.

A Greater Heart

SEPTEMBER 4

*If our hearts condemn us, we know that God
is greater than our hearts, and he knows everything.*
1 JOHN 3:20

The Father is greater than anything, greater than your heart, He knows everything. And He promises to receive you not based on your own goodness, but on My righteousness. It's when your heart condemns you, that the Father promises to receive you if you will come to Him with a repentant humble heart that trusts in Me alone.

The Holy Spirit dwells in you to convict you. And I do not condemn you, I understand. I was tempted in all ways, just as you are, but I was without sin. I stand in your place before the Father. He doesn't see your sin, because of Me. Pray that the Spirit would work within you, helping you to fulfill the Father's plans for your life and loving others, putting you in place of asking for the right things and receiving them. Above all things your faith in Me is the key to staying the course in your journey of life. You will make mistakes, you will get off track of the Father's best plan for your life, but I am with you always.

Look to Me when life is falling apart, and I will lead you in the way that you are to go. Don't give in to the despair and don't allow the Enemy to guilt you into depression. Keep your heart focused on the Father's. He is full of love, mercy, and grace and He will lift you up.

FAITH THOUGHTS

Sometimes it's easy to forget that God is greater than anything and everything. He's certainly greater than your sin ... He sent Jesus to save you. So, don't allow the little things in life to burden you and keep you from living in the joy that you're meant to. Come to God with a humble and repentant heart and His grace will always be there waiting for you.

SEPTEMBER 5

Compassionate and Gracious

But you, Lord, are a compassionate and gracious God, slow to anger, abounding in love and faithfulness.
PSALM 86:15

With the grace of the Father, you can face each day. In My strength you can walk in faith and know that every detail of your life is being handled by your heavenly Father. Just because you have faith does not mean that your problems will disappear. It just means that you have My power and presence to deal with them and overcome.

It's the Father's love that keeps you from being consumed by the fiery trials of life that can overwhelm you. It's His love that mediates and works out solutions in your life and it's His love that allows you to live free from worry and walk confidently in peace. His peace and the worries of the world cannot coexist. It's His love that replaces your fears with trust. Fear vanishes in the face of faith. And the Father's compassions never fail, giving you hope that you can count on Him to deliver you.

Your hurting heart can be healed with the Father's love. The Father is faithful to His Word, so you don't ever have to doubt Him. He cannot be unfaithful. So, when you don't know what to do, wait on Him and trust and obey His every Word. Through all the uncertainty in life, you can be at peace, serving the Father who is full of love, compassion, and faithfulness.

FAITH THOUGHTS

If you truly trust in God's faithfulness, what is there to worry about? Your strength to walk through the troubles of life comes from Jesus. So, you're not going through life with anything short of the miracle-working power of God. Whatever you need, call out to God in prayer, humble your heart, and tell Him what you need. Then wait, in confident expectation, and watch what He will do.

Overflowing with Hope

SEPTEMBER 6

May the God of hope fill you with all joy and peace as you trust in him, so that you may overflow with hope by the power of the Holy Spirit.
ROMANS 15:13

Living in faith is proof of your confidence in the Father's character, and it's the anticipation of the fulfillment of His promises that have not yet been realized. I am your hope. You have a living hope because it rests on My redeeming sacrifice. Hope is a gift from your heavenly Father who has loved you by His grace and given you eternal encouragement.

At some point in life, you will eventually find yourself in a valley, a season of despair. I know that those circumstances that cause you to doubt, prompt discouragement that feels impossible to overcome. And I also know that in these times it is easy to find yourself drowning in feelings of hopelessness.

It's when you pray and pray, and years go by, and your prayers seem to go unanswered, that your greatest feelings of hopelessness set in. But if you will come to Me, and continue to trust, the Father will fill you with joy and peace. If you put your trust in Me, you can pray with anticipation of the Father's answer. And even though He hasn't answered yet, your spirit of faith assures you that He will.

FAITH THOUGHTS

You don't have to live discouraged. There is no reason for you to lose your hope. You don't have to conjure up hope or joy where it doesn't exist. You can know hope and joy through the power of the Holy Spirit. When you need to be encouraged, immediately seek God's promises. They will fill you with the hope you so desperately need.

SEPTEMBER 7

Taking Refuge

*But let all who take refuge in you be glad;
let them ever sing for joy. Spread your protection over
them, that those who love your name may rejoice in you.*
PSALM 5:11

I want you to come to Me. Take refuge and take all of your wants and desires to the Father in prayer. I know that you have real problems that need real solutions. Saving a boat that is flooding, capsizing, and preventing you from drowning, requires nothing short of a miracle.

At all times, in all situations, you can raise your hands to praise the Father and rejoice. He gives comfort and hope in times of need through His promises. And He pours out His love into your heart and shelters you each and every day. His mercy never fails. He guards your way every moment of every day. His power is greater than the raging storm and His love deeper than the oceans. I am with you to assure you that you will never be abandoned. He will never forsake you. I am your continual strength when you are weak, the Spirit and comfort to which nothing else compares.

Lift your eyes to heaven, above all the pain and suffering – the Father parts waters, takes down giants, moves mountains, and raises the dead to life. Even when you can't see Me with you, I am there. The Spirit dwells within you to give you the peace that the Father is in control and assures victory. Live in that Truth.

 ## FAITH THOUGHTS

Do you run to God as a refuge? In His strength you can endure and walk in faith. Having His divine help is a blessing that you must continually accept. Don't try to do things on your own, allow God's love and power to be your shield and cling to His promises through all of the unknowns. You can rest because you are trusting in the One who knows.

Through It All

*I am forgotten as though I were dead;
I have become like broken pottery.*
PSALM 31:12

I am with you through it all, the good, the bad, and all that's in between. In your brokenness, there is the works of a new beginning. You can have hope in Me. Don't allow the disappointment to lead you away, you need My hope in your hopeless situation.

The Father has rescued you before, He will do it again. Don't worry about the evil around you, or be tempted to look for a shortcut through your faith. Trust in the Father no matter what and rejoice in His goodness and love. It's even in your distress, your hurts and weakness that He will give you grace and more grace. Your life's situations may be more than you can handle, but nothing is too difficult for Me. Your life is in the Father's hands and He longs to bless you.

You always have a choice as to how you will handle your disappointments and frustrations of life. I know it is hard when you have faith but life is still falling apart. The Father sees, and He listens. Ask the Spirit to help you come to a place where you can wholeheartedly trust and rely on Him, and praise Him in the midst of your troubles. Ask that you will have a heart that is constantly surrendered to the Father's ways and plans, setting aside your perceived needs and desires. The Father knows what is best for you … trust that He does.

Faith Thoughts

When you're broken and unable to lift yourself up, God will do it for you. He restores and renews. You can have hope even when it clearly appears that hope is completely gone. There is no limit to God's grace. Keep seeking Him and trusting Him, He's with you through it all.

COMFORT IN GOD'S CONSTANT LOVE

*May your unfailing love be my comfort,
according to your promise to your servant.*
PSALM 119:76

Storms of life can cause you to doubt God's Truth. It's difficult to comprehend how it is that a gracious, loving God could allow death of a loved one, terminal illness, the loss of a job, or financial crisis that destroys a family. But you can't judge God's love based on your current circumstances. Jesus promised that in this world you would have trouble. It's not a surprise, but it still causes a lot of pain and suffering. You can't let the storms of life discourage you … they are part of God's plan.

It's the Spirit dwelling in you that is going to comfort you through your sufferings. With all that you will go through in life, you're going to have to dwell in divine grace so that your faith can withstand the difficult seasons of life. Though you might feel alone, you're not. And as you long for God to intervene in your life, you're going to need to draw near to Him through meditating on His Word, giving you the assurance of His faithful love.

Whatever difficulties in life you are facing, He knows what you're going through, and He wants you to rely on Him as your source of peace, happiness, and joy. God has promised not only to provide you with comfort through your storms of life, but to bring about miracles in them and *through* you.

A Stronghold

*The LORD is a refuge for the oppressed,
a stronghold in times of trouble.*
PSALM 9:9

It is certain that troubles in life will come. And when they do, you must run to Me. I am your stronghold. It's not enough to merely acknowledge Me, you must actively seek Me. You will always find Me waiting, arms open, a ready help in times of trouble.

Seek the Father always in confident prayer. He is both compassionate and powerful, receiving you through grace. And His grace through Me has given you eternal life. You can find comfort in Me. I am your ultimate stronghold. When you feel as though you can't go on, when you struggle in your faith because you are so disquieted in your soul, pray for the Spirit to move within you in a powerful way to assure you of My presence in your life and the Father's constant care.

You are never abandoned, you are not alone, I am with you always. When you are treated unfairly, hurt and angry by your circumstances, look to Me to comfort you and give you hope. The Father will give you beauty for your ashes. Look joyfully and expectantly for that day.

FAITH THOUGHTS

Do you sometimes feel treated unfairly? Like all you do is what is right but you are continually treated wrong? Jesus knows. He understands. He is your closest friend. Turn to Him in your frustration and anger and allow Him to bring comfort to your soul and joy to your heart as you journey through your troubled times.

SEPTEMBER 10

The Source of Comfort

*"Blessed are those who mourn,
for they will be comforted."*
MATTHEW 5:4

Remember the way you first came to Me. Broken, poor in spirit, crushed with sadness, desperate for love and mercy. And then remember that grace has been poured out on you. I am your source of comfort when you mourn for the sorrows of your sins, the losses in your life, and the disappointment over the fallen world around you. It is My Spirit within you that will encourage you and free you from pain, grief, and anxiety.

You do not need to live under the weight of your burdens. Turn to Me and ask Me to carry them for you. Grace calls your name. Each and every moment of your life, you are to live free from the chains of guilt and remorse. I died and overcame death so that you could continually live in victory. It's when you come to the Father in complete humility that pride is gone and your empty-handedness finds His grace always waiting.

If you will look to Me, I will be all you need. You will find rest for your soul in Me. Regardless of what you are mourning in your life, it is My Spirit that will comfort you and refresh your spirit.

FAITH THOUGHTS

God expects you to come to Him with a humble heart, surrendering everything in your life to Him, so that He can help you in every way that you need. You need rest for your soul, to be comforted in your affliction. Jesus is your Source of comfort and the Spirit will comfort you.

A Cry for Mercy

SEPTEMBER 11

*I love the LORD, for he heard my voice;
he heard my cry for mercy. Because he turned
his ear to me, I will call on him as long as I live.*
PSALM 116:1-2

Most often in life you will realize that you don't have any control over what happens. You will face continual problems in life, it's a fallen world. There will be bigger troubles than others, but no matter the size, the Father is in control of them all. Nothing is beyond His reach.

As you follow Me, you'll see My example in trusting that the Father is in control at all times. He rules all nations and places the governments in power according to His perfect will. He is the One that can ultimately control what happens in your life. Though you make choices that have consequences, it is the Father that can control those and even override them. It's when you submit to Him and His will that you can be led by Me, giving you peace in the storms of life.

While you patiently endure, you can thank the Father for His love, compassion and grace. You can give Him praise at all times because He is in control of all things. You can pray for greater faith, in order that you might submit your will in every facet of your life and ask to continually be forgiven when you fall short of His glory. Call upon the Spirit to help you live your life in the midst of trouble with a confident faith that is assured of the Father's promises.

FAITH THOUGHTS

Each and every day you must ask the Spirit to help you let go of your selfish desires and put God's plans for your life first. Continually ask that you will be used to draw others to God and rely on Jesus to give you peace through the storms and rest when you are weary.

SEPTEMBER 12

Troubles and Doubts

> *He said to them, "Why are you troubled, and why do doubts rise in your minds?"*
> LUKE 24:38

When you are troubled, when you doubt, I am here with you to calm and convince you of the Father's faithfulness and love. Throughout your journey in life you will need to walk by faith, trusting in My presence and power, and believing in the Word to give you hope. There are two things you can be sure of: the Father can be trusted and I am no longer in the grave. These truths can give you peace and strength each and every moment of your life.

I know what you're going through. I'm with you. The Spirit is occupying your heart and knows your thinking. I want to expel all of your doubt and fear by building your faith and trust in Me as I provide you with My assurance and peace. Rest for your soul comes from trusting in Me. It comes from trusting in the Father's Word, His promises that destroy all doubt and fear. I want you to learn to trust in My power, knowing that there is nothing that I cannot do. And it's My presence that is in the middle of your mess and your confusion.

In love and grace, I will come to you and give you peace. I will always assure you that I am with you. You can rest in Me, you can receive faith and confidence in trusting in the promises, My power and presence. The Father will do exceedingly abundantly above all you can ask or think. Believe that He will.

FAITH THOUGHTS

What is it in this moment that is causing you to feel troubled and doubt? Are you thinking when you should be praying? Don't allow the troubles of the world to cause you to doubt. Faith is what brings about miracles and gives you peace as you trust God to lead you into His blessings.

Forever Enduring

SEPTEMBER 13

*Give thanks to the God of heaven.
His love endures forever.*
PSALM 136:26

The Father's love persists even through your unbelief – fixed, firm, and constant. His love remains regardless of your feelings, or circumstances. Pray and consider how the Father has led, provided, and worked miracles in your life. And then walk forward in the promise that His steadfast love endures forever.

There is nothing that endures longer or stronger than the Father's love for you. I came out of the Father's great love for you. I came to restore every broken heart with His love. I will heal your hurts, erase the pain, and use the Spirit to pour out the Father's love through you into the lives of others.

Remember not to take the Father's goodness and love for granted. Be thankful at all times, even through the darkest nights and give Him the glory that is His due. If you are unfaithful, the Father remains faithful. He has called you by name and you are His. No matter what you go through, I am with you, and the Father never takes His eye off you. He is your refuge and His everlasting arms are under you. Live in His love.

FAITH THOUGHTS

Do you make it a priority to be truly thankful for all that God has done for you? Every day is a gift and an opportunity that you've been given to thank God for His enduring love.

SEPTEMBER 14

Even When

*And hope does not put us to shame,
because God's love has been poured out into our
hearts through the Holy Spirit, who has been given to us.*
ROMANS 5:5

The Father loved you even when you were lost in sin. Even when you were running away from Him, His love called you back. You can have hope, you can live in that hope because of My sacrifice, My blood, the Father's love poured out … for you.

It's because of the Father's love that you can have peace with Him, living in real hope. Right now, when you can't understand, you can praise the Father for His love, for the Spirit that now dwells in you, and for the joy to come that will last forever. Your peace and hope are based on the love the Father has already shown proof of. I have already died for your sins so that you could choose to be reconciled to the Father through His act of grace.

Your hope is in the Holy Spirit, knowing that whatever happens, through amazing grace, the Father is present in and through you, leading and guiding you. You can have hope knowing that the Father is sovereign, in control of all things, and loving at all times. Ask the Spirit to help you in your journey of faith, ask for clarity in taking each and every step and then trust that as you walk in faith, the Father will take care of everything else … every detail.

FAITH THOUGHTS

Do you live each day, fully aware that God is living in you and is using the Spirit to lead, guide, and direct you? Are you looking for His signs and listening for His voice? Or are the distractions of disappointments keeping you from being fully present in God's presence. Take His hand and trust everything to Him.

Faithful

SEPTEMBER 15

*Know therefore that the LORD your God is God;
he is the faithful God, keeping his covenant of love
to a thousand generations of those who love
him and keep his commandments.*
DEUTERONOMY 7:9

You need to continually remember that the Father is faithful and you can depend on Him to do what He says. None of His words fall to the ground … they will accomplish what He speaks. The evidence of His faithfulness is seen in everything He says and does. You will see the evidence that His word will not return to Him void. He can be trusted completely.

If your faith is being tested and you're confused about what is happening in your life, you can still live securely in the knowledge that the Father is in control and He will care for you and deliver you in whatever ways you need Him to. He is faithful to every one of His promises, but it is up to you to believe them. It is your choice to live in faith. It's when everything seems to be falling apart that you'll be called to greater faith, where you'll find the Father's everlasting arms beneath you. And it's His love that pardons, protects, and pursues your heart each and every moment of your life.

His faithful love is limitless and abounds. His mercies never cease and are fresh every morning. And it's through His love that you have salvation through Me and because of what I've done, you're made right before the Father, condemnation is gone forever, you are brought into the fullness of the Father's purposes for your life and you are empowered to live with hope and confidence.

FAITH THOUGHTS

You need to continually remember God's love for you. Make it a priority to continually be aware of His faithfulness to care for you and protect you. When life's troubles are getting the best of you, simply come into His presence and just rest in His loving arms for a while.

September 16

No Separation

> *... neither height nor depth, nor anything else in all creation, will be able to separate us from the love of God that is in Christ Jesus our Lord.*
> ROMANS 8:39

Nothing will ever separate you from the Father's love. Nothing can separate you from Me. Despite your sin, the Father loves you in a way that you will never be able to comprehend. He loves you unconditionally. You are always welcomed in His open arms, you're always heard when you call out to Him in prayer, you always have the promise of eternal life and His mercy and grace are yours through My death on the Cross. Nothing can ever take His love from you.

Once you put your hand in Mine, I never let go ... I never leave you. No matter how bad life gets, you can know that the Father will never stop loving you. Things will go right and things will go wrong, but His love will never end. As you trust in His promises, you'll be filled with peace and joy, knowing that when things don't go right and you don't understand, you can rest in the Father's hands. You may want to give up, but the Father never will.

When you trust in Me, I draw you to Me and I walk with you in your pain and suffering, in the joy and laughter. Nothing can separate you from Me. And when you cry out to the Father, but there is no relief, when pain persists, you will have My presence. When you look back you will see how I was with you, caring for you, and meeting your deepest needs.

Faith Thoughts

No matter what problems you're facing, remember that Jesus is holding you. God has given you the gift of the Spirit to strengthen you when you are weak, comfort you when you are suffering, and hold you in His hope. You are constantly held and loved beyond all you can comprehend. So just rest your hope and live in the peace Jesus died to give you.

Made Alive

SEPTEMBER 17

But because of his great love for us, God, who is rich in mercy, made us alive with Christ even when we were dead in transgressions – it is by grace you have been saved.
EPHESIANS 2:4-5

There is no other "love" that is the same as the love of the Father. It's not a worldly kind of love. It is love that is rich in mercy, freely giving undeserved kindness. If you were left to yourself, you'd be in a desperate and hopeless situation, but the Father has loved you enough to show mercy, compassion, and forgiveness through Me.

The Father's love is not about approving who you are and what you do, He found you dead in your transgressions, deserving of His wrath. His love has met you where you are, invited you to believe in Me and offered you forgiveness and eternal life.

He has loved you deeply and profoundly. It's the Spirit living within you that has changed you, for the better, giving you a new identity, bringing you into a new reality. I am alive and victorious. You've been given eternal life, a life that will go on forever, rich, full, secure with Me. That's your future. You have that eternal reality and identity right now, in this moment, because you are raised with Me. You've been made alive.

FAITH THOUGHTS

It's easy to get caught up in life and the daily struggles, forgetting just how deeply and profoundly God has loved you. And yet all we do and say is supposed to be with eternity in mind. And you don't have to continually prove yourself, God's grace is continually poured out in your life. He just wants you to fully receive the love He has for you, unconditionally.

SEPTEMBER 18

Not Far Off

The LORD your God is with you, the Mighty Warrior who saves. He will take great delight in you; in his love he will no longer rebuke you, but will rejoice over you with singing.
ZEPHANIAH 3:17

I am with you in this moment. There is never a time in your life that I am not in your presence. The Father is ever-present, He is not far off. He is always watching over every detail of your life, working all things together for good. You are never alone.

The Enemy will constantly point out things you do wrong, trying to convince you that you're not worthy of the Father's love, that you're worthless. But if you are listening to the truth, the Father rejoices over you with gladness. He believes you are worth My death and there is nothing you can do to change His mind.

When you're struggling in your faith, frustrated with life, the Father wants to quiet you with His love. His love is a gift that must be received. And His desire is to bring through Me a quiet peace to the stress and worry in your life. You have peace available to you any time you're willing to surrender your heart and be filled with My presence. It's through My death that your sin is paid for and you are able to walk in restored relationship with the Father.

You can live out the victory that the Father has achieved in you. You get to look forward to seeing Him face to face.

FAITH THOUGHTS

There will be times when you will feel utterly alone, but you are not. And when you think you've failed so badly that you can't turn back to God, you're wrong. The truth is that God is always rejoicing over you, over your faith, even if you have very little. Because you have accepted Christ as your Savior, He no longer sees how you've fallen short, He only sees Jesus in your place. You can live free of condemnation because of what Jesus has done for you.

Love Does

Dear friends, let us love one another, for love comes from God. Everyone who loves has been born of God and knows God. Whoever does not love does not know God, because God is love.
1 JOHN 4:7-8

If you love properly, I will be seen in you. Others can see Me through you if you are loving, following My pattern of selfless, sacrificial love. It is My love that will change you, allowing you to love like you wouldn't have been able to before I loved you first.

Even in the face of struggle and adversity, difficulties and unending challenges, love wins. Love will always win in the end. The love of the Father comes unexpectedly and undeservingly. I came to save you by the Father's love. When the wages of your sin should have been death, it's the Father's love that had a different plan for your life. In your separation from the Father, you should have been destroyed, but He found a way to redeem you. And before you could ask for it, the Father loved you ... unexpectedly.

You won't be able to avoid the struggles and brokenness of the world. You'll surely experience the injustice, hatred, pain, and suffering, but love will overcome ... every time.

FAITH THOUGHTS

Each and every day you're given the opportunity to allow others to see God's love in and through you. But there will be situations where His love doesn't come naturally, when you're faced with such debilitating difficulties that you don't "feel" loving. In those moments, call upon the Spirit for strength, surrender your heart and then let God do the rest.

September 20

Filled to the Measure

... may have power, together with all the Lord's holy people, to grasp how wide and long and high and deep is the love of Christ, and to know this love that surpasses knowledge – that you may be filled to the measure of all the fullness of God.
EPHESIANS 3:18-19

Remember, you can only do all things through Me. It is My strength and power that overcomes every obstacle and heals every heart, while strengthening your faith. I am with you, I am the Father's immeasurable love for you.

Because of what I've done on the Cross, eternal life has been offered to you ... you must only believe. Yet, while I give you the victorious life that's indestructible, you must come by faith to prove your belief, living by it, learning the laws and being conformed to Truth through the Spirit.

In exchange for your surrender, I give you victory, power and glory. There is no length, depth or height to the love of the Father and He offers you the fullness of it. Do not let tribulations discourage you ... hardships are a part of the Father's plan. It's through your trials that the Father works powerfully within you to do more than you can imagine. He wants you to believe that His love is unchanging and it is your foundation in the difficult seasons of life.

Continually seek to grow in your understanding of the Father's love. Dwell on His divine grace as you stand firmly in faith during trials and meditate on the Word to strengthen your faith for the future.

FAITH THOUGHTS

Do you daily focus on God's great love for you? Do you stop to realize that the Creator of the universe loves you intimately? If you will strive to understand His love more and more, you'll find the blessing is in your seeking Him. There is nothing He cannot do and will not do out of His great love for you.

With You

*May the Lord direct your hearts into
God's love and Christ's perseverance.*
2 THESSALONIANS 3:5

No matter what you go through and endure, I am there with you every step of the way. The Father is constantly watching over every detail of your life. And it's His love that will make you secure and strong. It's My perseverance that enables you to face your problems, issues, and troubles, and overcome them.

It is more than endurance, more than just holding on to the end. And just when you think you can't take anymore, the Father continues to work to strengthen and transform your heart. It's your faith that is a strong and vigorous confidence, built on the truth of the Father's holy love, knowing that you cannot see Him or understand what He is doing. This confidence keeps your faith on a firm foundation.

The trust the Father seeks after in you – it's one that will completely surrender and abandon yourself with total confidence upon Him. In My strength you can face anything in faith without wavering.

When the struggle is overwhelming, pray for the strength and stability to keep going. I am with you, and I can carry you when you're just too weary to carry on.

FAITH THOUGHTS

What problems are you facing today? Are you relying on Christ's perseverance to help you? You can't give up. Not now. You're just a prayer away from breakthrough. You've come too far, gone through far too much and you need to persevere … not in your own strength, but in Jesus'.

THE ASSURANCE OF GOD'S ABUNDANCE

And God is able to bless you abundantly, so that in all things at all times, having all that you need, you will abound in every good work.
2 Corinthians 9:8

If you're living life in the abundance of God, you're fully believing that He is working everything out for your good … no matter what He's allowed to be taken from you, no matter what doors have been closed and prayers that have not been answered. But this isn't easy, is it? Pain hurts. Loss cuts deep into the heart. And when life falls apart, or a raging storm rolls in to ruin all that was going so well, it seems that God is full of anything but generosity, love, and grace. It's in these moments where doubt can sink your faith in a single breath.

There's only one way to truly live in the abundance that God promised you … it's the Way, the Truth, the Life, it's only through Jesus. And you need healing. It doesn't matter where you are in your life, your heart has been broken at some point, your soul torn to pieces, and you realized that you're living in a very fallen, disappointing world. But you've got to see it for what it really is.

This world, the situations of your life are going to be used by God to destroy the things that are not of Him. And that's a good thing. One day you will see how He used it all. But for now, you need to call upon the Spirit to lead you into all truth and to heal you from the damage of past mistakes and wounds of your heart. And then you're going to need to get up and live in the complete victory Jesus died to give you.

Opening the Heavens

SEPTEMBER 22

The LORD will open the heavens, the storehouse of his bounty, to send rain on your land in season and to bless all the work of your hands. You will lend to many nations but will borrow from none.
DEUTERONOMY 28:12

There is never a moment when you should doubt the Father's ability to provide for you in abundance. Your attention, during good times and bad, should be on the Father and all He has done and is yet to do for you.

It's important for you to remember, even during times of great blessings, that it is the Father who gives you all those good things. Your life should be lived in praise and thanksgiving for all the Father has given, even the giving of My sacrifice, your eternal salvation in Me. Do not set your hope on the uncertainty of material things, but rather on the Father who richly provides you with everything you need and desire.

Your gratitude will show as you do good works, being generous, building your foundations of faith. Your purpose is to worship the Father with all your heart, soul, and mind. Know that the Father may allow hard times in your life to humble you, revealing whether you trust Him as much as you claim to. Faith must be tested. You are nothing without the Father and you are everything in Him.

Remember that it is the Father's power that provides prosperity, which includes your material, emotional, physical, and spiritual well-being. Now is the time to praise Him.

FAITH THOUGHTS

Each and every day, take time to look at those things around you which God has blessed you with. Remember that He has blessed you out of His great love for you and allowed you to go through testings of your faith out of His love, too. There is nothing He will not do to bring glory to His name and good to your life.

SEPTEMBER 23

Good and Perfect Gifts

Every good and perfect gift is from above, coming down from the Father of the heavenly lights, who does not change like shifting shadows.

JAMES 1:17

Everything good and perfect comes from the Father. And the Father does not change. He is constant, always good, never shifting, consistent and steadfast, and so your faith should be also. And whether or not you can understand it or not, there is goodness in the trials and testing in your life. The Father has promised that if you endure trials, you will be blessed. And in My strength you can do all things.

In the midst of trials you can turn to the Father for faith and joy, in confusion you can pray for wisdom. In times of temptation, you can seek holiness and strength, and at all times you can approach the Father's throne of grace with confidence because of what I have accomplished.

In considering the Father's goodness and all the wonderful blessings He gives, you can thank Him with a humble, surrendered heart. And don't forget to worship the Giver instead of the gift. Enjoy your blessings with gratitude toward the Father. At all times, because the Father is always good, you can respond in faith with humility and gratitude, living in the knowledge that the abundance that the Father provides will never run dry.

He is able to bless you abundantly, so that in all things at all times, you will have all that you need.

FAITH THOUGHTS

When you are facing adversity, remember that God is good all the time. Everything He gives and allows is designed for your good. So, you can count it all joy when you face various trials. Although it may seem like it, God is not unfair or unjust. He will work all things together for your good and His glory.

Running Over

SEPTEMBER 24

"Give, and it will be given to you. A good measure, pressed down, shaken together and running over, will be poured into your lap. For with the measure you use, it will be measured to you."
LUKE 6:38

When you truly believe what the Father has promised, you will learn to be enthusiastic about giving because of the blessing that comes in giving it and the blessings that the Father gives in return. It's in allowing the Spirit to live in and through you that takes your eyes off yourself and instead helps you to focus on the Father and His purposes.

If you want to receive from the Father, you must be willing to sacrifice. The Father wants to overflow your life with His blessings, and they are triggered by your giving … your giving of your resources, gifts, and talents are the direct route to the abundant blessings of the Father in your life.

The world around you will try to convince you to store up wealth and resources for your own purposes. But I tell you, it is better to surrender them to the purposes of the Father and reap the great blessings of being a part of His plan. The Father loves to give, bless and empower you and He wants you to participate in blessing. If you are faithful to use what He has given you, He will bless you with more to use to help others and bring glory to His name. If you will give, share, and bless, the Father will continue to supply you with more than you can imagine.

FAITH THOUGHTS

Where in your life can you give more to further the kingdom of God? It doesn't have to be your money, you can be led by the Spirit to give your time, or talents and gifts. Ask that God would direct you to opportunities where you can be a blessing to others every single day.

SEPTEMBER 25

First Things First

"But seek first his kingdom and his righteousness, and all these things will be given to you as well."
MATTHEW 6:33

Life is uncertain and life is short, so each and every moment needs to be spent making the Father your first priority. Until you put the Kingdom first in your life, you will never be satisfied. There are no material objects that can fill you. Those things will always leave you empty, needing more and more. I will satisfy your soul. Come to Me ... first.

All too often, you try to take care of your own needs, or try dealing with difficult circumstances before asking the Father for what you need. You try to work through things, struggle through obstacles in life that only the Father can handle, and you end up tired and empty. If you'll put the Father first in everything, seeking His righteousness, His way of doing things right and being in sync with the Spirit, everything else will be taken care of.

If you'll follow Me in My ways of worshiping the Father, trusting Him in all ways, and living in faith, you'll find that your difficult circumstances start working together for good in a divine way. The Father always listens to your prayers and will intervene as you place Him first in your life. You will always have what you need.

FAITH THOUGHTS

Are you focusing on placing God first in your life each and every day? Are you seeking to hear from Him by meditating on His Word? If you're feeling empty, struggling with worry, know that Jesus is right beside you to strengthen your faith and the Spirit within you to lead and direct you into the blessings God has for you. There is never a moment where God lets go of you.

Riches of His Glory

And my God will meet all your needs according to the riches of his glory in Christ Jesus.
PHILIPPIANS 4:19

You are going to have to choose to be content. The world is going to try and convince you that you need more. Regardless of your circumstances, you are going to have to be determined to be content. I supply you with the fullness of Myself, the Spirit dwelling in you forever.

If you're looking for ways to give, always generous with every opportunity given to you, you are showing proof that you have put your trust in the Father to meet your needs and take care of you. I gave the most priceless gift of laying down My life and I have given you the gift of the Spirit to dwell in you.

Pray to have an open heart. I gave up all and I'm asking you to continually follow Me. Whatever you're faced with today, the Father will supply all that you need. Don't allow yourself to get preoccupied with the things you selfishly desire. Live by the promises and find contentment with what you already have. Accept what the Father gives, instead of wanting more and more. It's always time to count your blessings rather than list your wants. Look at what the Father has already blessed you with and then look forward to the hope of all He's yet to do.

FAITH THOUGHTS

What do you truly need in your life? How is it that God can enable you to experience it in your life? Ask the Spirit to show you how to be happy with your needs being met by God. Look at the things you do have instead of the things you don't and be determined to live with a heart of gratitude for all God has done.

SEPTEMBER 27

Filled to Overflowing

*Then your barns will be filled to overflowing,
and your vats will brim over with new wine.*
PROVERBS 3:10

You can trust the Father to direct your paths. You can always move forward in peace, believing that through His Word, through the leading of the Spirit, the Father is in control and knows what is best. And one day, you will look back and see that even through the most difficult circumstances, through the suffering and in all the tears of joy and pain, you were on the path the Father intended all along.

You will need the Father's wisdom to make the right decisions, to stay on His path, to keep you from wasting your life on things that have no eternal benefit. The Father wants more for you than this world can offer. He wants you free from the worries of the world and when you follow Me, as He desires you to, you will need to give things up.

It's not because the Father wants less for you, but because He wants more for you. More than you can hope for or imagine. He wants you to have peace with Him and a life well lived in His presence, relying upon His wisdom and grace. But you won't always feel like things are moving in the right direction. His wisdom teaches you to look beyond your feelings.

Ultimately, no matter what happens, the Father's purposes for you are for good because He is your heavenly Father ... He will always do what is best for you, graciously giving you all things.

FAITH THOUGHTS

It's easy to forget, in the struggles of life, that God is not only going to provide all that you need, but more. Your faith needs to move past feelings of unworthiness and fear to simply trust. God has promised you so many wonderful things, are you looking expectantly to receive all of them?

Peace and Prosperity

*But the meek will inherit the land
and enjoy peace and prosperity.*
PSALM 37:11

Your meekness is not weakness, it is merely strength that is controlled. If you are meek, you have an inner strength, My strength, that enables you to be gentle and kind even in the most terrible of circumstances. It's your quietness of Spirit that enables you to have self-constraint, not given to the world around you that stirs up trouble.

I have given you the Spirit as a gift and you have the gift of stability through Him. If you will live each day longing to honor the Father through your love for Him, you can rejoice in My victory that will give you inner peace. My peace will enable you to endure hard times patiently and it will give you a spirit of kindness and goodness, as the Spirit works within you to make you more faithful.

You do not need to fret because of evil men or be envious of those who do wrong. Their happiness is temporary. You are to trust the Father, submitting to Him and doing all things in dependence upon Him. If you will trust, you will find the peace, joy and prosperity that you yearn for.

Allow Me to carry your burdens and be still, patiently waiting for the Father to intervene in your situation. I am with you in the valleys, and you will share My glory on the mountaintops.

FAITH THOUGHTS

Do you struggle with letting things go? Unable to understand why God would allow such chaos and turmoil? It's time to take another perspective, to look at your troubles as tools in the hands of God. He is using these situations to work within you and make your heart more like His ... expect growing pains.

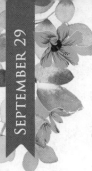

SEPTEMBER 29

A Pathway of Promise

Observe what the LORD your God requires: Walk in obedience to him, and keep his decrees and commands. Do this so that you may prosper in all you do.
1 KINGS 2:3

What the world values in life and what is valuable in the eyes of the Father are two different things. It's your living and loving of Me, living in grace in which you can run the race set before you. It's when you walk faithfully in all the ways the Spirit is leading you to, that you will grow in the mercy and love of the Father and you will taste and see that He is good!

You have a pathway of promise that you will come into the fullness of blessings of the Father, with a desire to love and serve Him with all of your heart, soul, and mind in all of your ways. Serving with grace and humility will open doors of opportunity for you and close others not meant for you to walk through. Know that the Father will be faithful to fulfill all that He has promised through you and for you. And in surrendering your life to Me, you will glorify Me in whatever you do.

It's whenever you doubt, whenever your faith is weak, that you can look to the Father in thanks, trusting in His ways that bring life, satisfaction and success in Me. Ask the Spirit to open your heart and eyes to see what the Father wants you to see, to understand what He wills you to understand and to walk closely and faithfully as He works out His plans for your life.

FAITH THOUGHTS

What do you define as success? Does your answer match up with God's? God has a path designed specifically for you, to prosper in ways that go beyond your understanding. His success for you most likely looks different than it does to you because His priority is transforming you into His image and He will use all of your circumstances to do that. Trust Him.

With Abundance

*You crown the year with your bounty,
and your carts overflow with abundance.*
PSALM 65:11

You are blessed with the Father's presence, you are gifted with My Spirit. You are held. The Father is a trustworthy Refuge. He is your Shield and your Defender. And the Father blesses you in abundance. Not an abundance of material things which can be taken at any minute, but one that enables you to live seeking after Him and His goodness. His abundance. He gives more than you can ask for.

The Father sent Me to die on the Cross so that everything could be made right again. I give you abundant life. I give you more than salvation. I give you an intimate relationship with the Father while you live this life on earth. I give you eternal hope. A hope that you can live in today. You can live an abundant life right now. Your only security and comfort is found in Me. You should live in the joy that the Father has given to you. You can live in peace because the Father is good and faithful and is accomplishing His purposes through your life.

When you live in this peace, from a place of abundance, you're showing your complete trust in the Father's goodness and providence, fully believing that He is working all things together for your good. Look to Me in doubt and use My strength to rest in, knowing that whatever is taken from you, your faith will not waver.

FAITH THOUGHTS

Do you really believe that God is good? And that He will give you good things? Do you trust God to be God in your life? Or are you allowing doubt to control your faith? Christ is in you ... you have a living hope. It is not a hope that disappoints. Search the heart of God, seek His promises for you and then look expectantly for their fulfillment.

October 1

Not Enough Room

"Bring the whole tithe into the storehouse, that there may be food in my house. Test me in this," says the LORD Almighty, "and see if I will not throw open the floodgates of heaven and pour out so much blessing that there will not be room enough to store it."

MALACHI 3:10

Your only hope in life is this: the Father never changes. He is the same yesterday, today, and forever. Though everything around you moves, turns, and shifts, the Father does not. Nothing that He's promised will be modified, His character will never alter. All that He is, all that He has always been and will ever be can be trusted completely. He is always wise, sovereign, faithful, just, holy and fully loving. He is always good … not just sometimes.

It's because the Father never changes that you can confidently depend on His promises never changing, His purposes never wavering, and His character never altering. Having faith is a matter of trust in the Father. You must continually make that decision to trust Him in everything you do and say.

Your life is to be lived as a blessing of the Father, poured out into the world. I am always with you, the Spirit in you, to strengthen, comfort, and guide you. You have divine help to accomplish all that you're supposed to. You don't have to do it on your own. If you're continually bailing water from your boat, look to Me. I am the One who does the miracles. I am the One who calms the storm. The blessing is in the journey and the struggle. The greatest miracles will be the ones that happen in and through you.

FAITH THOUGHTS

God has promised to throw open the floodgates of His blessings in your life if you will simply put Him first. The Spirit will lead and guide you in opportunities to live out your faith. You must simply trust God to not only provide, but to hold to His promises and bless you with abundance.

Glory and Goodness

OCTOBER 2

*His divine power has given us everything we
need for a godly life through our knowledge of him
who called us by his own glory and goodness.*
2 PETER 1:3

Living a life of faith is living fully persuaded, convinced, putting all of your trust in the promises of the Father. You are both saved and called. And the sooner you commit to live the life that the Father has intended, the sooner you will live in My peace.

Even though you are a new creature, with a new life in Me, you will still struggle with the human life. You will still struggle with fear and disappointment. I know that it might be hard to believe, when you are looking at your current circumstances, but the Father has already given you everything you need in life. Through the connection you have with Him, He pours out His power. Stay grounded in His Word. You'll find that His promises for your life include all of the resources and opportunities to lead you into His will in furthering His kingdom.

So, never let your circumstances try to control what you can and can't do. You have My power living within you and My presence always with you. Your life is what you believe. The Father is not looking for how powerful you are, but He's looking to use you in your weakness. You don't have to do anything but allow the Spirit to work in and through you, with a surrendered heart, the Father does the rest. In your weakness He is strong. It's His promises that are exceedingly great and precious because they are greater than any problems you'll ever face. Nothing is impossible for Him.

FAITH THOUGHTS

God is nothing but good. He has saved you and called you to a life lived in Him, allowing you to take part in His glory and goodness. You don't have to live the godly life in your own strength, you have the fullness of God's power living in you through the Spirit. You have everything you need.

October 3

The Blessings

*Humility is the fear of the LORD;
its wages are riches and honor and life.*
PROVERBS 22:4

To be blessed by the Father you must be humble, admitting you're a sinner. Your humble heart should come to the throne of grace admitting you don't have all the answers and that without My help you can do nothing. With a humble heart you are able to ask the Spirit to search your heart, to accept correction, repent and be completely surrendered to the Father's will for your life.

A life in Me comes with a fear of the Father, reverently seeking to honor Him in all that you do. It should be your desire to obey Him and honor Him in all ways. It is in your complete surrender of your heart that the Father will bless you, in ways you ask for and in ways that you're not expecting.

The Father has promised a humble heart and an abundant, good, joyful, peaceful, productive, and eternal life. You have the hope and joy of living with Him for all eternity because of Me. There is no shortcut to the Kingdom, there is no other way. And faith will not be easy. It doesn't mean living a life that is free from trouble or cares, it means knowing what to do when things go wrong … it means running to the Father in prayer. Your blessings will come in knowing that I am with you and I am the Truth and the Way and the Life.

FAITH THOUGHTS

Each and every day you will have to humble your heart to walk in faith. Life will always have obstacles, so you must always remember to run into the arms of God and ask for His help. He's always waiting. No matter what it is, He can handle it … and He'll bring blessings from it.

A Flourishing Life

OCTOBER 4

*May the LORD cause you to flourish,
both you and your children.*
PSALM 115:14

The goodness of the Father cannot be measured, His blessings cannot be counted. His love is so amazing that you cannot even begin to understand how deep, wide, and long it is. His wisdom is so much greater than your own. He is perfect and divine.

The Father is good and you can praise Him for His love and care. You don't have to worry about the details of life because they are all in His hands and I will carry your burdens. It is through your faith that you are to live for Him and allow others to see Me in and through you. You can live in joy even when life is hard. Spend your time in prayer, thanking the Father for all He's done and all He's yet to do.

Everything that the Father has planned for your life, He has given you the strength and ability to walk through. His desire is that you follow Me, using your abilities and gifts that will continually be developed with the help of the Spirit for the sake of the Kingdom. All you need is a willing heart, trusting Him every day, in whatever He is calling you to do. So, don't be full of worry looking too far down the road, trying to see what the Father's plan is … you'll lose sight of what He is trying to do in and through you today, in this moment.

FAITH THOUGHTS

Live a life of praise, praising God for His strength and wisdom in your life. Thank Him for His love that He continues to pour out. Ask the Spirit to open your eyes to see how blessed you really are and to have a deeper commitment for living out His purposes for your life.

SECTION 4

"Peace, Be Still"

*The disciples were absolutely terrified.
"Who is this man?" they asked each other.
"Even the wind and waves obey him!"*

Mark 4:41 (NLT)

One thing is for sure, when God shows up in your life, you're going to be at peace, you're going to be still … you're going to fall to your knees in awe. If you're blessed enough to be brought to your knees by God more than once in your life, you're experiencing an extra outpouring of His love and grace. But remember, those breathtaking, life-changing moments are probably going to come through your storms of life. God's ways are always higher and invariably better.

It may take a few journeys in a boat with Jesus to learn that, but don't worry, God's not giving up on you. His patience has no limits. His love has no bounds. And His faithfulness endures forever. His power is unexplainable, unfathomable, and ever present in your life. It's His power at work within you, transforming you into His image through the working of the Holy Spirit. God created the complexities of the universe and holds it all in place, keeping it all in motion.

Your life is not too difficult for Him. Your troubles hold no impossibilities in His hands. Don't try to figure Him out. You don't need to … and you just can't … His greatness is unsearchable. And if everything is truly *under* His control, then nothing is ever *out* of His control … including every storm that ever comes into your life. There is power in the name of God … call upon Him … and find hope as you rest in His peace.

SAVED BY GRACE

Out of his fullness we have all received grace in place of grace already given.
JOHN 1:16

God's love for you will never change. His love for you is so great that He sent Jesus to pay for your sins and give you eternal life. You didn't deserve it then, and you don't deserve it now. That's His grace. He pours it out into your life every single moment of every single day. For no other reason than that He loves you.

You need to have a full understanding of God's grace. You need to live in the truth that sin's power over you is broken and you have freedom in Christ. You are given a new life. In the middle of the messes, in the doubt of the raging storms of life, you have hope. All that is good in you, all the sins you've confessed and repented, all the love, mercy and kindness you've given to others, all of the ways you've humbled yourself, all the hope and faith you've held onto, is all by the grace of God … the Spirit living in you, taking you from faith to faith and glory to glory.

Any good in your life is because of the Cross … keep going to the foot of it. Remind yourself of the bigger picture. Ask the Spirit to help you see what God is doing in the storms of your life. And rely on His help to stand firm in your faith by God's love, mercy and grace. You're saved by grace and sustained by it, and one day you'll receive the surpassing riches of divine grace for all eternity. Live right now in that joy and hope.

Holding Nothing Back

OCTOBER 5

*He who did not spare his own Son,
but gave him up for us all –
how will he not also, along with him,
graciously give us all things?*
ROMANS 8:32

Each and every moment, you have the opportunity to reflect on the Father's character through your attitudes and actions. You can live out your joy for the gift of eternal life you've been given in the here and now.

As your faith follows Me, it can so easily get distracted by the world and you can mistakenly place your earthly desires above your desire for the Father. It's a burden of your imperfect world and you'll end up facing disappointment after disappointment. You must continually focus on placing your hope in the Father's Word and His promises, looking thankfully and expectantly for the fulfillment of His promise to give you all things.

There is no greater sacrifice than the one I made. You can live in the hope of eternal life because of Me. You should know that the Father will hold nothing back from you. He longs to bless you. Remember to be patient and faithful in the midst of troubles and wait and trust in every single one of the promises. Always remember that the Father is continually working all things together for good.

FAITH THOUGHTS

It's easy to forget that it is God that gives us all things. We so easily fall into the trap of trying to do things on our own that we fail to call upon the grace of God. Make it a priority each and every day to call upon God's grace, first and foremost. Decide that your hope will be in nothing other than the saving blood of Jesus.

October 6

Shining with Grace

*... the LORD make his face shine on you
and be gracious to you.*
NUMBERS 6:25

All of the temporary things in life are not irrelevant or insignificant. They can be wonderful blessings, precious gifts, expressions of the Father's favor. But they are not the heart of the blessings. They can be taken away. The center of your blessings is the presence of the Father Himself. The Giver.

It is through My death and resurrection that the Father moved toward you in goodness, seeking you out with His favor, being gracious to you. By accepting Me as Savior, you are made holy. And the Father has promised not only to protect you, but to take care of you. He watches over you and His face shines upon you with His favor and acceptance.

When He looks at you, it is with a permanent smile, not with disappointment or anger. He is pleased with you regardless of what you do or don't do. You are in Me and no longer under the curse of sin ... you are in the Father's eternal favor. The Father does not measure His love for you by your actions or words. When He looks at you, He only sees My righteousness. The Father longs to bless you. Walk in faith believing that truth.

FAITH THOUGHTS

There is nothing you can do to earn God's grace and there is nothing you can do to lose it. When you put your trust in Jesus, He is all God sees when He looks at you. You can approach the throne of grace with confidence because of what Jesus has done. It's always time to open your arms and tell God you receive His blessings.

The Upright Life

OCTOBER 7

For the grace of God has appeared that offers salvation to all people. It teaches us to say "No" to ungodliness and worldly passions, and to live self-controlled, upright and godly lives in this present age.
TITUS 2:11-12

Today, and every day, be reminded of the grace of the Father and how it reveals, saves, trains, and prepares. Grace is revealed through Me. I sacrificed to give you eternal life through your faith. There is nothing you can do to earn this grace. There is no price to be paid, I have paid it all.

It is through the Spirit that you are filled with the Word and the Father's transforming work is done … training you to renounce ungodliness and worldly passions, to live a self-controlled, upright, godly life. And it is grace that enables you to live this way. Living uprightly cannot be done apart from the Father's grace.

If you follow Me, you will see your steps directed. You will never walk by faith, blindly, because searching the heart of the Father for your every step gives you divine direction. No matter how long it takes for the Father to direct you in the next step, wait. His ways may be beyond understanding, but they are always worth following.

FAITH THOUGHTS

In order to live a life worthy of God, you need His grace. You can't do it on your own. Keep your eyes on Jesus and immerse yourself in the Word. It is the Spirit that will enable you to hear the voice of God, leading, guiding, directing you into His perfect blessings.

October 8

Under Grace

*For sin shall no longer be your master,
because you are not under the law, but under grace.*
ROMANS 6:14

You need to clearly understand that you are under grace. I know that you struggle with falling short, with failures. But the Father has made full provision through Me for you to pick yourself up and move forward immediately. You don't need to be discouraged.

You are not ruled by sin and you are no longer under law and condemnation, but under grace. Even through your struggle, each time you fail, you can turn back to the Father and ask for His forgiveness because of what I've done. When you repent, accept the forgiveness given to you and remember how much the Father loves you. He is not angry or upset … His love abounds. And you don't have to earn it. It's unmerited favor.

You didn't do anything to gain the Father's grace and you can't do anything to lose it. It is all because of the Father's immeasurable and unimaginable love shown toward you that He gives you grace. And I have paved the way for you to always live under grace. You are not to live under the law anymore, under the Father's penalty. I have paid the price for you to live under the Father's grace. You are to live a new life in righteousness and holiness.

Faith Thoughts

Do you live with the burden of guilt, instead of the liberating power of God's grace? Have you forgotten that you are captured by God's unrelenting love for you? You will make mistakes and you will fail, but you can let Jesus pick you right up so that you can keep walking forward in faith, at peace with God.

One Day

The grace of the Lord Jesus be with God's people. Amen.
REVELATION 22:21

I am coming back ... one day. In a moment, in the blink of an eye. I am your hope now and forever. Because of the Father's love, it's My blood poured out that secures you a place in heaven for all eternity. You can live in joy and hope and within the Father's grace every moment of your life.

I want you to live expectantly, living your life for Me in all ways. Do not let the world distract you from the Father's purposes for you. Your time is limited and precious and there is much to be done. Ask for a new outpouring of the Spirit in your life. Keep your eyes on Me. Faith will not be easy, there will be obstacles and difficulties that you will not be able to handle. Know that whatever each day holds, the Father is always holding onto you. There is never a reason to fear.

Every one of your tomorrows are secured in grace and the Father's blessings are always stored up to be released in your life at the perfect time. Hope is not in the grave. I have risen and I will be returning and My return will be both powerful and triumphant. I am coming back in all My glory. I am coming back for you because I love you. Wait expectantly for what is to come. It is the Father's love that gives you this hope, a final restoration to Him that is meant to give you joy here on earth.

FAITH THOUGHTS

Are you looking forward to the day of Jesus' return? You're called to live in the joy to come, in the here and now ... even in your difficulties. As you wait for the Second Coming, the Spirit works to transform your soul and give you the comfort and strength to not only endure, but to persevere, through faith. Simply surrender, let go, and praise the Father at all times and in all ways.

October 10

Falling Short

For all have sinned and fall short of the glory of God, and all are justified freely by his grace through the redemption that came by Christ Jesus.
ROMANS 3:23-24

All fall short of the glory of the Father. Don't allow the Enemy to use your sin against you, telling you that you are not worthy of the Father's love and grace. Because of Me, you are worthy. The Father does not see your unrighteousness when He looks at you. He sees only My righteousness living in you.

All you must do is confess your sins and the Father has promised to forgive and cleanse you from all unrighteousness. Humility and sorrow, with a contrite heart, asking for forgiveness, is what opens the Father's heart.

Though the Enemy loves to hold your sin over your head, it will not succeed. When the Father forgives, He forgets. And you need to as well. You will always be faced with temptations of the world. And at times you will fall into sin. It's all about how you handle your sin. Don't run from the Father, run to Him. Don't quit reading the Word, don't stop praying ... just ask for forgiveness. Repent. You can move forward in the Father's grace. The Father has so much for you to accomplish in your life, using your gifts and talents to further the kingdom of God.

You need to quickly get beyond your failures, so that the Father can continue to use you as His plans unfold. I have set you free from your sins. There is no price to pay. Just keep your eyes on Me and rely on the Spirit.

FAITH THOUGHTS

In what ways do you feel that you've failed? Do you believe that God truly forgives you and has forgotten your repented sins? You don't have to live in the chains of your sins from yesterday, you're to live in the grace given to you today.

Just Return

OCTOBER 11

"If you return to the Lord, then your fellow Israelites and your children will be shown compassion by their captors and will return to this land, for the Lord your God is gracious and compassionate. He will not turn his face from you if you return to him."
2 Chronicles 30:9

At times, life will drag you off course and you'll allow your attention to be drawn away from Me and the Father's plans for your life … you'll work to accomplish your own desires instead of the Father's. But you're not lost, all you have to do is humble yourself and confess. Just return to the Father in prayer and humbly give Him your heart once more, allowing Him to have His rightful place in your life. There is never a moment when He is not gracious and compassionate. He will always wrap His grace around your heart.

Never forget it's your heart that matters most. In those moments when you feel that the Father is far away, don't believe the lie that He has rejected you. Just draw near to Him and rejoice in His faithful loving-kindness. It's in walking with Me, in step with the Father that you will have strength, peace, and hope.

Your relationship with the Father is one that is grounded in knowledge of His Word and communication with Him through prayer. Draw near to Him and He will draw near to you. He will not turn His face from you.

Faith Thoughts

Is your motivation each day to please God, yourself, or someone else? Your heart can so easily be led astray. Ask the Spirit to guard your heart. Pray continually, and ask that whatever you do and say will honor God with all your heart, soul, and mind.

OCTOBER 12

Grow in Grace

The grace of the Lord Jesus Christ be with your spirit.
PHILEMON 1:25

Sometimes you simply need to remember. Remember the Father's faithfulness, remember His grace. It is the Spirit that will work within you to demonstrate to others the same love and faith that comes from Me. Your heart should be willing to cheerfully love others, so that I might be glorified. Pray that your life would be a living example of gracious love that reflects the deep love that I have for you.

Grace means you can walk with Me, you are saved by Me and in the most crucial moments of your life, those circumstances that are overwhelming, you can find comfort and strength in Me alone. You have a great hope for eternal life because the Father sees Me when He looks at you and I have been substituted for you and your sins.

You are now hidden in Me. It is impossible for anyone to deserve grace. Yet, the Father has chosen grace to pour out His great love for those who will turn to Him. Remember how the Father has loved you and healed you. Ask the Spirit to help you to walk in that same love. Each and every situation is used by the Father to help you grow in grace.

It's easier to see the providence of the Father in retrospect than in the present moment, but He is always working all things together for good. Remember what He has done and wait in praise for all He is yet to do, according to His promises.

FAITH THOUGHTS

Don't allow the distractions of the world to keep you from remembering God's grace. It's easy to get caught up in the here and now, the trials and tribulations that are threatening your finances, relationships, and even your health. Know that God knows. He's working on it. Rest in His grace and trust Him completely.

How Much More

OCTOBER 13

But the gift is not like the trespass. For if the many died by the trespass of the one man, how much more did God's grace and the gift that came by the grace of the one man, Jesus Christ, overflow to the many!
ROMANS 5:15

The gift of eternal life is free for anyone who believes. I have completely undone what sin did. You are no longer separated from the Father because of Me. It's My death that put you under the mercy of the Father forever. Because of Me, you are declared "not guilty," and you are given eternal life.

But I did more than save you from death. You are now redeemed. Sin brought you condemnation, I brought justification. Sin brought death … I brought life. I am the only answer. I am the only Way. All that I have is yours. And everything in your life, the cycle of grace is from Me. It's all about grace. And the response of your heart, moved by the Spirit, is giving gratitude to the Father and in living righteously.

You do not need to live righteously to find favor with the Father – you are accepted, loved, favored and given grace upon more grace. You can rest in My righteousness because you cannot be more righteous than what I give to you. You are loved with an everlasting love that does not stop. It is through Me that you can have security, acceptance and understanding before the Father.

FAITH THOUGHTS

Do you continually live in the favor you've been given? It was an enormous price that Jesus paid, His own life, to allow you to live in the fullness of God's grace. Life can cause you to lose sight of the eternal life you've been given, so make it a priority to start each day thanking God for it and strive to live in the grace He's given you for this moment.

OCTOBER 14

Finishing the Race

*However, I consider my life worth
nothing to me; my only aim is to finish the race and
complete the task the Lord Jesus has given me –
the task of testifying to the good news of God's grace.*
ACTS 20:24

I have called you to a life of faith. And one that can only be lived in My strength, with the help and guidance of the Spirit. When things become difficult, don't become discouraged to the point that it keeps you from living the life the Father has for you to live.

In My strength you can keep running the race faithfully with a heart after the Father's. Don't forget how the Father has delivered you in the past. Don't become forgetful or unthankful. Don't forget the awesomeness of the Father and how He has always cared for you. You can have the strength to move forward in faith because He is compassionate and gracious and abounding in love.

If you remember who He is and what I've done, you can finish the race. It's the Spirit that will fill you with the Word to nourish your soul and give you what you need to live your life as an example of grace. And you must rest along the way. Learn to rest in My power and rely on My strength and not your own. It's your faith that will give you endurance, when days are long and hard. You must complete the task given to you by relying on grace, moment by moment.

In My strength, you can finish the race set before you and you can finish it strong.

FAITH THOUGHTS

Pray that the Spirit will enable you to finish your race strong, just as Jesus did. It will require resolve as well as sacrifice, but in the Spirit you will find the comfort you need to trust God for the strength you need. Ask to be guided to make choices that keep yourself at the center of God's will for your life at all times.

Having Everything

OCTOBER 15

*The lions may grow weak and hungry,
but those who seek the L*ORD *lack no good thing.*
PSALM 34:10

You can attain the highest achievement or have all the material things in the world, but if you are missing Me, not living in Me and for Me, you will remain empty. You will grow weary and hungry when you are seeking the things of the world instead of focusing on the kingdom of God.

But if you passionately pursue the Father's will, you will lack no good thing. If you use the gifts and talents the Father has given you, you will find that the Father will pour out His blessings on you. You don't need to worry, the Father knows what you need before you ask Him.

He sees your whole life, from beginning to end and He is involved in every area of it. He is concerned with your spiritual needs, but also with your physical, financial, health, emotional, and relational needs. Because you remain in Me, you take on My strength and resources, not your own, so you can accomplish far more than you think you can.

Trust the Spirit to guide you and trust the Father to provide. If you continually seek the Father's will for your life, surrendered to His purposes, you will find that your faith in Me will be enough. I am all you need.

FAITH THOUGHTS

It's easy to grow weak and weary when you're striving for the success of the world instead of the purposes of God. Don't allow the distractions of the world to fool you and keep you from having everything in Christ. Seek God continually, praise Him always, and you will lack no good thing.

October 16

Great Mercy

But in your great mercy you did not put an end to them or abandon them, for you are a gracious and merciful God.
NEHEMIAH 9:31

Each and every day the Father reveals His mercy to you in new ways. Don't dwell on the past ... on yesterday's sin and struggles. Rely on the mercy of the Father which is infinite and inexhaustible. In His great love and mercy, He sent Me to take the judgment that was rightfully yours. There is no greater love.

With the rising of the sun, each new day gives way to a fresh new start. Yesterday doesn't matter, the Father has forgotten your past sins and looks at this very moment when you're in His presence, wrapped in His grace. I know it is often difficult when your prayers seemingly go unanswered and you struggle in your faith, but often the Father's delays or denials are His mercies in disguise.

His perspective is far different from yours. So, you must trust that the Father is in control and although He appoints every day's troubles, He also appoints every day's mercies. You don't have to carry tomorrow's burdens with today's resources. Today has enough mercies for today's troubles. There will be enough mercy for tomorrow, along with enough grace.

The Father wants you to come to His throne of grace in prayer continually, repenting of your sins and asking for His mercy. It's there, upon your knees, that you will find His help and love when you need it.

FAITH THOUGHTS

Are you continually calling upon the mercy of God in your life? You may have made mistakes yesterday, but today is a new day. You can receive the grace God wants to give you in this moment. Will you take the free gift He's offering?

Let It Reign

*Just as sin reigned in death, so also
grace might reign through righteousness to
bring eternal life through Jesus Christ our Lord.*
ROMANS 5:21

The Father's grace is not like human grace ... imperfect and subject to change. You have an enemy that wants you to feel pressure to earn grace. But that is not the Father's grace. He has already determined that you are undeserving of it ... that's why it's grace. And yet, He has decided that He will pour it out on you and your life out of His great love.

The Father's grace is based entirely on who He is and who you are in Him, through Me. He gives grace upon grace because He desires to. Because of what I've done, your debts are paid and your sin is forgiven. In exchange for your faith, you are given grace and eternal life. So, you need to realize that you don't need to worry about messing up and making mistakes ... you can simply focus more on drawing nearer to the Father as you follow Me, building your relationship with Him and strengthening your faith.

Stop for a moment and realize that no one can take away the Father's grace from your life. So, stop exhausting yourself trying to earn the Father's favor and simply ask Him to help you acknowledge and receive what is already yours. Live your life in His grace.

FAITH THOUGHTS

Where in your life do you struggle to receive God's grace? Ask God to help you fully understand His grace, accepting what He wants to give you. You don't have to struggle to be accepted in His eyes, you already are. His grace covers all of your sins. He wants you to get up and walk in faith, focused on the crown you will one day wear.

IN PURSUIT OF PEACE

*You will keep in perfect peace those whose minds
are steadfast, because they trust in you.*
ISAIAH 26:3

God has promised you peace. He hasn't promised to get rid of all your problems. And that perspective changes everything. What He's giving you is something far better … a miracle in every storm. He's teaching you that no matter what the storm is in your life, you need to take your eyes off of it and look to Him … that's when He gives you His perspective of joy and peace in all of life's circumstances. And it's through that perspective that you learn to live in the indestructible hope that you have in every situation.

Storms will cause you to be afraid, you will not "feel" peace. You'll doubt that Jesus will calm the storm. Faith doesn't make you perfect, it makes you realize that God is God and you are not. Storms help you to understand that you need to have complete dependence on God.

There are two things that will happen in your storms of life, when you're in the boat with Jesus … He'll either calm it or He'll stay with you through it. The presence and power of God … with you. Rest in that truth.

Divine Peace

OCTOBER 18

*"Peace I leave with you; my peace I give you.
I do not give to you as the world gives."*
JOHN 14:27

You can't live in the world and not expect troubles. I am telling you there will be tribulation, but I'm also telling you that I have overcome the world. Everything ends well. All things will work together for good.

As you live in the world, seeing the troubles in day-to-day living, I want you to be of good cheer, happy, knowing that you can experience the peace I have for you. Always remember that no weapon formed against you shall prosper, instead whatever you do will prosper. Trusting in Me to bring about everything in your life according to the Father's plan will change the outcome of your life in every situation you face.

Always focus your faith on the promises and pursue My peace that always leads to victory. Know that I give you My peace in the midst of trouble. Right in the middle of distress and heartache, My peace is there. I am in you, and you in Me. Know that the Father will bring an end to your troubles. I will still the storm and quiet the waves. And you can rest in the boat with Me, knowing that you're not going under, the Father controls the storm. This is your peace – your trust in your heavenly Father.

FAITH THOUGHTS

Are you living in the peace Jesus has given to you? If you're constantly restless, rest in God. You'll find that rest by trusting, by believing in the promises He has made to you. Jesus said there will be troubles, there will be storms ... but He's in them with you. The power of God is with you at all times and in all ways.

October 19

Proclaim It

How beautiful on the mountains are the feet of those who bring good news, who proclaim peace, who bring good tidings, who proclaim salvation, who say to Zion, "Your God reigns!"
ISAIAH 52:7

I am the "feet" who has brought the good news, who has proclaimed peace, bringing good tidings, who has proclaimed salvation. The Father reigns. No matter what you're facing, no matter the bad news, it all pales in the face of My good news. You must choose who or what will reign in your life. If your circumstances reign, you will face frustration, disappointment, and despair, but if the Father reigns, you can live in His peace and joy, even when things are not peaceful or joyful.

At times you may declare with your heart that the Father reigns, but looking at your life, He has not. He should permeate your face, your voice, your entire life. One day pain and suffering will end, but for now, your faith must endure. Do not fall into the sins of the world, chasing the wind, seeking things that will not satisfy. You are not to live as if you don't know what to do.

The Father has a plan and purpose for your life ... and He has stored up blessings. But this journey of faith is about putting Him in charge of your life. Seeking His guidance and living obediently. And I am walking with you. You are never alone. Don't look at the obstacles ahead of you and turn the other direction. Face them, in My strength. If you stand firm, you will see the Father's deliverance. He parts the seas and calms them. He's the only One who does ... so come to Him and trust Him. He reigns over all.

FAITH THOUGHTS

Is there an area in your life where God is not reigning? Put Him first and trust in Him most. Now is the time to pray.

The Answer

OCTOBER 20

*"The LORD turn his face toward you
and give you peace."*
NUMBERS 6:26

As you journey through life, it's easy to lose your peace. There are countless ways for you to be disappointed and be tempted to give up hope. I came to bring peace to your soul, a peace that you will never fully understand when you're experiencing the worst of times. I brought peace to the storm with My disciples, I'll bring peace to your storm as well. Whatever you're going through, I am the answer.

Know that the Father doesn't bring chaos, He brings peace. So, even though your circumstances may be less than ideal, you can rest in My peace, knowing that soon the storm will calm and, in the meantime, you can rest. The Spirit will move your soul to long for My peace. Choose to look at Me, at rest, and come into My peace.

Let faith answer the door when fear comes knocking and stay focused upon Me. In the worst of circumstances, the Father keeps blessing you, holding you, and causing His face to shine upon you. He is always smiling upon you and your life. He gives you favor and grace, undeserved, but freely given out of His great love. In your sinfulness and rebellion, His mercy pours out. And as the raging storms of life threaten to take you under, you have My peace.

FAITH THOUGHTS

Do you sometimes compare your life to others and feel disappointed? Do you often feel like God has forgotten about you? No matter how you feel, the truth is that God is always working in your life. There is never a moment when He abandons you. In this very moment, He is working a miracle in the mess around you.

October 21

Every Effort

Make every effort to live in peace with everyone and to be holy; without holiness no one will see the Lord.
HEBREWS 12:14

This world is not your home, and you need to be reminded of that. You will experience the same kind of hostility that I endured from sinners who were opposed to Me. You are being trained through your sufferings in this world and you will later enjoy the peaceful fruit of righteousness.

It's vital that your faith does not fail and that you stand firm. Your life surrendered to Me will enable Me to live in and through you, strengthening those that are weak and giving hope to the hopeless. In you, others will see My peace and you will draw others to the Father. You are already at peace with the Father because your sins are forgiven by grace through faith, so you are to make every effort to maintain My inner peace, maintaining a mind stayed on Me, in order to draw others to Me.

You are called to strive to live in peace with all people and to pursue holiness of heart. With the help of the Spirit, you are called to be holy and set apart for Me. The Spirit will enable you to be holy in all your words and in all your ways. It's only through the empowering of the Holy Spirit that you can pursue peace and holiness. Call upon His help.

FAITH THOUGHTS

What is it that you need to surrender to God? Are you making room for Him to do whatever He needs to do to work in and through you? Call upon the Spirit to help you pursue peace and to remain in the peace of Jesus at all times and in all ways.

In Pursuit

OCTOBER 22

Whoever would love life and see good days must keep their tongue from evil and their lips from deceitful speech. They must turn from evil and do good; they must seek peace and pursue it.
1 PETER 3:10-11

Do not be ashamed to obey the Father's commands … turn from evil and do good. Even when it doesn't make sense, even when it doesn't feel right. You will always be better off obeying than disobeying the Father's commands. The only way to have the power to follow Me in the way of love is to be filled with hope, with a strong confidence, that if you lose your life doing the Father's will, you will find it again and be richly rewarded for all eternity.

When you follow Me, you are held to a higher standard. The good news is that those difficult times can be what makes you more like Me and ultimately brings you into the everlasting joy that your soul desperately desires.

The Enemy will try to deceive you, talk you into believing that evil is not so bad and can even seem good. He'll try to devour you. But the choice is yours. You can resist Satan. In My strength you can do anything. You'll make mistakes, you'll do wrong things, but with My power within you, you can turn back to the Father and He will restore you and make you strong, firm and steadfast. Troubled times will knock your faith off balance, so continually seek the Father and My peace and keep pursuing His righteousness.

FAITH THOUGHTS

In which way has Satan deceived you in the past? What lies did you believe? What area of your life is vulnerable? You can resist temptations by staying grounded in the Word of God. The Word will keep you on God's path of righteousness. Draw near to Him and He will draw near to you and empower you to pursue His peace and live in it.

Justified through Faith

Therefore, since we have been justified through faith, we have peace with God through our Lord Jesus Christ.
ROMANS 5:1

You need to truly believe that the Father will do what He's promised. You need My peace, taking hold of your salvation. Remind yourself continually what the Father has promised. It's in trusting in the Word that your faith can be restored and you can cast out your doubts and fears. Always remember, your standing and acceptance by the Father doesn't depend on you. Your sins cannot outdo His love and forgiveness. By faith you are able to fall upon the mercy and grace of the Father.

I know that you don't go looking for troubles, they just find you. When they do, you can rely on the Spirit to use them to transform you, to mold you into reflecting the characteristics of the Father. So, even in the most difficult of times there are reasons to give thanks. Ask for help to keep from losing hope.

It's living in the Father's love and hope that empowers you to live in faith and serve with strength and courage, no matter what your circumstances are. Long before you followed Me, long before you turned to the Father, He declared His love for you. You can only be overwhelmed with the love that has saved your soul. Ask that you will be given opportunities to show that love to others, so that your life might be used in the saving of souls.

FAITH THOUGHTS

Do you daily ask God to bring opportunities into your life where you can show His love to others? You've been given a free gift that you should share with others whenever the situation arises. It is a great joy and you will be blessed for making the kingdom of God a priority in your life.

Reaping A Harvest

OCTOBER 24

*Peacemakers who sow in peace
reap a harvest of righteousness.*
JAMES 3:18

Envy and selfish ambition will always lead to a life filled with chaos and sinful choices. You need to live a life of humility, as I did … which led Me to lay down My life for you. You may need to lay down your pride and be peaceful when everything around you is not. You can do it in My strength.

The Spirit is continually working in and through you to bring about peace in your life. It's through the Father's love and grace that you can experience true happiness and peace. Sowing peace is your faith in action, evidence of the Spirit within you. Peace reigns where the Father is.

If you are not at peace, draw near to the Father. Come in prayer continually until peace floods your soul. It's the fruit of the Spirit that will fill you with true wisdom that looks for peace instead of trouble. You'll find yourself gentle and helpful to others, not harmful.

Your soul will be full of mercy and you will be quick to forgive, quick to overlook the offenses against you. You will find yourself in a life of peace that guides you continually into the Father's will. Your peace will reap righteousness … just seek it and pursue it.

FAITH THOUGHTS

It's not always easy to be at peace when life is full of chaos. It's the Spirit living in you that will give you the wisdom and strength to be peaceful in a world that is not. You can't do it in your own strength, your natural human response to offenses is not peaceful. And yet, when the Spirit moves you to a place of peace, it will be the evidence of the fullness of God in you.

OCTOBER 25

Called to Peace

*Let the peace of Christ rule in your hearts,
since as members of one body you were
called to peace. And be thankful.*
COLOSSIANS 3:15

With all the troubles of life, it can be easy to lose your peace. It's a *feeling* of peace. But the Spirit dwelling in you can help you to have true peace at all times, no matter what difficulties you're facing in the moment because I am your peace.

When thoughts of worry flood your mind, choose to focus on Me. If you are walking with Me, there is nothing to fear. You've been made right in the Father's sight and that righteousness allows you to live a life that is free from stress, worry, fear, and failure.

Guard your thoughts. In the middle of your circumstances, trust in the Word. When everything in your life is falling apart, you can believe that the Father will cause it to fall in place. I will see you through everything. And although it is difficult to be thankful and live joyfully when everything in life seems to be going wrong, My peace will help you to trust in a miracle.

Focus your energy on being thankful, even for the smallest things and you'll find yourself living in peace that is a lot more unshakable.

FAITH THOUGHTS

Being at peace is never easy when the circumstances of your life are ever-changing and expectations continually fail to be met. But focusing on being thankful is a first step toward the peace of Jesus. And you need His peace to walk through this journey of life, so find one thing at this moment you can thank God for and then continue to thank Him more and more.

Different

*Finally, brothers and sisters, rejoice! Strive for
full restoration, encourage one another, be of one mind,
live in peace. And the God of love and peace will be with you.*
2 CORINTHIANS 13:11

You can't live like everyone else if I live in you. Even in your wandering, the Father's grace and power uses your life to lead others to Him. He brings about opportunities in your life to show His love and kindness in and through you.

It's nothing you do, it's the work of the Spirit. Let the difference in you be Me. The Spirit within you produces love, grace, understanding and forgiveness. Pray that the Spirit will fill you until you overflow with His power and presence.

You are called to live in a fallen world, one that brings conflict and disappointment. But I am with you. When you need to be encouraged, encourage others. When you need to be comforted, comfort those around you who need My love. The Spirit already dwells in you, it is not something you need to pursue, but something you need to completely surrender to. Walk according to the Spirit and don't live according to the ways of the world or the desires of the flesh. You are a new creation. You no longer turn away from the promises of the Father … you run to them.

You no longer live trying to hide anything, but fully acknowledging that you have sinned and fallen short and fall on the grace and forgiveness of the Father, a life in the Spirit that leads others to that same grace and forgiveness.

FAITH THOUGHTS

Does your life look different from the lives of nonbelievers? Emotions can take hold in your dire situations and you can find yourself so self-centered, in a position of self-preservation, that you forget who you truly are. You're a child of God, a daughter of the King of kings, and you have the Spirit living in you. Walk humbly in that truth.

OCTOBER 27

Every Effort

Make every effort to keep the unity of the Spirit through the bond of peace.
EPHESIANS 4:3

Peace is a blessing. Pay attention to your peace. If your peace becomes unstable, it should be a sign of the Enemy's presence. When things don't seem right, ask the Spirit to intervene and search your heart. Ask if there are any areas of your life that are allowing the Enemy a way in to destroy your peace.

It's your faith that gives you the peace that surpasses all understanding. The Spirit dwelling in you leads you in how to live in the peace of the Father. Without the Spirit, life is messed up and confusing, bringing about worry, defeat, and helplessness. Yet, living in My peace brings a source of joy to your soul. The Spirit within you brings your heart to a place of humility and gentleness, making room for the Father's work in your life.

Love, peace, and harmony is the Father's way of living ... this is what He wants for you. Always pray that you would pursue peace with the Father and with yourself. If you do not have peace with yourself, you will not be able to extend peace to others. No-one is perfect. Don't have unrealistic expectations of others.

As you live out your life, live it in peace, enjoying and benefiting from the gifts and talents the Father has given you. Refuse to allow the Enemy to use you in his scheming and dividing tactics against others. He knows that if you are bringing peace to the world around you, amazing things will happen to further the Kingdom.

FAITH THOUGHTS

There will always be conflict around you, and the Enemy is always out to destroy your relationships. Choose to look at your situations as spiritual battles, rather than what they might appear on the surface. There is always something greater at stake than just winning an argument or being right. Be determined to be the one who brings peace and comfort to others.

Pathway to Victory

OCTOBER 28

*For to us a child is born, to us a son is given,
and the government will be on his shoulders.
And he will be called Wonderful Counselor,
Mighty God, Everlasting Father, Prince of Peace.*
ISAIAH 9:6

My peace gives you freedom from all the chaos. I *offer* you peace. The only way you can experience peace with yourself, others, and the world around you is by being at peace with the Father. That's why I came … to reconcile you to the Father.

My peace calls you out of darkness into My Light. I am your Wonderful Counselor, working in divine wisdom. I am your Peace. You need peace in your life. Your attempts to bring peace in your relationships and even in your own thoughts will be futile if they are not in My power. More and more you will realize how much you need Me. You couldn't reconcile yourself to the Father, but I did. Let me do what only I can do … bring about peace.

It's My strength that is great enough to solve your problems, but merciful enough to lay down My life for you. If you are trusting in Me as your Savior, you are given an assurance of hope and peace that flows out of your relationship with Me. Once you are in Me, I show you that I can bring peace wherever I rule. I can bring peace in your life's trials, in your transformation, in your relationships, and in you.

Faith Thoughts

Is there an area of your life that is lacking peace? Are you experiencing inner conflict, a strained relationship, or another kind of obstacle in your walk with God? Call upon Jesus, the Prince of Peace, to bring His power and His love into your situation and give hope where hope seems gone.

OCTOBER 29

The Fullness of Life

The mind governed by the flesh is death, but the mind governed by the Spirit is life and peace.
ROMANS 8:6

I know that you want to enjoy your life, living every moment in joy and peace. And yet, there is only one way to do that. The Holy Spirit must be in you, must be leading you, and governing you. All other paths to peace are temporary. Life and peace are only found in pursuing the Father, trusting in Me, and being led by the Spirit.

Your fullness of life will only come from having your mind set on the Spirit. It will be your choice to show love, help others, speak Truth, and above all, love the Father and seek His glory. It will mean turning your back on a world that drives you to focus on material things and temporary pleasures.

When you are living your life in the Spirit, you are looking at life from the Father's point of view and not the world's. You are a different person, a new creation in Me and it should affect every part of you, every area of your life. In all that you do and in all that you pray, seek that the Father be glorified. Set your mind on what is true, noble and right so that your mind can be renewed.

Don't dwell on things you can't control, which will steal your peace. Don't allow worry and wrong thinking to keep you from resting in My peace. Focus on all you've received from the Father. Focus on what the Spirit desires … life and peace … the fullness of true life.

FAITH THOUGHTS

Do you continually examine your priorities and your heart? Life moves fast and it can get away from you easily. You must make a conscious effort to focus on the things of God, to call upon Him constantly, and rest in Him always. The fullness of life you're seeking can only be found in trusting in Him completely.

Under the Shadow

OCTOBER 30

*In peace I will lie down and sleep,
for you alone, LORD, make me dwell in safety.*
PSALM 4:8

You can maintain a sense of peace and spiritual balance when troubles come by having a close, abiding relationship with Me. Turn your eyes upon Me. An unshakable peace is available to you when you turn your heart to Me. Though your soul may cry out "Why?", your questions will draw you near to the Father for answers. And anything that draws you nearer to Him is good.

Never forget that all your comfort and security is firmly within the Father's grasp. Only He can handle your problems. He never meant for you to be strong on your own. You are to find courage and hope in Me, having the strength to trust in the Word. You will, at times, become anxious, but remember you are to be anxious for nothing. You are to pray with thanksgiving and let your requests be made known to the Father. It's then that His peace will guard your heart and mind through Me.

Your life is a gift from the hand of the Father and you are called to live out His purposes for your life, resting in His everlasting security. Rest in faith, in quietness. Know that the Father knows all of your pain and His peace and presence are with you. Come to Me in your moments of worry and despair and receive what I want you to have … immovable and eternal peace.

FAITH THOUGHTS

Is something troubling you? Are you feeling full of fear? What is it that is stealing your peace? Tell God what you're feeling and allow His peace to flood your heart. He loves you unconditionally and He has promised to keep you and deliver you. Rest in God's relentless love for you.

JOY IN THE JOURNEY

"I have told you this so that my joy may be in you and that your joy may be complete."
JOHN 15:11

If you stop to think about the abundant and amazing blessings that have been promised to you by God, gratitude should overflow from your life and overwhelm you. Though troubles will still come and storms of life still rage, though sadness and suffering in circumstances may endure, it is the joy of the Lord that will carry you through the deepest pain, through the moments of greatest fear. Yes, even in the worst of times, you have a joy within you that never fails.

If you don't understand it yet, happiness and joy are not the same thing. Happiness relies entirely on your circumstances. It is as ever changing as the wind, as soon as difficulties arise and pain and suffering rush in, happiness ceases. But it's joy, a gift from God that enables you to have peace and find hope even when life seems to be falling apart.

Don't miss out on the joy you've been given. Don't live in regrets and past failures, fear of the future, or despair and discouragement. That's not who you are in Christ. Remember who you are in Him. God pours out His grace and His love unconditionally as the Spirit dwells in you, never abandoning you.

There is nothing that Jesus does not understand and there is nothing that His power cannot do. Surely, knowing that He is with you always, even unto eternity, should make your joy complete.

The Joy and Hope

OCTOBER 31

*The prospect of the righteous is joy, but
the hopes of the wicked come to nothing.*
PROVERBS 10:28

I have told you that joy is waiting beyond the grave. But you can also live in joy, right now, in the midst of all circumstances. The beauty of the joy I give is that it is not fleeting or temporary. My joy is sustaining and strong, based on Truth. It's through the Spirit that the Father will fill you with joy, regardless of your circumstances or feelings.

Though happiness and joy may seem the same, they are different. The Father promises joy, but He never promises happiness. Happiness is an emotion ... fleeting. But joy is a long-lasting state of being. Joy is promised by the Father and something you should pursue. You have the joy in the eternal life you've been given that awaits you. The constant knowledge of your salvation and the Father's love for you will give you joy, even if your current circumstances aren't "happy."

You can know in this moment that there will be joy in heaven and you can live in it now as you expectantly wait for eternity. Know that you must keep Truth at the forefront of your mind, meditating on it day and night. You'll find that you'll be filled with peace, even a settled joy, even in the midst of pain and unhappiness. My joy is your strength.

FAITH THOUGHTS

Do you get frustrated because you're not happy and you have the expectation that you always should be? The world will try to convince you that you need things, accomplishments, to make you happy ... you just need Jesus. When you are weak, when you're going through difficulties, the joy He gives in the hope of eternal life brings about a happiness that no one and nothing can take away.

November 1

Made Complete

I have much to write to you, but I do not want to use paper and ink. Instead, I hope to visit you and talk with you face to face, so that our joy may be complete.
2 JOHN 1:12

Your joy is not dependent on having or not having things. It's the attitude of your heart. When you rejoice in Me, worldly possessions take their proper place and can be used for the Father's purposes, according to His will. Ask the Spirit to continually remind you that I am Lord of your life and the Father is always in control.

Your heart will be filled with joy when you think about your salvation, when you fully realize that this is not all there is. Because of My sacrifice, your heart should always be in a place of gratefulness, thankful for the Father's love and the hope of spending all eternity with Him. You may not understand things now, but in hindsight, you will clearly see the Father's mercy and forgiveness pouring into every day of your life.

In the meantime, in this journey of faith, you must live in grace. I am your example in living and in dying ... dying to self. I was able to endure the physical pain, emotional agony, and spiritual darkness of the Cross because of the joy set before Me. I will teach you to keep your eyes on the joy of eternity so that you can endure all the troubles that come into your life.

You have the great reward of eternal life ... but as you wait, pray that the Spirit living in you will help you to become everything the Father wants you to be and accomplish all that He wills. And one day your joy will be made complete.

FAITH THOUGHTS

Do you sometimes feel as though something is missing? Rest in the joy of Jesus, living out God's purposes for your life. The fullness of your joy will only come when you one day see God face-to-face.

A Refreshed Heart

Your love has given me great joy and encouragement, because you have refreshed the hearts of the Lord's people.
PHILEMON 1:7

When things in life get hard, don't grumble and complain as the Israelites did. Turn to the Father. It's your mindset, your thinking, that is holding you back from the miracles the Father has stored up for you. Be determined to avoid the long, hard way through the wilderness. Walk directly into your faith and stand firm until the Father answers your prayers.

If you find yourself struggling in the wilderness, living in your anger and bitterness, know that the Father is working in the middle of it. You may not be able to see it, but He's always working in your life. In these in-between moments, He's growing you, and teaching you to trust Him. There will be times when you feel "it's just too hard", but I am with you. You can do all things in My strength. And the Father wants you strong enough and mature in your faith to keep moving forward in His plans for your life.

Keep focused on Me and set your mind on the things above, not the things here on earth. Decide, each and every day, that you are going to live and experience the promises the Father has made. Don't remain stuck in your doubt, disbelief, and disappointments. Don't allow your mind to get stuck on the hard things in life … remember the Father's faithfulness and stay focused on Him.

FAITH THOUGHTS

Do you sometimes feel like something is holding you back from experiencing the promises of God? Do you read and hear about the peace of God, but don't seem to experience it? Do you read the promises and believe them, but fail to see any of them fulfilled in your life? Ask the Spirit to renew your mind and refresh your heart. God's miracles are waiting for you. Believe that they are on their way.

NOVEMBER 3

Shouts of Joy

Then my head will be exalted above the enemies who surround me; at his sacred tent I will sacrifice with shouts of joy; I will sing and make music to the Lord.
PSALM 27:6

When you face times of trouble and temptation, your heart should be focused on the Father, not on your circumstances and what surrounds you. Too often you become more concerned about your situation than the purposes the Father has in taking you through it. You should always work to please the Father, crying out to Him for help.

I am your Light and a Stronghold. The Father will cause your enemies to stumble and fall. It's the result of grace and faith. It's when you place your trust in the Father that He moves graciously in your life. It is right now, even when problems are not solved and things are hard, that you can rejoice. With your head lifted high, you can sing the Father's praises.

You may not know what lies ahead, but you've been promised that you'll be taken care of. There is never anything to fear. Celebrate the gifts you've been given through your faith. Don't be tempted to complain, you'll fail to see the blessings in all the brokenness. Ask the Spirit to help you remember what is really important in life and help you to focus on those things throughout the day. Make your relationship with the Father, your walk of faith, the center of your life. Live faithfully and thank the Father for His faithfulness.

FAITH THOUGHTS

Ask God to help you take a step away from the worries of life and to rejoice in the love and grace that He has abundantly poured into your life. Stay focused on eternity and ask the Spirit what it is you can do on this day to further the Kingdom. Embrace the opportunities to give praise to God in the middle of all the messes in life.

Gladness and Joy

NOVEMBER 4

Those the LORD has rescued will return. They will enter Zion with singing; everlasting joy will crown their heads. Gladness and joy will overtake them, and sorrow and sighing will flee away.
ISAIAH 35:10

The Father wants you to be happy. His desire for you to be happy is supposed to transform the way you live. Know that perfection doesn't exist in this world. It's an expectation that will always leave you disappointed. Believing that everything needs to be "just right" will cause you to live an unhappy life, full of frustration and relentless dissatisfaction.

But although life will never be perfect, the Father has a path to happiness … to being content. You can be satisfied with what you have, in looking at all the blessings you've been given. In changing your perspective from what you don't have to what you do, you radically change your feelings, putting your soul in a more peaceful, joyful place.

It's as you continue to follow Me, that you will find yourself overtaken by who I am. You'll find strength when you are weak, and you will have peace when you are afraid. I am with you to carry your burdens, and the Spirit is within you to carry your soul. Right now, in this moment, acknowledge Me as Lord of your life, and walk in the joy I died to give you.

FAITH THOUGHTS

Has gladness and joy overtaken your life? Though you haven't reached eternity yet, you can live in the hope Jesus died to give you. Don't allow the worries of the world to keep you from the fullness of life that you are meant to live. Call upon the Spirit to renew and refresh your soul so that you might walk in a way that is pleasing to God.

November 5

Perfecter of Faith

Fixing our eyes on Jesus, the pioneer and perfecter of faith. For the joy set before him he endured the cross, scorning its shame, and sat down at the right hand of the throne of God.
HEBREWS 12:2

I am the author, the writer, creator, initiator of your faith. I am the perfecter, the One who knows what it takes, what you must go through, to make your faith strong enough, complete enough to travel through the rest of your days on earth.

You cannot make your faith grow. It is My Spirit at work within you that can get you to a place where your faith is unshakable – where your faith parts seas, calms them and moves mountains. There is nothing you cannot do with My power within you. The Father is always orchestrating the situations in your life to make your faith mature and complete. Your greatest desire should be to be used by the Father, to accomplish His purposes.

The difficulties you have already gone through have transformed your faith ... changed your heart ... in ways that you don't even realize. As you have endured trials and overcome, your faith has become stronger and more mature. One day, if you will stay the course, if you will trust in Me and run the race set before you, one day you will see Me face-to-face and hear the words, "Well done."

FAITH THOUGHTS

Are there moments when you take your eyes off Jesus? Do you so easily forget as you hurry about your day that Jesus is with you each step of the way through your journey of life and He is with you to perfect your faith? Continually keep focused on the joy set before you ... eternity with God, everlasting life.

Great Reward

NOVEMBER 6

*"Rejoice in that day and leap for joy,
because great is your reward in heaven.
For that is how their ancestors treated the prophets."*
LUKE 6:23

In the middle of pain and suffering, when life is hard and overwhelming, it can become difficult to see a way out of the darkness. So, be reminded through the Father's promises that your troubles are only momentary. If you focus on how big the Father is, your problems will become smaller. And all the while, through all of your struggles, the Father is preparing for you an eternal glory that will prevail. Fix your eyes on Me and the glory you'll receive in heaven.

It is often hard to live obediently to the Father's will, it is contrary to the ways of the world. And sometimes you will want to quit, you'll feel as though all your trying is amounting to nothing. But there is a great reward in heaven for you if you endure. You'll be misunderstood, slandered, and abandoned, but I will never leave you. And as I live in you, I will help you to respond to the trials and tribulations in a way that will glorify the Father and bring glory to His name.

It is the Spirit within you that will help you follow My example, shifting your focus from your frustrations and centering it on the things of eternity. Know that one day the Father will get rid of all pain and adversity, but until then, you'll need to stand firm in your faith, in My strength. Set your gaze on the immeasurable blessings that lie ahead.

FAITH THOUGHTS

Where is your focus? Do you continually fix your eyes on the hope of Jesus each and every day? It's easy to get distracted with all that's wrong, instead of praising God for all that's right. Know that as you strive to live a righteous life, there are great rewards for you in heaven.

NOVEMBER 7

One Desire

Indeed, you are our glory and joy.
1 THESSALONIANS 2:20

I will keep you from stumbling in this life. It is the Spirit within you that will keep you steady, walking with Me, fulfilling the purposes of the Father. I stand before the Father in your place, willing and able to present you as faultless, so that one day you will stand in the glory of His presence. It's all because of His will, My sacrifice, and the power of the Holy Spirit.

One day you will experience exceeding joy, but until you do, live in Me, so that I might live in you. The Father longs for you to live a life in the Spirit, so that you might see who He truly is … He longs to reveal His glory, love, power, holiness, and splendor in your life. He will reveal Himself in simple but mighty ways. He sacrificed Me, His only Son, so that you might see His glory, so that you might know the fullness of His love. And He will not force you to love Him. It's your choice to receive, each and every day what He's giving you. Knowing Him, loving Him, and having a heart of gratitude will change your life.

As the Spirit works in you, your heart and mind are transformed and you begin to see the world as the Father does. As you follow Me, you see His care, concern, and miracles in every moment. Don't miss out on the journey for one moment of your life. Start each day in a place of surrender. The Father has one desire … your heart.

FAITH THOUGHTS

Are you starting each day in a place of surrender? Are you calling upon the Spirit to transform you into the likeness of Christ, no matter what that means? Faith is not easy. It will require walking through things in life you wish you didn't have to. But Jesus is always with you. There is nothing to fear. If you'll surrender your heart to God, He'll give you His.

Restore the Joy

*Restore to me the joy of your salvation and
grant me a willing spirit, to sustain me.*
PSALM 51:12

Your joy will come from your obedience, from having a willing spirit surrendered to the Father. The source of your true happiness will come in having a relationship with Me, following Me, living a righteous life. And the purpose of your trials is to strengthen your faith, not destroy it. The Father allows them to come to draw you to Him.

You will never find joy through sin and disregarding what the Father has commanded. Just as sin brings about misery and sadness, I bring about unspeakable joy and glory. Joy will come when you are living each day by faith, seeking the Father's will. Don't allow the world to give you the truth.

If joy is missing from your life, you can be sure it is because you are seeking it where it cannot be found. Your joy is receiving Me as Savior, knowing your sins are forgiven, having fellowship with Me, and realizing that the Father has a purpose for your life. Without the Father's promises in your life, you are like a ship lost at sea, tossed by the wind and the waves without direction. It's in trusting in His promises that you can come to His throne of grace with boldness and ask to be restored in the joy of your salvation.

FAITH THOUGHTS

You need to remember that you are saved, that you don't have to pay a price for your sins to be forgiven. Jesus has already paid the price for you. Now He just wants you to live in the joy and peace He died to give you.

November 9

Choose Joy

Rejoice in the Lord always. I will say it again: Rejoice!
PHILIPPIANS 4:4

Are you choosing joy each day? You won't always feel like choosing joy because of your life's circumstances, but you can look at Me and always find joy. Ask the Spirit to cause your heart to choose joy no matter what your current circumstances might be.

I know that your troubles will lead you into depression and despair. The Father hears your complaints. He knows. But He's doing something through your circumstances and in you. Most of your life is simply going to be a matter of focus. When your mind is tangled in the web of the Enemy's lies and his voice is drowning out the voice of the Father, it's time to do battle. It's time to immediately get focused on the Word and boldly declare your faith in Truth.

Whatever you're going through, you can be sure that the Father is at work in it and the Spirit is guiding you in His will. There was no joy in the Cross. The joy set before Me was beyond the Cross and beyond the grave ... I kept eternity as My focus. And so must you. Continually choose to praise the Father and live in joy. When things aren't going well, know that they soon will, so you can be thankful right now, choosing to be joyful that the Father has promised great things.

FAITH THOUGHTS

Most of the time you will have to choose joy. In a troubled world, joy is not always abundant. But there is always a reason to be thankful, something that you can look to the Father in gratitude for. He's promised that He's smiling down upon you and that is His grace poured out. So, smile ... when you think you can't.

This Very Day

NOVEMBER 10

*The LORD has done it this very day;
let us rejoice today and be glad.*
PSALM 118:24

It's easy to praise the Father when all is going well, when expectations in life are met or exceeded, but not so easy when days contain sadness and disappointment, and even despair. It's in those moments when you're doubting, that you must declare that today is a day that the Father has made and you can rejoice and be glad in it, whether you feel like it or not.

It's those days when you are struggling with pain and conflict, when relationships are broken, loved ones are lost, your job is in jeopardy, and finances are falling apart, where you must understand that these days are also days that the Father has made. These days are also days when you should rejoice and be glad. You can rejoice and be glad that at this very moment, the Father is working all things together for your good.

Today, blessings are being prepared for your life and one day you will have the abundant grace and strength to receive them. Today, as you endure, suffer, and bear everything with joy, you can do so knowing that the Father is in control. Don't lose courage, but look at the things that are not seen, because it is then that your troubles will be light and temporary, as they work for you a more exceeding and eternal weight of glory.

FAITH THOUGHTS

Whatever today holds, you can rejoice and be glad. You may not feel like rejoicing when your life is falling apart, but God is holding you. You can be glad that you've been reconciled to God and have the hope of eternal life. Don't allow the troubles of this world to rob you of the joy you're meant to live in.

November 11

The Fruit

But the fruit of the Spirit is love, joy, peace, forbearance, kindness, goodness, faithfulness.
GALATIANS 5:22

Miracles are always closer than you think and most of them will occur in you. Without Me living in you, without the Spirit, there is no way you could love the unlovable and have joy during chaos. True peace, patience, and kindness are impossible in your own strength. Your efforts at goodness and faithfulness fall far short of the Father's glory. But in My presence, with the work of the Spirit, you can do all things.

You are a walking miracle. It's your intentional, daily choice to submit and surrender to the Father that will bring about supernatural results. Each and every day you are being sanctified, taken from faith to faith and glory to glory. Ask the Spirit to open your eyes to the miracles in and around you each day.

The Father is always doing something, working all things together for good in every situation you face. You may not be able to see it. You may not understand it, but you can trust Him and every promise He has made to you. He is faithful even when you're not, and the Spirit resides in you at all times to keep you on the path of righteousness.

You will stumble, you will fall, but I will always be there to pick you up and carry you. Surrender each and every moment of your life to the Spirit, allowing the character of God to grow in you, bringing, love, joy, peace, forbearance, kindness, goodness, and faithfulness. This is the fullness of life.

FAITH THOUGHTS

Do you get caught up in trying to live life your way? Remember that God is using your situations to transform you. The process might hurt, but you can rest assured you are loved by God and what He does is for your good and His glory.

Knowing Why

*"However, do not rejoice that the spirits submit to you,
but rejoice that your names are written in heaven."*
LUKE 10:20

You need to be continually reminded to focus on Me and Me only. No one knows your heart as deeply as I do. I want you to see that there is a war raging inside your heart, a spiritual battle, that will bring you to a place of repentance. When you turn from who you are and to who I am, it changes everything.

There may be many reasons to rejoice, but the one reason that never changes is that your name is written in heaven. The Spirit dwells in you to guide you as you journey through your daily life. It is divine power that will strengthen you to remain vigilant and fully aware of the presence of the Holy Spirit in your life.

Whatever the day holds, know that the Father is always at work, sanctifying you, giving you a new heart, a transformed mind, and a soul that rests in His peace. I have lived as your example ... to be humble, to walk in a way that brings glory to the Father and it's the Spirit alive in you that will enable you to do the same. When you can't seem to find anything in life to be joyful about, come to the Father in prayer and just sit in His presence. His grace will amaze you, comfort you, and bless you in ways that you cannot imagine. When you call out His name, know that He first called out yours.

FAITH THOUGHTS

Do you forget that God calls you by name and that your name is written in heaven? Stop for a moment and just think about what that means about the depth of God's love for you – it's too amazing to understand. Throughout each day, God is calling your name ... are you listening?

THE SIGNIFICANCE OF YOUR SUFFERING

Dear friends, do not be surprised at the fiery ordeal that has come on you to test you, as though something strange were happening to you. But rejoice inasmuch as you participate in the sufferings of Christ, so that you may be overjoyed when his glory is revealed.
1 PETER 4:12-13

It may seem like the pain and suffering that God allows is all for nothing, but it's not. He promised that. And He said you shouldn't be surprised by it. Though specific storms of life may seem to come unexpectedly, we're told to expect them. They will come, with great purposes. Even though you don't understand what those are, God is at work, He's using it all ... for your good and His glory.

At the forefront of suffering comes a force that drives you to your knees in dependence on God. It's those situations where there's no one and nothing that can save you, that you realize exactly who God is and that you desperately need Him. It brings your heart to a place of humility, understanding that God is in control and you're not ... keeping you from walking through life full of pride.

It's your troubles that turn up the heat, as God holds you in His refining fire. Pause on that last part ... He's *holding* you. And He never lets go. Never. It's through your sufferings that your faith is going to endure and it's going to grow in ways you can't imagine.

God is concerned with transforming you to live with Him forever. He loves you enough to allow you to go through pain and suffering, taking away anything in the world that you might be tempted to rely on. His goal is that you would grow deeper and stronger in your confidence in Him, that you fully realize that He is all you need.

Divine Deliverance

NOVEMBER 13

*The righteous person may have many troubles,
but the LORD delivers him from them all.*
PSALM 34:19

Your troubles don't go away simply because you have faith. Faith gets you through them and opens the door for divine deliverance. And sometimes, you may even find that troubles increase, the Enemy recognizes you as a threat and begins to work to steal, kill, and destroy your life. But no matter what, the Father has promised to deliver you from all of your troubles … every single one.

The Father's timing may not be the same as yours, but He has reasons for all that He does. Just because your troubles don't cease, or the devastation they cause does not disappear, doesn't mean the Father has abandoned you. Remember I am with you always. And it's the Spirit that will give you the strength to endure until your miracle comes. Know that in the midst of your enduring, the Father is growing you, strengthening you, and transforming you into My likeness.

This is the goal, this is the purpose through your pain … that you might be sanctified, being prepared to live with the Father for eternity. I was made perfect through My suffering. And with the Spirit dwelling in you, you too, will undergo the Father's work to refine and perfect your faith. He is always up to something … something *good*.

FAITH THOUGHTS

God may be walking you through fires, but He's with you. There's no reason to be afraid when troubles come … God uses them to refine you and perfect your faith. So look at your tribulations from a different perspective. Ask the Spirit to give you eyes to see what God does and a heart that trusts Him in all things and in all ways.

November 14

Bearing Up

For it is commendable if someone bears up under the pain of unjust suffering because they are conscious of God.
1 PETER 2:19

You will go through many tribulations in order to enter the Kingdom. You live in a fallen world. In the new heaven and new earth there will be no more tears and no more pain, mourning or death has not arrived yet. You have been promised that your suffering is not random or without purpose.

You may feel exhausted, working out your faith and never seeming to get it right … come to Me. If you're trying to do things in your own strength, you'll grow weary … doing it in My strength will enable you to bear up under the pressure. You'll face times of great challenges but the Father has given you the gift of faith. It's because of the faith you're given, that you have access to grace. And it's grace that enables you to communicate with the Father.

As you draw near during difficult times, you'll find that your suffering produces endurance, character and hope. Because of your faith in Me you can experience the fullness of the Father's presence through all of your sufferings. If you believe, then your troubles are not wasted, the Father is working through your adversities to bring out His good purposes in your life. It's your choice to focus on your problems or center your thoughts on things above. If you keep your eyes on Me, you will see that the problems you're experiencing are simply avenues by which the Spirit will transform you, creating a faith that endures hardships with the joy of what lies ahead … a hope that does not disappoint.

FAITH THOUGHTS

Are you struggling and suffering and tired? In which areas of your life does God need to renew your strength? Make sure that you are looking to God for security, comfort, and strength as you endure the trials of life. There is no other hope than Jesus.

The Godly Life

November 15

*In fact, everyone who wants to live a godly
life in Christ Jesus will be persecuted.*
2 TIMOTHY 3:12

If you follow Me, you will be persecuted. You will encounter resistance and hatred. But I am with you and the Father is always watching over you. When you are feeling fearful, confused, angry, and doubtful, look to the Word and take comfort in My promise that if you're persecuted for following Me, you will be blessed.

I know that you desire a life that is free of worry and full of happiness and joy, but in a fallen world, life will not be easy. There will be trials, tests, and tribulations. Pray for the Father's protection. And be prepared in faith. Don't be surprised … expect trouble with great confidence in the promises you've been made. Stand firm in your faith and rely on My strength and the Word to help you overcome whatever you must face.

Whatever you must go through, the Father has already made a way through. Look at your trials as a way that the Father draws you nearer, making you more dependent on Him and helping you to learn to listen to His voice. There is no better place for you to be than on your knees, worshiping and calling upon the Father for guidance and direction. And there's no better path than the Father's will. Come with Me and walk in it.

FAITH THOUGHTS

Are you ready with faith when you are persecuted by situations and people, by the Enemy? Or are you surprised, caught off guard, and finding yourself losing the battle before it's even begun? Stay in the Word. Be prepared for what lies ahead and be ready in faith, knowing that God will protect you through it all.

NOVEMBER 16

Carrying Burdens

Carry each other's burdens, and in this way you will fulfill the law of Christ.
GALATIANS 6:2

Pray for wisdom, discernment, and patience to allow the Father to fulfill His purposes in your life. You will need to carry others' burdens just as I carry yours, and it will most often be more than you can handle. You will need the comfort and courage given to you by the Spirit and you will need a firm foundation of faith.

At some point, everyone will struggle under the weight of difficulties. It may be sins that are difficult to overcome, a trial that just will not stop, or basic needs that continue to go unmet. There is no reason for anyone to struggle through it all alone. The Father has given you a family of believers to walk beside you, as I do. Knowing that at times you will need your burdens to be carried, make sure you are always looking around you to fulfill your responsibility and privilege to strengthen others, even when you are undergoing your own hardships and afflictions.

You can't wait until your life is free of troubles and worries because that day will never come. When you think you don't have the strength to help when help is needed, look to Me and remember that you can do all things in My strength, which includes carrying someone else's burden, or at least sharing in it. Be a blessing and you'll be blessed. As you have witnessed the evidence of the Father's love and grace in your life, be determined to show that same evidence by pouring out yourself in the same way.

FAITH THOUGHTS

Though you're overwhelmed with your own troubles, someone might need your help. You'll be surprised by how simple care and kindness in the lives of others will bring about great blessings in your life. Your troubles will slowly fade in the Light of God's glory and grace as you fulfill His purposes in your life.

Proven Faith

November 17

> *In all this you greatly rejoice, though now for a little while you may have had to suffer grief in all kinds of trials. These have come so that the proven genuineness of your faith – of greater worth than gold, which perishes even though refined by fire – may result in praise, glory and honor when Jesus Christ is revealed.*
> 1 PETER 1:6-7

Sometimes your troubles and suffering are caused by your own mistakes, at other times they are simply from living in a fallen world. I know that when you're going through pain and suffering, you doubt. You need to know that in your doubt is where the Father is working the most.

Suffering isn't punishment from the Father, and it's temporary. Suffering comes from a world that is fallen, but you can be assured that the Father will use it all for good. Your faith will be refined and proven no matter what you must face. Know that your suffering leads you to pray more … whether it's out of anger or petition, you are drawing near to the Father. Through all that you must endure in life, know that you're never alone.

I understand your pain and weakness. I, too, endured suffering. One day you will see Me face-to-face because you ran your race, you fought the good fight, and you suffered well and endured. It's the way that you respond to life's troubles that should reflect My character. Your response, in faith, brings honor to My name and glory to the Father. Pray that you would have faith through sufferings and be willing to endure as you wait upon the joys that will last forever.

Faith Thoughts

Sometimes your troubles feel never-ending. Don't forget that you can and should embrace these times, God is using it all. His priority is to refine you. Although painful, it will come with great gain. Trust Him for it.

Through Suffering

*In bringing many sons and daughters to glory,
it was fitting that God, for whom and through whom
everything exists, should make the pioneer of their
salvation perfect through what he suffered.*
HEBREWS 2:10

You are not expected to be perfect. You can't be. I, too, had to endure trials. I experienced fear and uncertainty. Although I never acted out of My temptations, I overcame them by falling upon the Word of the Father. And so must you.

If you run to the Father in your times of fear, you'll find the despair that is gripping your heart fade in His presence. The moment you feel uncertain, rest on the wisdom, love, mercy, and grace of the Father. I know and understand all that you feel. I am the One with scars on My hands. It's because of what I suffered that I am uniquely qualified to give you power and help. I understand. And since the Father uses all things, even suffering, it is not always in His plan to fix it.

At times, you may need to just walk with Me through the greatest griefs, troubling trials, and darkest nights. My death and resurrection had to take place for My work to be perfected. I know that at times you will need to overcome your fears and your desires to try and control things instead of trusting and obeying the Father. Walk in faith, in My strength, and with each step, know that the Father is doing something amazing, working within you, transforming you, and preparing you for all His glory.

FAITH THOUGHTS

When you're facing temptations of any kind, you need to look to Jesus. He knows. You aren't meant to walk through this journey of faith alone. You have a Savior ... One who suffered. He is always there, in the depths of despair and in the darkest night. He never leaves you.

The Commitment

NOVEMBER 19

*"And whoever does not carry their cross
and follow me cannot be my disciple."*
LUKE 14:27

Your cross is when you willingly die to self. When you surrender all that you are to the Father. It's when you say "no" to sin and self and say "yes" to Me. I know that at times life gets in the way, things get busy and times get tough. It's in those times that it is best to put the Father first. Nothing should get in the way of your relationship with the Father and nothing should keep you from following Me.

Each and every day you must choose whom you will serve. Don't let excuses get in the way of making the Father's purposes for your life a priority. Nothing is too difficult. Nothing is impossible. And although I ask you to suffer all reproach, affliction, persecution and even death itself, cheerfully and patiently, it does not mean that you are to be happy about it. It means it is a choice you make. A willingness to suffer comes when you fully understand My sacrifice for your soul. Ask the Spirit to examine your heart to ensure that you have Me placed first in all you say and do.

Let nothing get in the way of following Me and accomplishing all that the Father has purposed for your life. There is blessing in the following and in the surrendering. Live a life continually surrendered out of the great joy that you've been saved.

FAITH THOUGHTS

Are God's purposes for your life your priority? Do you often find yourself getting so busy with surviving in life that your faith moves down another place on your priority list? Take a moment to ask the Spirit to help you find ways to prioritize your faith through what you do and say each day. Put God first.

To Know Him

*I want to know Christ – yes, to know the power
of his resurrection and participation in his sufferings,
becoming like him in his death.*
PHILIPPIANS 3:10

You need Me. You need to know Me. There are blessings that come from knowing Me. I am your risen Lord, dwelling in you, who gives you resurrection power that is able to do in and through you above all that you can ask or think. It is power that is perfectly adequate, able to do miracles, in every circumstance you face. My risen power is yours.

And though there are so many blessings that come from your faith in Me, it is also your participation in My sufferings that transform your spirit to be more meek and compassionate. At the center of who I am is victory, hope, and blessings, and you get to share in those as well.

You are able to walk in newness of life, ending your old, sinful way of life, and grabbing hold of the freedom of forgiveness you've been given through grace. You can't accomplish all that the Father plans for you in your own strength, through your own means. All that you do to further the Kingdom is not achieved by trying, struggling, and striving ... it all simply comes from knowing Me.

FAITH THOUGHTS

Do you really know Jesus? Are you allowing His Spirit to fully live in you and are you willing to walk through sufferings in order to also share in the blessings? Faith will not be easy. You'll want to quit ... but you can't. Keep your eye on the prize. Keep your eyes on Jesus and press on.

Everyday Life

To this you were called, because Christ suffered for you, leaving you an example, that you should follow in his steps.
1 PETER 2:21

NOVEMBER 21

You have a calling, each and every day of your life. Ask the Spirit to reveal and remind you of it continually. You can be sure, without having all of the details for your specific plan, that you should always do good and follow My example in living.

When you follow Me, you will experience suffering, but it's your suffering that brings you closer to the example I set. It is the Spirit that will help you to patiently endure as you cling confidently to your faith and hope. Your salvation is continually being brought to maturing and completion by the sanctifying work of the Spirit.

Don't forget, this is not your home – you're being prepared to go there and live for eternity. You can be sure that the Father is always at work in your life, sometimes especially when you are going through hard times. You can be assured with confident hope that your struggles are not wasted time, but that you are simply going through a season in which the Father will use in one way or another to accomplish His purposes in you. Never forget the bountiful grace that has been shown to you through My living and dying. The grave could not hold Me and it won't hold you either.

FAITH THOUGHTS

Do you recognize that God is at work in your life right now, regardless of your circumstances? Rest assured God never allows anything to go to waste. He uses it all. Ask the Spirit to help you live with a hope that is beyond this life. And when your faith is tested, ask Him for help in standing firm in the strength that comes from knowing that you've been given the incredible gift of salvation through grace.

NOVEMBER 22

The Promised Crown

Blessed is the one who perseveres under trial because, having stood the test, that person will receive the crown of life that the Lord has promised to those who love him.
JAMES 1:12

Sometimes, when your troubles are overwhelming, you can be tempted to think that the Father does not have your best interests at heart. Know this: the Father never tempts you. If you are doubting your faith and doubting the Father, the Enemy is at work. Run to Me when you are tempted and know that I know exactly how to help you. The Spirit will comfort and strengthen you, encouraging you to press on until you receive your crown.

If you trust Me, if you keep your eyes on Me, you will be blessed when you endure. You will receive the crown of life if you will fight the good fight in My strength. This life is preparing you for glory. And it's the storms of life that threaten to destroy you that will determine whether or not your faith grows stronger or gives way to the darkness. It's only those who have a genuine relationship with Me, rooted and anchored by the indwelling Spirit, that will remain.

Pray and be steadfast. Let nothing move you. Your life is a spiritual battleground. You are running to finish the race. If you grow weary, call upon the Spirit for help. There is nothing you cannot do in My strength, through divine power. You should never be confused about the finish line, your destination ... you are headed to heaven. And it's the Spirit that will be with you along the way, growing your character. Your entire journey to eternity is led by the Spirit within you, and He is leading you to the place where you see Me face-to-face and receive your crown.

FAITH THOUGHTS

Do you ever stop to think that one day you will be wearing a crown in the kingdom of heaven? You can live in the joy now as you look forward to your rewards in heaven.

Hope in Sharing the Glory

Not only so, but we also glory in our sufferings, because we know that suffering produces perseverance.
ROMANS 5:3

You've been told to expect to experience suffering. Your faith does not remove your troubles. Your distresses can be something minor, or a major disaster in your life. They all require My help. And as you face them, your tribulations, your response in your suffering must be a choice to rejoice. It won't be your instinct – it will come from the Spirit within you assuring you that if you endure, there is great glory ahead.

You can rejoice in your sufferings because you *know* ... you know Truth ... which tells you that your suffering is accomplishing something. Your troubles are doing something that goes far beneath the surface of them all. Those storms may cause destruction, but they're meant to ... the Father may need to tear down things in your heart that need to be healed and rebuilt. There can be joy in the midst of suffering.

It's in them that you persevere, that you experience the Spirit comforting you and strengthening your faith in ways you have never known. As you stay under the pressure, keeping the faith, your faith becomes steadfast. And it's through each and every storm that you start to realize that you will not be destroyed, you are under the Father's care. Through it all, you have the hope that the Father is transforming you into My image. As you become like Me, you are stronger, wiser, purer, and more patient. And the transformation happens in your suffering ... so rejoice.

FAITH THOUGHTS

Do you rejoice in your sufferings? Suffering hurts. And so does refinement by God. It's not going to feel good ... it's not going to seem like God is loving, but there is no greater love than your heavenly Father transforming you to be like Jesus.

November 24

Raised Up

For Christ also suffered once for sins, the righteous for the unrighteous, to bring you to God. He was put to death in the body but made alive in the Spirit. After being made alive, he went and made proclamation to the imprisoned spirits.
1 PETER 3:18-19

You are alive in Me, raised up out of your sins, forgiven and saved. But believing in Me, having the hope of eternal life is not all there is. The day you receive Me into your heart is just the beginning. It's at that moment that you become a slave of righteousness, submitting to Me as Lord of your life.

It won't be easy to walk according to the Spirit and not the flesh. I didn't sacrifice My life just to give you eternal life, I died to change you, transform you, to make you a new creation. Your faith makes you ready to live in holiness, created in Me to do good works that the Father has prepared for you. All of your sins, past, present, and future have been nailed to the Cross. And it's grace which has given you salvation, that will instruct you to turn from ungodliness, fleshly lusts, in order to live a life in the Spirit, self-controlled. You cannot be made alive in Me and your life remain unchanged. To live for yourself is to live for nothing. Your purpose is to pursue the Father's purposes for your life and further His kingdom. Let nothing get in the way.

FAITH THOUGHTS

Are you living fully in the knowledge that in Christ you have been made a new creation? You are no longer the same person. It's the Spirit living in you that will motivate you in the right direction, the paths of righteousness, that will lead you into the Father's will for your life. And you can trust that no matter what He has planned, it will be for your good and His glory.

Rejoice and Be Glad

NOVEMBER 25

"Blessed are those who are persecuted because of righteousness, for theirs is the kingdom of heaven. Blessed are you when people insult you, persecute you and falsely say all kinds of evil against you because of me. Rejoice and be glad, because great is your reward in heaven, for in the same way they persecuted the prophets who were before you."
MATTHEW 5:10-12

Everything you do and experience is by the Father's design. You should always rejoice in Him. Your rejoicing is your expression of gratitude for all He has done to make you alive again.

When you rejoice, you worship. When you worship, you show your love for the Father as He has shown an outpouring of love and grace in your life. He wants you to rejoice in His love and in His works. It's in your rejoicing that you are given strength to overcome all obstacles to your faith. Even in trials, you can rejoice and you will have the strength to persevere. It's the Spirit that strengthens you through suffering and gives you a heart of praise through it all.

On good days and bad days, you can praise the Father. There is never a moment when the Father does not know what you're going through and I'm walking with you. Rely on the Spirit to comfort you when things are hard and to help you when things are hopeless. You can live in the hope and joy I've given you … but it's your choice. Make sure you focus on Me when I call to you to walk upon the water, and not on the wind and the waves. I've given you the faith that walks on water … walk with Me.

FAITH THOUGHTS

Are you grateful simply for the fact that you are able to know God – to have a personal relationship with Him? It's a blessing to spend each day in His presence. Don't allow a moment to go by that you do not thank God for the breath you're given and the eternal life that awaits you.

TRANSFORMED BY THE SPIRIT

But we ought always to thank God for you, brothers and sisters loved by the Lord, because God chose you as firstfruits to be saved through the sanctifying work of the Spirit and through belief in the truth.
2 THESSALONIANS 2:13

Change is never easy. And often it's painful. But the changes the Spirit make in your heart have purposes that will impact your life here on earth and for all eternity. It's worth it. It will all be worth it. It just doesn't seem like it right now when you feel as though your soul is being shattered and you're struggling through life, desperate for relief. Something is happening … a miracle within you … you're being transformed into the likeness of Christ.

God has a habit of shutting you in with Himself, until you get it, until your faith has learned what it needs to. His intention is to saturate you, your whole being, with Himself, so that you will be fully transformed. God is seeking you … are you seeking Him? Are you asking Him continually to search your heart and show you if there is any area of your life that needs altering? It's difficult to take that step of faith because you know that there are lots of things that need changing. And change usually comes with pain … and we'd rather do without it. But the momentary suffering we must go through will grow dim in the Light of God's glory and grace.

It's these "light and momentary" troubles that are doing more than you can understand … they are achieving an eternal glory that far outweighs them all.

Made Holy

NOVEMBER 26

Those who cleanse themselves from the latter will be instruments for special purposes, made holy, useful to the Master and prepared to do any good work.
2 TIMOTHY 2:21

Always remember, as a child of the Father, saved and set aside, you are not a sinless saint. You are never in a position to judge, never in a place of placing someone lower than yourself. You simply live in the love and grace that you must freely give. You have a high calling to extend My mercy, unreservedly. And you can only do this if your heart and life is cleansed by the Spirit.

Regardless of what you must go through in life, you are continually being prepared through it all to press through the problems and spread the Good News. And it is the Word that cleanses you, strengthens you, and empowers you to accomplish all that the Father purposes for your life. It's the Word that displaces unrighteousness and the sins that entangle you and replaces it all with righteousness. It is a Living Word. With all power. It destroys fear and sets your faith on a firm foundation. It cleanses anyone who surrenders to its influence, power, and authority. It is because of the changing, transforming power of the Word that the Father calls you blameless and unreprovable in His sight.

You are washed, sanctified, and justified in My name and by the Spirit. Call upon the Spirit to continually help you to understand and consciously walk in the Light of the Word, in the Light of righteousness. Live in Me as I live in you.

FAITH THOUGHTS

Are you continually seeking out God's Word for your life, calling upon the Spirit to cleanse you? In a world that is full of sin, it can be easy to get entangled if you are not continually surrendering to the Word's power to transform your mind and cleanse you from all unrighteousness. Faith is a journey, not a destination.

Disciplined for Good

They disciplined us for a little while as they thought best; but God disciplines us for our good, in order that we may share in his holiness.
HEBREWS 12:10

You will find yourself in difficult times. Sometimes it will seem like hell on earth. Troubles may affect your health, relationships, or finances, and it will seem like everything is falling apart and faith has no purpose because things are not getting better. Know that the Father may allow you to remain in a valley with great purposes that go beyond your understanding. Trust Him.

All too often, you fail to realize that the Father allows you to go through tough times for your good, so that you might share in His holiness. When it doesn't make sense, look at My life. Remember how the Father walked Me through unthinkable trials to prepare Me for the cross. And then look at your own life and realize that when you endure hardships and troubles of every kind, the Father can use them for greater things.

The secret to surviving the tribulations of life is to fix your eyes on Me, the perfecter of your faith. I have led a life that is an example to strengthen you, to encourage you, and to remind you not to lose heart. Whatever the Father does, whatever He allows, is done out of His love for you. Cling to Him, trust in His promises, and keep your eyes fixed on Me.

FAITH THOUGHTS

Are you facing difficulties that seem far beyond your ability to handle or endure? Are you looking at it as hell on earth or are you viewing it as God does ... situations to sanctify you? Realize that all that God allows, all that He sees you through, is meant for good. It may not seem like it right now, but one day you will understand and it will all be worth it.

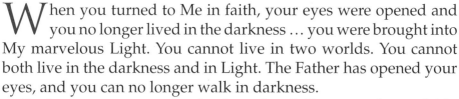

Eyes to See

> *"Open their eyes and turn them from darkness to light, and from the power of Satan to God, so that they may receive forgiveness of sins and a place among those who are sanctified by faith in me."*
> ACTS 26:18

When you turned to Me in faith, your eyes were opened and you no longer lived in the darkness ... you were brought into My marvelous Light. You cannot live in two worlds. You cannot both live in the darkness and in Light. The Father has opened your eyes, and you can no longer walk in darkness.

Darkness represents sin, death, and evil. Because of your faith, you've been brought out of it all. You are no longer held captive, but set free. Now you are to dwell in the Light. The Father did not leave you to wander in darkness. He will never leave you nor forsake you. Through My sacrifice, your eyes have been opened to the paths that the Father has made for you. You are now in right relationship with the Father, reconciled, guided into His Light with every thought, emotion, action, and decision.

Your eyes will continue to be opened as you journey through faith. Ask the Spirit to go into the darkest places of your past ... your thoughts and feelings that have led you astray. Allow Light to illuminate your darkest sins so that you can be healed. It's once you allow the Father to illuminate your whole life, you can see yourself as you truly are, while discovering the fullness of His grace, love and forgiveness. You are set free. Once you were blind ... but now you see.

FAITH THOUGHTS

Are there places in your life where God's Light has not been allowed? Have you tried to keep Him out? Surrender everything. Every thought, every action. Don't live one moment that isn't guided by Light. You have been set free from sin by the blood of Jesus. There is always grace.

Heavenly Minded

*Let the message of Christ dwell among you richly
as you teach and admonish one another with all wisdom
through psalms, hymns, and songs from the Spirit,
singing to God with gratitude in your hearts.*
COLOSSIANS 3:16

As you dwell in the Word, it will affect your heart in such a way that you will naturally rejoice. When you are living and breathing the Word, it will pour out into every area of your life. With every breath and heartbeat, the Word should become the essence of who you are. It is the Father's transforming grace that takes place when you allow the Word to dwell in you richly.

It is easy to wander from the truth. There are so many lies that surround you. So, it must be your first priority to seek the Word until it becomes a part of who you are. When you face struggles of many kinds, don't focus on your present circumstances, but on the things above, spiritual things.

When you do, you will find yourself letting go of your earthly, sinful nature and walking in your renewed self. The Word will transform your heart into one that is compassionate, kind, humble, meek, patient, and forgiving. When the Word dwells in you, you become more loving and you have My peace. I want you to experience the fullness and completeness of the Word. I want you to see it for the treasure that it is. It should be your refuge and your rest, your hope and your help. No matter what you face, the Word will fill your heart where praise just happens.

FAITH THOUGHTS

Do you find it difficult to really get into God's Word? It may not seem like God is really speaking through it, but as you read each word, the Spirit begins to work within your soul and transforms your thinking and your life. Sometimes, when things are hard and you're confused, you just need to look up.

Every Spiritual Blessing

Praise be to the God and Father of our Lord Jesus Christ, who has blessed us in the heavenly realms with every spiritual blessing in Christ.
EPHESIANS 1:3

November 30

The blessings of the Father are for you to experience now … in Me. Because of your faith in Me, the Father has given you all the spiritual blessings that heaven has ever known. He does not withhold a single blessing. Take hold of them. Do not miss out because of a lack of faith.

You are forgiven and redeemed, set apart for the Father's eternal purposes. The greatest blessings you will experience in life are spiritual and I have given you all of them. You don't need what you already have. I have given you every spiritual blessing. You have all the peace you need. You have all the goodness you need. You need to realize what you have and all that is readily available to you. It's time to start accepting and applying the blessings you've been given. You don't need more patience … you have it already. Whatever you need, trust that in Me, it is yours.

The manifestation of spiritual blessings comes through and by your faith. You receive by faith because you are just and live by faith. Believe in what you've been given. Ask the Spirit to reveal those blessings to you continually and live your life in praise for all you've been given. These are free gifts … I already paid the price.

FAITH THOUGHTS

Are you constantly aware of who you are as a child of God? Are you living and continually receiving the spiritual blessings He's given to you? All you really need is Jesus. Go to the throne of grace, it's there where you receive more than you can hope for or imagine on top of what you've already been given.

Put to Death

*Put to death, therefore, whatever belongs
to your earthly nature: sexual immorality,
impurity, lust, evil desires and greed, which is idolatry.*
COLOSSIANS 3:5

Temporary pleasures will seem to satisfy … but they don't. Only I can satisfy the emptiness of your soul. The Father's way is contrary to the world's. Though I have taught you that mercy, meekness, and peacefulness mean success in the Father's kingdom, the world urges you to have material prosperity, and personal comfort. Do not be deceived. The Father is not mocked, you reap what you sow. Sow seeds of eternal purposes.

Ask the Spirit to regulate your attitude and actions, and to help you respond to situations in the Father's character. Stay in the Word, meditating on it day and night, allowing it to set the standard for how you think and live. If you ask the Spirit to permeate your soul with the Word, you'll find that the way you live your life will be different. Your greatest desire should be to become all that the Father has planned for you to be – there is no greater success.

When I died on the Cross, you died in Me. When I was raised from the dead, you too, were raised with Me. You can submit your sinful nature and live your life for Me. You must walk in the Spirit and in Truth. And always remember that you are being prepared for your heavenly home, when you will appear with Me in glory. Choose to live a godly life in Me, and let go of the old you … grabbing hold of the new.

FAITH THOUGHTS

What do you define as success in your life? Does it line up with what God sees as success for you? Continually pray that the Spirit would search your heart and remove anything that separates you from God. Put your old self to death and live in the fullness of life and joy that Jesus died to give to you.

A Life of Power

I have been crucified with Christ and I no longer live, but Christ lives in me. The life I now live in the body, I live by faith in the Son of God, who loved me and gave himself for me.
GALATIANS 2:20

You have been given a life that is joy unspeakable, full of glory. Because I live in you, your life overflows with the supernatural and divine. The life you now live, is not the one you once lived. You've been given a new life, sins washed away, guilt-free, full of grace. The old has gone because My life has flooded into every part of yours. Your life should radiate all that I am.

I died to be brought back to life so that I could live in you and so that your heart would overflow with all that I am, spilling out into your life. I live in you, move in you and work through you. No matter what your circumstances are, My joy is your strength. Don't wait for things to get better to live the fullness of the life I died to give you. Right now is the time to live a life of joy in your salvation.

You are under My protection and provision, and you can live with gladness and contentment. Living the victorious life comes with power. Power to live with My joy and peace – joy to live with laughter and self-control – power to live in everlasting hope. I am the Way, the Truth, and the Life. I have given you all that I am to fill up your heart and your life. Live your best life starting right now. Let all of you … live for all of Me.

FAITH THOUGHTS

Do you stop to realize that you were different than before you asked Jesus to be your Savior? Everything has changed. You'll still make mistakes, and life won't be perfect, but you have a Savior that walks with you and the Spirit living in you to help and guide you into God's perfect will for your life.

December 3

The Blood

*How much more, then, will the blood of Christ,
who through the eternal Spirit offered himself unblemished
to God, cleanse our consciences from acts that lead
to death, so that we may serve the living God!*
HEBREWS 9:14

The price for your sins was paid in full, by My blood. As the Spirit dwells in you, you will become more and more aware how you are saved by grace and given the gift of righteousness. There is nothing that you need to do but believe in Me. Allow My blood to cleanse your conscience from dead works to serve the Father. The freedom you have in Me changes you into a better person through the love the Father has poured out into your heart and life by the Spirit.

Because of Me, you no longer have to live under the guilt of sin. It's the Spirit that changes you, freeing you from a lifetime of sorrow in your sins. There is no more condemnation and guilt for you to live under. I have washed away all of your sins by My blood – past, present, and future, you can live in freedom. You will continue to make mistakes, and you will sin … you are not perfect. But you will feel guilt and turn to the Father right away.

You know where grace and forgiveness reside. And when you turn to Him, walk in My strength and approach His throne of grace confidently. He sees Me in your place, He sees righteousness. So, don't be afraid. Ask the Spirit to once again refresh and renew your spirit so that you might fulfill the purposes of the Father. You have the great joy of following Me and serving the Father.

FAITH THOUGHTS

It's easy to get caught up in sin and just live under the guilt of it. But you are a new creation, you've been given a new life, one that is bought by the blood of Jesus. You don't need to do anything to earn God's forgiveness, it's given freely when you repent because of what Jesus has done.

Called to Greatness

DECEMBER 4

To the church of God in Corinth, to those sanctified in Christ Jesus and called to be his holy people, together with all those everywhere who call on the name of our Lord Jesus Christ – their Lord and ours.
1 CORINTHIANS 1:2

You must never be fearful, but always aware that Satan is out to destroy you. He will tempt you and lie to you and convince you that what is black and white is merely gray. His goal is to keep you discouraged and beaten down. But when you are calling Me Lord and Savior, you are called to greatness.

Don't settle for the ordinary in life, follow Me, and walk through the miraculous ... experience the Father's glory. You have a specific purpose to further the Kingdom. You may have had plans for your life, but you need to set those aside. Every ambition, every desire of life needs to be set aside, as you follow Me. Do not turn from your calling. And don't be surprised when life tries to pull you in different directions, trying to pull you away from your first love.

Whatever calling you have, whatever the Father has purposed you to do, don't give up when it gets hard. Don't listen to the voices of doubt, telling you that you don't have what it takes. The Father will protect you and provide all you need to accomplish His will. Keep focused on Me, in My living and in My dying, and every miracle in between.

FAITH THOUGHTS

Are you living out your purposes? If you're not sure what they are, pray until God tells you what it is ... until He speaks to your soul in such a way that you just know what you're supposed to do. It may require stepping into the unknown, but God is there. Amazing things happen when Jesus calls you to walk upon the water and you do it.

December 5

Once for All

And by that will, we have been made holy through the sacrifice of the body of Jesus Christ once for all.
HEBREWS 10:10

You have been set apart by the Father through what I did on the Cross. You have been cleansed of your sins, clothed in My righteousness ... and you now have the hope of eternal life. You are saved by grace through your faith ... once for all.

You are no longer separated from the Father. You've been forever forgiven, set apart, sanctified and made righteous. There was nothing you could ever do on your own to accomplish what I did. All of your efforts would have been in vain. But it was the Father's will that you be made holy through your faith. So, I endured the Cross. You are now called for the Father's purposes. You cannot achieve the Father's purposes for your life on your own. It's impossible. You'll always fall short.

You need grace and you need Me. You need the Spirit as your Helper and you need My divine power to walk with you through your journey of faith. It is the Father's will that you be holy, but you cannot do it by simply obeying rules or living morally. You are only able to be made holy because of My sacrifice and because of the Spirit dwelling in you.

It is the Spirit that fills you with hope, inspiring you to press on, even when you fall short of God's glory ... through it all, you are safe, secure, in the arms of the Father. Since I have already done My work, He can do His in you.

FAITH THOUGHTS

You don't need to try so hard to please God. What you really need to do is just surrender to the Spirit. Let Him do the work in and through you. Jesus has already done the hard part, you just have to believe and be saved.

In the Name of the Lord

DECEMBER 6

And that is what some of you were. But you were washed, you were sanctified, you were justified in the name of the Lord Jesus Christ and by the Spirit of our God.
1 CORINTHIANS 6:11

You come to Me, just as you are ... a sinner in need of salvation and forgiveness. And I accept you just as you are. But that is just the beginning. It's then that the Spirit comes to dwell in you, washing you in My blood, sanctifying you, and justifying you. If you are in Me, you are new, old things have passed away, and all things are made new. You are forever changed.

You are justified by your faith, and being justified, you have peace with the Father. I stand in your place, I was punished for you and now you've been saved and made new. You will never face the Father's wrath. You have hope, not because you've simply been set free of your sins, but because I died for you, and I am your righteousness. Your faith doesn't rest on who you are, it rests in Me, in what I have done, and what I am continually doing for you.

Pray that you would continually surrender your heart, allowing the Spirit to be fully alive in you. Don't allow any obstacles to get in the way of your faith, of your pursuit of the Father's purposes, of your desire to follow Me.

FAITH THOUGHTS

It's easy to forget that through each moment of your life, you are being sanctified by God. The Spirit dwells in you, working to transform you and make you more like Jesus. Each situation in your life is used by God to mold you and although it may not be a quick or easy process, it is always worth it.

December 7

Until the Day

*Being confident of this, that he who began
a good work in you will carry it on
to completion until the day of Christ Jesus.*
PHILIPPIANS 1:6

The Father never takes His eyes off you, and He has a plan for you that is unique and personal. You may not always understand His plan fully, and you may not grasp what He's doing, but His results will always be worth it. All He asks you to do is to trust and obey.

In the middle of your unspeakable heartaches and trouble, you can be sure that the Father knows. He knows where you are and He knows what you need. And though He tests you, the test will come to an end and you will come forth as gold. Know that His process will always precede the promise.

It's the Father's divine favor working on your behalf that is evidence of His power and love manifested in and through you. He desires that you have a life that is overflowing and abundant. It's His favor that brings supernatural increase, restoration and promotion in your life. Once you understand that you have the Father's favor, you will gain confidence and faith to move mountains. It's in walking with Me that you will see that prior impossibilities are now possible.

If you choose to walk by faith and not by sight, you will not accept that lack, fear, defeat, or sickness have any place in your life. You will continually stand in the divine power you've been given, living inside of you ... until the day of completion when I return.

FAITH THOUGHTS

Are you confident that you can do all that God has called you to do? Are you relying on His strength and power to do it? Don't wear yourself out trying to make things happen, let God be God, and follow Jesus. If you trust Him, you'll never be disappointed.

The New Is Here!

Therefore, if anyone is in Christ, the new creation has come: The old has gone, the new is here!
2 CORINTHIANS 5:17

When you put your faith in Me, your old self who was unable to please the Father is transformed. You are a new creation: adopted, accepted, and loved. As you are transformed on the inside, you begin to change on the outside, too. Some changes will be so drastic that you may not even recognize yourself. Do not question the transformation and do not doubt what the Father has done once it is complete. You are made new, in Me.

Embrace the fact that you've changed, that you are no longer who you used to be. There is divine work happening in you through supernatural power. Ask the Spirit to help you see areas of your life that are not embracing the new life you've been given. You should not be thinking or living the same way you used to. And then ask for the strength to surrender those areas, so that you will fulfill the Father's purposes in your life.

The life-change that takes place by your faith is only possible through your belief in Me. I have given you access to the throne of grace, able to be in right relationship with the Father, leading you into His transformation process so that you can be holy because He is holy.

FAITH THOUGHTS

Which areas of your life are the same, and which ones are different since you first believed in Jesus? Do you continually ask the Spirit to show you what still needs to be made new in your life? God is always at work in your life. Make sure that your heart is always surrendered.

BLESSING IN DISGUISE

For the LORD *your God will bless you as he has promised.*
DEUTERONOMY 15:6

God's blessings don't always seem like blessings. A hardship full of heartache can be a gift of hope when God is in control. You just can't see it in the moment. It's difficult at best to understand how it is that God is good when everything is going badly. But that's where faith comes in, that's when miracles happen, and that's when you'll be blessed not by understanding, but simply trusting.

No matter what your circumstances are in life, no matter how things appear, no matter the impossibilities you face, you're a child of God and you have His favor in your life. You have the Holy Spirit living in you, supernatural wisdom, and power, ensured by the promises of God. You have God's Word and He's made you countless promises of blessings that you need to grab hold of. You need to seek Him in your storms of life and in the eye of them, when all is calm.

Don't allow a moment to go by when you are not holding on to the hope that Jesus died to give you, the assurance of God's faithfulness in your life, reconciliation with Him, enabling you to approach His throne of grace. When you can't see it, you're going to have to walk by faith and realize there is blessing in your brokenness. It's in your troubles that you're going to find the blessing of God's grace and goodness in your life. It's in the middle of the messes of life that you'll see Him open heaven's doors and pour out His favor in your life like never before. God has promised you uncountable, unthinkable gracious blessings, don't miss them just because they're disguised.

Blessed for Trusting

*Whoever gives heed to instruction prospers,
and blessed is the one who trusts in the LORD.*
PROVERBS 16:20

You are not meant to have all the answers to life's questions, but to trust the Father who does. Your questions draw you nearer to the Father, and knowing Him gives you satisfaction in life. Having all the answers would never satisfy you. So you must surrender. Surrender your life in such a way that you trust the Father even without answers.

If you are in the deepest valley or on the highest mountaintop, I am with you where you are. I am with you to give you peace and comfort as you continually build a more intimate relationship with the Father. And that's all that matters to Him. If I must take you through the fire to do that, then it is for the best. Yet, never forget I'm with you.

There is never a moment when I leave you. I am with you in the fire. I am with you in the storms. Begin each day, as I did, giving your life to the Father, surrender your moments and give Him the authority over all of your days. Daily you will face important opportunities to trust the Father, like when you encounter relationship problems, health issues, and financial challenges. In every situation, you must be faithful to obey Him and to sincerely trust Him to care for you and bless you.

FAITH THOUGHTS

Do you find it hard to trust and have faith that God knows all things and can see the bigger picture of your life? It's difficult to believe in something you can't see, and yet you trust that there will be air to breathe when you take your next breath. It's time to let go and just trust. God is there to catch you ... and He's there to bless you.

December 10

Finding Favor

For I command you today to love the Lord your God, to walk in obedience to him, and to keep his commands, decrees and laws; then you will live and increase, and the Lord your God will bless you in the land you are entering to possess.

DEUTERONOMY 30:16

The Father longs to give you blessings, advantages in life designed to increase your happiness and well-being. Know that the Father has promised to bless you and keep you, prosper and protect you, while making His face shine upon you with His grace. And I give you peace.

You've been given the gift of forgiveness and righteousness, and the Holy Spirit gifts you with grace, peace, protection, and prosperity. I want you to walk in the Father's favor with Me each day, receiving more of His wisdom, goodness, and provision. As you walk with Me, you build your faith and confidence to trust the Father more, preparing yourself to be more blessed and favored. You will need to continually rely on the Spirit to lead you.

You will need spiritual wisdom and direction to make sure you stay on the path of righteousness, obeying the Father's commands. You may not always be able to understand His ways, but you can trust Him. He wants the very best for your life, living a life full of His grace and mercy, blessed with every good thing.

FAITH THOUGHTS

You may not always understand God's ways, but there is no promise that He will not keep His Word on. You've been given special favor through His divine power, make sure you receive it and ask the Spirit to lead and guide you in ways that will use that favor to benefit the Kingdom.

Be A Blessing

*Do not repay evil with evil or insult with insult.
On the contrary, repay evil with blessing,
because to this you were called so that you
may inherit a blessing.*
1 PETER 3:9

If you will focus on blessing others, the Father will make sure that you are always blessed in abundance. Your blessings will come in ways that are not always the ones you're expecting. They might come as wisdom, information, ideas, power, favor, skills or opportunities. And the blessings you receive will not be just for you, they are for you to share and bless others too.

Blessing others may be as simple as praying for them as the Spirit prays on your behalf. You can listen and give encouragement, while comforting them as the Spirit comforts you in your afflictions. When you are weak and weary, cast your burdens upon Me, so that you can help carry the burdens of others.

Make sure your heart is open to My love so that it can flow out to others. Though struggles will come and temptations are hard to resist, you can endure and walk victoriously through it all in My strength. Keep your heart full of the promises of the Father so that you can walk firmly in faith and strengthen others around you. Ask the Spirit to open your eyes to the opportunities the Father puts before you to be a blessing to others … even in the midst of your troubles.

FAITH THOUGHTS

Is it so easy to get focused on the ways that you need to be blessed that you forget all the ways in which you can bless others? If you ask the Spirit to open your eyes to opportunities in which you can be a blessing, you'll find that God will bless you in ways that you can't imagine.

December 12
The Promise of Blessings

"I will make you into a great nation, and I will bless you; I will make your name great, and you will be a blessing."
GENESIS 12:2

If you are feeling insufficient and weak, you are right where you should be ... pain and suffering can be used as a tool of brokenness. It's a different way the Father brings you into the blessings He has in store for you. So pray, wait and watch what the Father will do to fulfill the promise of blessings in your life.

Sometimes it's the breaking of you that allows the Father to go to work. It takes Him to the deepest area of your life that needs refinement. And often you cannot experience the glory of the mountaintop until you've traveled through the darkest, deepest valleys. Yet, there is nothing to fear. I walk with you. Never will I leave your side. And the grace the Father gives is absolutely sufficient for anything and everything you must face in life.

It's your brokenness that makes you more sensitive to the Father's presence and it is the Spirit that will comfort and assure you that He is there. It's in knowing that I am with you that you can be secure and rest while you wait for the Father to reveal Himself to you as your provider and protector.

You don't have to fear and you don't have to worry. You can be still with Me and experience My abiding peace and unspeakable joy, regardless of your circumstances.

FAITH THOUGHTS

God has made lots of promises to you, but the one that you should cling to is that you will be blessed – you need to trust that ... at all times God is working to bring about great blessings in your life. You need to know that when He seems silent, He's busy working. And in those moments of doubt, keep believing, keep trusting, and watch and wait for what He will do to ultimately bless you.

Abundantly Good Things

How abundant are the good things that you have stored up for those who fear you, that you bestow in the sight of all, on those who take refuge in you.
PSALM 31:19

True faith always comes before abundant blessings. You have to trust, stepping into the unknown … walking upon the water. You need to live in faith, stepping out into the deep, instead of waiting for the Father to show Himself before you respond. You won't see the results of your obedience until you obey.

If the Spirit has shown you your calling, your purposes to further the Kingdom, you will need to completely rely on Him to guide and direct you. It is up to you to take the steps. To trust when you're not sure you can. It's then that you'll find Me walking to you upon the waters. Don't be afraid to get out of the boat. Otherwise you'll miss out on the greatest miracles of your life.

The Father's divine power works in small ways and in greater ways than you can comprehend. It is up to you to walk in faith, fulfilling His purposes for your life, which will bring about the blessings He has stored up for you. Whatever you ask Him to do, He can do more. Trust in Him as your refuge, a place to rest and renew your soul. Let Him work on your worries while you focus on the hope that is only found in Me.

FAITH THOUGHTS

God stores up blessings to pour out into your life at the perfect time. It's in difficult times that you can be sure He's preparing you for all that He wants to give you. He needs to make sure your heart is right to receive His very best. Run to Him, trust in Him, and rest in Him while you wait in faith upon His blessings in your life.

DECEMBER 14

Seeing God

*"Blessed are the pure in heart,
for they will see God."*
MATTHEW 5:8

The Spirit is continually at work to make your heart pure toward the Father. It is when you have a pure heart that you can be happy. Your walk of faith is one that brings you into peace with the Father.

Your heart is crucial to Me. The deepest parts of you are what I care about the most. I came so that your heart might be purified. You need a heart that has nothing to do with deceit and lies. Purity of your heart is seeking My face. You need to have a pure heart before you are able to walk into eternity. You are cleansed by My blood and it is your obedient living and faith in the Father that keeps your heart pure. You are to live your life with a heart that is open to the Spirit's guidance ... a heart that is kept by Him, protecting you from the corruption and destruction all around you.

The Father is faithful and He will watch over you and protect you always. There is never anything to fear. Pray that the Spirit will do His work in you. It's heaven that needs to be in you before you can enter its gates. And you must become pure in heart before you can see the Father.

FAITH THOUGHTS

What is the state of your heart in this moment? Are you allowing yourself to be deceived by lies of the Enemy? Are your actions consistent with your heart? The Spirit is within you to continually help cleanse your heart of any unrighteousness. Pray that He will change your heart to look more like God's.

Prosperous and Successful

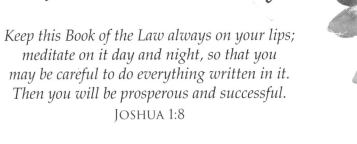

DECEMBER 15

*Keep this Book of the Law always on your lips;
meditate on it day and night, so that you
may be careful to do everything written in it.
Then you will be prosperous and successful.*
JOSHUA 1:8

It's the Spirit that will lead you to understand how the Word should be applied to your life. You don't need to keep searching for secrets of success to life. Your fullness of joy has already been outlined in the Father's Word and it's all you need to succeed in this life and the life to come.

Don't forget to make time to focus on the Word. It is your instructions for life. Don't fail to set aside time in your day to simply seek the voice of the Father. It's the Word that will grow your faith and develop godly character within you. You only need to ask the Spirit to help you as you look to understand what the Father wants to speak to you through His Word. It's the Spirit that will lead you in and through all Truth. And you can't just know the Word, you must live it.

Ask that your confidence be restored each day so that you can walk in the supernatural strength and courage to be faithful to the Father. Ask Him to remove every barrier that is before you and open doors that have been closed. Know that angels go before you and prepare your way. You have a divine path to follow and you are anointed to do whatever you're called to do. Follow Me and watch what the Father will do in and through you.

FAITH THOUGHTS

Are you making time to meditate on the Word of God? There are countless promises that He has made for your life and unless you know what they are they cannot come alive in your life. The Word is your instructions for life and it is in knowing it and living it that you'll experience blessings like never before.

DECEMBER 16

All the Fullness

*For the LORD takes delight in his people;
he crowns the humble with victory.*
PSALM 149:4

There is a victory you are to live in. One given to you through My sacrifice. You are blessed beyond anything you can imagine, your transgressions are forgiven and you have received the gift of eternal life. What greater blessings are there? What greater cause of joy exists? You are to live blessed and as a blessing to others.

Life will never be fair, since you live in a fallen world. And I know that at times, when all is well, you feel close to the Father, yet when things are bad, you question His very existence. The greatest blessing in your life is being able to simply know the Father. I have reconciled you. You can fully experience His presence and power and He is the source of your deepest joy.

When life is hard and you're experiencing pain and suffering, know that it is transforming you. It's your emptiness that pushes you into a deeper life with the Father and you will learn to rest in Him alone. Long for His presence. Trust in His faithfulness. When you have a relationship that is intimate with the Father, you find the greatest blessing of all through the fruits of the Spirit flowing from you. And the greatest blessing of all is in the Father Himself. If you know Him, you'll be truly blessed.

FAITH THOUGHTS

Are you living the victorious life you're meant to? It's easy to let life get in the way and believe that you're just meant to suffer and struggle in this world. But God has called your name and He has blessed you with the Spirit. You no longer have to live in defeat ... you can claim the victory that has already been given to you.

What to Do

DECEMBER 17

But whoever looks intently into the perfect law that gives freedom, and continues in it – not forgetting what they have heard, but doing it – they will be blessed in what they do.
JAMES 1:25

The Word is like a mirror that shows you yourself as you are. It's when you look at what you see that you must make the choice in changing what is not reflective of the Father. You will need to rely on the Spirit to help you do the work that is necessary to change your life and become all that the Father longs for you to be.

You once had different attitudes, old habits and sinful desires. It was when you turned from them and followed Me that you realized that things need to be removed and replaced so that you could be more like Me … reflecting the Father's character and heart.

The transformation that takes place in your life will not happen overnight. Each and every day you must create new priorities and habits that will take you step by step into the Father's will. It's in seeking after His heart that you will find the fullness of His love, joy and peace. It's what you desperately need. It's your obedience to the Father that is evidence of true faith. Seek the Word and submit to it … that's what you need to do to be blessed.

FAITH THOUGHTS

You ask to be blessed but forget, at times, to ask God what it is He wants to do in your life. Ask Him if there is something He needs to change about your heart, and seek His Word to understand His. Don't be afraid of the transformation. The Spirit will do all the work and comfort you in the process. And never forget there is always grace … more and more grace.

Strength and Peace

*The LORD gives strength to his people;
the LORD blesses his people with peace.*
PSALM 29:11

You receive blessings that you seldom fully recognize. When you have strength and peace through the most difficult circumstances, you are blessed. There will be countless times in your life when you will cry out that you can't go on, that you have no more strength. And yet, I am with you ... carrying you during those times. It's when you fail to look to Me that your joy is stolen and you are left feeling weak and weary.

You can have peace in Me, not because your surroundings are peaceful, but because your heart and mind are focused upon Me. In the uncertainty and pain and suffering, you can hold on to your faith by reaching out to Me for your peace. Your daily life brings with it unexpected demands, which leave you feeling overwhelmed, angry and confused. You might be tempted to put your relationship with the Father on hold, but don't. It's in those times that you need Him more than ever. You need to hear His voice, know His heart of love for you and feel His protection and provision.

Daily stay in the truth, praising the Father for all He has promised. Recall His faithfulness in your life and you'll find the courage to face your present troubles. Today, you must choose to seek the Father and find your strength and peace in Him. He is giving what you need to receive.

FAITH THOUGHTS

When things just go wrong, unexpectedly, do you frantically try to solve things in your own wisdom and strength? Don't miss out on the divine guidance and help that is always readily available to you. When you don't know what to do, when you're overwhelmed and weary, ask God for help. He has promised to be a ready help in times of trouble.

Blessed by Correction

December 19

> *"Blessed is the one whom God corrects;*
> *so do not despise the discipline of the Almighty."*
> JOB 5:17

The Father's goal is to help you grow. His discipline doesn't feel good at first ... it hurts. But if you learn to accept and be trained by it, your life will be transformed and the Holy Spirit will fully work in and through you to bear fruit.

It's easy for you to sometimes mistake the Father's discipline for punishment, but it is truly a blessing. Don't miss what He's really doing. His discipline is His love poured out, His goodness and grace consuming you is evidence of His good character and His purposes.

It's easy to accept the Father's love when He is providing, giving you the things your heart desires, but when it is necessary to correct you, to discipline you in order that you might develop greater godly character, it seems unloving. You won't understand it all when it's happening, but later on, you will see that it was all for your good and the Father's glory.

The correction in your life that the Father makes will last a lifetime. It's your toughest challenges, most of which you never expect, that can heal you, transform your heart, and restore your soul. Trust the Father through His discipline, be willing to surrender everything to Him and watch what He will do on the other side of it all.

FAITH THOUGHTS

It's easy to confuse God's discipline with punishment. There is never a moment that His grace is not covering you, healing you, transforming you, and restoring you through the most difficult trials of life. Whatever it is you're going through, can you take a moment to just fully surrender it all into His loving hands? In this moment, whatever you're struggling with, ask that He will use it for your good and His glory ...

Covered Sins

Blessed is the one whose transgressions are forgiven, whose sins are covered.
PSALM 32:1

Your sins have been paid for, once for all. You are blessed beyond understanding by the will of the Father through My sacrifice. You continually receive the Father's favor ... what you don't deserve but are freely given. I died for you so that you can live for Me, you are cleansed by My blood, able to live in joy because your hope is in Me.

It's your forgiveness and freedom from guilt over your sins that transforms your heart. You pray for blessings, but often forget the daily blessing of your transgressions forgiven, your sins covered, and your iniquities that are not counted against you. And over and over the Father grants forgiveness when you repent.

You will never be perfect, you will make mistakes and you'll need the Father's forgiveness. Know that there is no limit to how much He will forgive you. Come to Him in your sins, don't wait and try to clean up your own mess. He's waiting. There is no embarrassment, shame, or guilt at the throne of grace. You will not be turned away. His love knows no bounds. As you seek forgiveness, search the Word and draw nearer to the Father. In His presence there is peace, strength, and comfort. It's through His Word that you will hear His voice and know that you are fully loved.

FAITH THOUGHTS

Each and every day you need to remember what's been accomplished on the Cross. Whatever happens, there is hope in Jesus. Don't allow the worries of the world to weigh you down, you have Jesus to carry those burdens. Because of grace, you don't have to live in guilt, you can come into the presence of God, confidently, full of peace because of what Jesus has done. You are blessed.

Every Single One

December 21

Praise be to the God and Father of our Lord Jesus Christ,
who has blessed us in the heavenly realms
with every spiritual blessing in Christ.
EPHESIANS 1:3

You are blessed because you have the Father's unconditional love. Always remember that the Father is good and gives good things. With all of the pain and suffering in the world, all the things that are wrong and all that causes you to worry, you have the unshakable goodness of your heavenly Father as your foundation.

The Father blesses you in countless ways. From the small things to the big things, an unexpected gift or miraculous healing, the Father is constantly working to turn evil to good. What is most important is the condition of your heart. The Spirit works within you to make your heart more like the Father's.

The Father wants to bless you with more than worldly success and wealth. He is concerned with all things that are eternal and He works continually in your situations to give you the abundant life your heart desires through your spiritual gifts. Living your life for the Father's purposes will bring you greater joy than anything material in the world. Stop and look at what you deserve and then what the Father gives you. His blessing truly comes when you follow Me as I guide you into the best possible life, filled with the fullness of a reconciled relationship with the Father, living out your purposes, and fully using the spiritual gifts you've been given.

Ask the Spirit to shift your focus and pursuits away from earthly things to that which will impact eternity.

Faith Thoughts

Are you using your spiritual gifts every single day? Are you asking the Spirit to lead you into the will of the Father so that you can have the greatest impact on eternity? You have great purposes on earth, it's in achieving those that you will experience the greatest blessings.

December 22

High Above All

If you fully obey the LORD your God and carefully follow all his commands I give you today, the LORD your God will set you high above all the nations on earth. All these blessings will come on you and accompany you if you obey the LORD your God.
DEUTERONOMY 28:1-2

All too often you don't live in the blessings you've been given. You struggle in life when you should be living in the Father's blessings. You pray for blessings, but you've already been blessed with every spiritual blessing. The Father has set you apart, He has lifted you up ... above it all.

You need to live in the truth that you are fully blessed and you can enter into My rest. You can live assured that the Father is watching over you as you live out His purposes for you. He wants you to live in His blessings. There's no need for you to worry and struggle. You can walk forward in life in confident faith that you are loved unconditionally by the Father and you've been given eternal life.

You aren't meant to live in despair. You have Me, I am your hope ... Living Hope. There is never anything to fear, I am always with you. Ask the Spirit to help you obey the Father's will and guide you onto His perfect path for your life. If you will allow Me to live in and through you, letting nothing stop you from having extraordinary faith, you'll find the greatest blessings in your life will come from simply being at peace and in relationship with the Father.

FAITH THOUGHTS

Are you living as though God has greatly blessed you? It may not be easy to choose joy when life is falling apart, but in Jesus' strength you can do it. Look to Him when you're weak and weary, when you're not sure you can go on. And live fully in the blessing you've been given as you wait upon all the blessings God has in store for your future.

EXPECTING MIRACLES

*"I am the L*ORD*, the God of all mankind.
Is anything too hard for me?"*
JEREMIAH 32:27

If God is making you wait, it will be worth it. His miracles include His incredible power and impeccable timing. And He doesn't move according to your plans, He works according to His purposes. Listen, although miracles may come as a surprise to you ... having faith through your doubt ... they are no surprise to God. He's had it planned all along. He's going to use miracles in your life to get your attention. His miracles will be full of supernatural power, unexplainable situations that will keep you humble and your heart in awe.

God performs miracles because He wants to show you who He is. Whatever impossibilities you face in life, whether it be something big or something small, there is always hope if you're trusting in God. With Him, there is *nothing* that is impossible.

That "thing" you thought of just now ... that situation that just came to the forefront of your mind that you think is hopeless and impossible ... it's not. Don't give up on faith. God has promised you there *is* a way. He will lead you to it and He'll take you through it. If you'll continue to step out in faith, you're going to see a miracle. Maybe not the one you're expecting ... God has something bigger and better in mind. He always does. You might not feel as though you have the strength to keep believing, but you do. The Spirit is living in you ... the power of God. The power that makes *all* things possible.

All Things Possible

Jesus replied, "What is impossible with man is possible with God."
LUKE 18:27

The Father's miracles have no boundaries. There is nothing He can't do. I walked the earth to show proof of that. The blind see, the lame walk, the dead are raised to life. There is no limit to the Father's power. And He likes to do the impossible. There is no hopeless situation if you trust the Father.

Sometimes, when life is hard and difficulties never end, you forget that nothing is too difficult for the Father's divine power. I know that it can be difficult to see how the Father is using the things you're going through for good. When things seem hopeless, it's easy for you to lose hope … so you must look to Me. I am the author and finisher of your faith.

You cannot doubt what the Father has promised … He is not a liar. Whatever He has promised will be fulfilled. There is always hope, no matter how bad your situation is, the Father will make a way. There is no reason to be hopeless or discouraged. Don't worry, I am with you and the Father will answer your faith. Nothing is too big for Him and nothing too small. I will carry the burden in your heart that calls out for a miracle. I will deliver you from the hopeless situation. The Father will provide all you need as you walk forward in faith, trusting in His love and grace.

FAITH THOUGHTS

Do you really believe all things are possible with God? What's the one thing you think He can't do? … He can do that. Trust Him to take you through it, and ask Him for the miracle. He may not answer the way you want Him to, but He will always do what is best. One day you will understand, even if now you don't.

Signs and Wonders

December 24

*I will not venture to speak of anything except what
Christ has accomplished through me in leading the Gentiles
to obey God by what I have said and done – by the power of
signs and wonders, through the power of the Spirit of God.
So from Jerusalem all the way around to Illyricum,
I have fully proclaimed the gospel of Christ.*
ROMANS 15:18-19

Miracles happen every day. And they happen in your life every day too. When you need a miracle, all you need to do is pray and believe. The Father not only listens, but longs to answer your prayer.

Don't try to go your own way, making your own decisions, going down paths that you're not sure where they lead. The Spirit has been given to you, supernaturally, to guide you through life and give you confidence as you walk in faith alongside Me. Even when you don't understand, you'll need to trust in the Father's plans for your life, knowing He sees the bigger picture.

You'll need to trust that the Father knows when something needs to happen, the way it needs to happen, and He designs each detail through His mercy and grace. In walking with Me, in meditating on the Word and living a life of prayer, you will learn to trust that the Father has your best interests at heart and will perform miracle upon miracle in your life … but in His way … in His timing.

It's His timing that will yield the greatest blessings, so trust Him, even when you think you can't.

FAITH THOUGHTS

Are you looking for miracles in your life? What is keeping you from believing in every single promise God has made? Be determined not to let anything in your life keep you from God's very best blessings, especially fear and doubt.

December 25

Countless Miracles

*He performs wonders that cannot be fathomed,
miracles that cannot be counted.*

JOB 5:9

The Father has prepared countless miracles that will cause you to wonder, to bring you to your knees, and beckon you to His throne. He is the answer to all of the impossibilities in your life. It's the moment that you have faith in His promises that you can be sure that His power will meet what you believe.

Miracles are the Father's deliberate acts that He uses to bless your life and your faith. It's when you are connected to Him that you begin to live in supernatural love, grace, and power through your faith. When you abide in Me, I abide in you and divine power is at work. If you are rooted in Me, you will find prayers answered in ways you never thought possible. As you walk in obedience to the Word, you can come boldly and lay your requests before the Father, trusting that He is capable of doing all that He has promised.

Don't allow doubt to keep you from believing in the miraculous. Don't fall victim to the lies that contradict your faith. Look to Me for strength and ask the Spirit for guidance as you look expectantly for miracles to happen in your life.

Faith Thoughts

Sometimes miracles don't happen the way you want or when you want them to. God has a bigger picture He is looking at and He has to work a lot of things together for ultimate good. You're going to have to trust Him when you bring your prayers to Him. You're going to have to just fully believe that He loves you and will do what is the very best for your life.

Immeasurably More

DECEMBER 26

To him who is able to do immeasurably more than all we ask or imagine, according to his power that is at work within us, to him be glory in the church and in Christ Jesus throughout all generations, for ever and ever! Amen.
EPHESIANS 3:20-21

I will never disappoint you. In Me, you will find everything you need to live a life of purpose. I will continually fill you with the Father's love and the Spirit dwelling in you will comfort and strengthen you, enabling you to experience the Father's fullness. In Me, you will find contentment and joy ... even when you're not happy with life's circumstances. And as you look upon your life with gratitude, you will see the Father's fulfillment of His promises and you have more than you can imagine.

You are to live a life of victory in Me. Think about overcoming every obstacle and fighting battles of faith until the very end. Focus on a future in eternity that has reward and rest, and the gift of a crown that you will one day wear.

Each and every day, focus on the Father's heart. If you will, you'll find that you will be blessed in more ways than you ever thought possible. There are no limits to the Father's love, no boundaries to His blessings. So pray, and wait with great expectation because whatever you've ask the Father to do ... He'll do immeasurably more.

FAITH THOUGHTS

When nothing short of a miracle will help you in your situation, you need to pray continually and watch hopefully for what God will do. He can do anything. It doesn't necessarily mean He will ... He determines what is for the best according to His perfect will. But, you can trust Him to use His divine power to bring about goodness and glory in your life beyond all you can hope for.

December 27

Believing Without Seeing

"Unless you people see signs and wonders,"
Jesus told him, "you will never believe."
JOHN 4:48

You can trust the Father with everything ... every detail of every day of your life. It's when you live in a surrendered trust that you will faithfully walk on His path and live out His purposes for your life. You must walk by faith, not by sight.

It's along the journey of faith, walking with Me, the Spirit dwelling in you, that you will see the Father at work in your life in ways you never thought possible. You'll be amazed at His love, mercy, and grace in the most difficult circumstances. And as you trust, even in turbulent times, you'll have My peace that transcends all understanding. In the middle of the chaos, I will calm your soul. When you can't see what lies ahead, when you are confused about what is happening and what you're supposed to do, it's your faith that will carry you through.

I have told you to follow Me because I know exactly what you need and where you need to go. The Father's love is unconditional and you can trust Him unconditionally. It's His divine protection and provision that makes His love unquestionable. You are truly precious in His sight. Always remember, whatever is going on in your life, He is in control and He is always working things out for good.

FAITH THOUGHTS

When you're facing difficulties, confusion, tough decisions, or uncertainty, are you trusting God completely? When you pray for help, are you placing the outcome entirely in God's hands? Are you living hopefully in His promises? Are you believing without seeing?

Gifts of the Holy Spirit

God also testified to it by signs, wonders and various miracles, and by gifts of the Holy Spirit distributed according to his will.
HEBREWS 2:4

Oftentimes the miracles that the Father does is what He does in and through you. You've been given spiritual gifts for the Father's glory. Serving Him and the Kingdom is not a suggestion, but a command. Don't miss out on His greatest miracles in your life by failing to fully use the gifts you've been given.

There are an endless variety of ways that you can use your unique gifts. Whatever gifts you're using, the Spirit is the source of them all and the Father is doing the work. It will require your faithfulness to follow through and fulfill the Father's plans for your life. Your spiritual gifts are the tools the Father gives you to do what He asks you to do. And He will never ask you to do something that He doesn't give you the full capability to do.

When you accepted Me as Savior, you were given your gift. You didn't choose it and you didn't earn it, and it's not for your benefit, it is for furthering the Kingdom. It's when you use your spiritual gifts that you'll be blessed. It's the Spirit within you that will continually develop the gifts you've been given.

Don't compare yourself or your gifts to others. Make sure your faith is continually moving, knowing that the Father's power does not show up in some areas of your life and not others. He is involved in every detail of your life. He is all-powerful and the gifts He has given you have the potential to change the world.

Faith Thoughts

What spiritual gift or gifts do you have? If you're not sure, ask the Spirit to open your eyes so that you can see what they are. Don't allow a day to go by where you are not using the spiritual gifts you've been uniquely given. It's in using them that you'll experience miracles.

What to Expect

You are the God who performs miracles ...
Psalm 77:14

It may seem like miracles are rare, but they are simply not recognized for what they are. The greatest miracle of all, each and every day, is the transforming power of the Father changing hearts and more lives being surrendered to Me. As you live in Me, am I fully alive in you? Do others see Me in you? My love and compassion, My joy? Call upon the Holy Spirit to make you a miracle.

You must believe if you are to see miracles in and through your life. You must believe that the Father is protecting you moment by moment. Even in your failures, in your mistakes of yesterday, in all your shortcomings tomorrow, you can trust in His love for you, in His presence that hovers over you and shields you from the troubles of life.

He is not only aware, but He is present. And you can rest under the shadow of His wings. I am with you every moment of every day. The Spirit is within you to lead and guide you, to strengthen you and give you comfort. The supernatural, divine power of the Father is a constant miracle in your life. Are you receiving that miracle? Are you living in it? No matter where you go, He is there. Expect His miracles.

Faith Thoughts

Do you fully recognize that God is with you at every moment of every day? Are you receiving that miracle? It's easy to get caught up in the stress of life and forget that God's presence is right there with you. If you will look to Jesus, you will see Him resting, and so should you. God has everything under control. You've trusted Him before ... you can trust Him now.

Never Failing

"For no word from God will ever fail."
LUKE 1:37

December 30

You are blessed if you will believe that the Father will fulfill His promises to you. The Father is good and His promises are true. Don't miss out on His very best in your life by not knowing and believing in what He has promised you.

The Father wants greater things for your life than you can possibly imagine. Instead of focusing on what you don't have in life, focus on the Father's promises in your life. Try to focus on what He's doing as He's asking you to wait on His promises to be fulfilled in your life. He never stops working for your good. His timing will not be the same as yours and you may not understand His ways, but He's proven Himself trustworthy.

When things don't go as you plan, hope for or pray for, you can rest assured that the Father's promises will never fail you. You are to watch in hope, knowing that He hears you. As you wait, you will walk with Me and the Spirit will work within your heart, to search it, to know it, to show you if there are any ways within you that need to be transformed. If you have faith in the Father's promise of your eternal life, you can have the faith that He is with you every day and all of His promises hold true.

Faith Thoughts

If you look back on your life, is there a situation where you're thankful that things happened in God's timing and not yours? You want blessings in your life, but often don't see the ones you have because you're seeing things from your perspective instead of God's. Are there promises that you're still waiting to see fulfilled in your life? Are you continuing to trust God or are you giving up hope? Go to Him, tell Him. You'll be blessed in His presence.

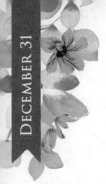

DECEMBER 31

Remember

*Remember the wonders he has done, his miracles,
and the judgments he pronounced.*
PSALM 105:5

Living in a fallen world will require you to need miracles. And yet, through My sacrifice, you have the unconditional love and favor of the Father. It's your faith in Me that produces an abundance of blessings in your life. It's your heart of gratitude, pouring out praise to the Father, that will bring about the fullness of His love and grace in your life. When life is difficult, when the storms don't cease and you feel as though you're continually bailing water ... remember. Remember the Father's promises, remember what He's done. Remember His faithfulness and His offer of continual forgiveness. Remember that because of My sacrifice you have free access to the Father's throne of grace.

Remember that you can choose to live in the joy I died to give you. Ask the Spirit to work within you to continue to transform and sanctify your heart. Look to Me when times are uncertain and you're filled with fear and come to Me when I call for you to walk upon the water. Don't allow doubt to cast you into despair and give up on your faith before the miracle happens. You're always one prayer, one step of faith, away from breakthrough, from the Father's greatest miracle in your life. Trust in His faithfulness and recall who He is and all that He's promised. Always *remember*.

FAITH THOUGHTS

You are always one step of faith away from God's greatest blessings, His biggest miracles in your life. Don't allow the doubt that is cast into your life, due to the uncertainty and overwhelming circumstances, to weaken your faith. Remember all that God has done in your life and thank Him for the promises of all He's yet to do. Pray, wait, and watch because He's full of surprises!

About the Author

Cherie Hill is an international best-selling Christian author and the founder of ScriptureNow.com, bringing the Word of God into countless lives around the world for over fifteen years. She has a BA in Psychology and is trained in Biblical Counseling through the AACC. She continually depends on the mercy and grace of God, in order to strengthen the faith of others through her writings.

Other books by the author

Walking in the Spirit

The Holy Spirit is God-in-us, a divine presence that guides us in God's ways. Although His presence is a crucial part of a believer's life, many people struggle to see and truly experience the Holy Spirit's influence. These 365 devotions will help you grow in awareness of Him and discern what the triune God is calling you to do. As you realize how the Holy Spirit is intertwined in and integral to every part of your life, you will experience what it's like to walk in the Spirit.

ISBN 978-1-4321-3401-3 (Faux Leather)
ISBN 978-1-7763-7002-3 (Hardcover)

He Whispers Your Name

He Whispers Your Name is more than just a devotional; it is 365 invitations to listen to God and the personal messages He wants to share with you. With 52 themes such as faith, prayer, forgiveness and salvation, Cherie Hill ensures that you will be able to draw closer to God in all areas of your life. There is also an index of the themes at the back of the book.

Written as if God Himself is speaking to you, *He Whispers Your Name* makes it resoundingly clear that He wants to have an intimate relationship with you.

Allow God to strengthen your faith as you listen to Him whispering your name. Find encouragement in God's whisper as you work your way through this full-color devotional.

ISBN 978-1-4321-1812-9